'An adroit and hugely enjoyable study of American counterculture. Christopher Gair moves fluently and perceptively across fiction, music, painting and film, and demonstrates with great skill the contradictions and tensions internal to countercultural forms and the degree to which they become assimilated to the imperatives of pre-existing ideologies. Gair negotiates the canonical and non-canonical in each of his fields with an adventurousness that is wonderfully informed, lively and stimulating.'

Professor Ian F. A. Bell, University of Keele

The American Counterculture

Christopher Gair

EDINBURGH UNIVERSITY PRESS

© Christopher Gair, 2007

Edinburgh University Press Ltd
22 George Square, Edinburgh

Typeset in Linotype Sabon and Gill Sans by
Iolaire Typesetting, Newtonmore, and
Printed and bound in Spain by GraphyCems

A CIP record for this book is available from the British Library

ISBN 978 0 7486 1988 7 (hardback)
ISBN 978 0 7486 1989 4 (paperback)

Contents

Introduction

A functioning police state needs no police.
William Burroughs, *Naked Lunch* (1959)[1]

Look out kid
It's somethin' you did
God knows when
But you're doin' it again
Bob Dylan, 'Subterranean Homesick Blues' (1965)[2]

It is tempting to start this book with a tidy narrative of origins that identifies one seminal moment as the countercultural Big Bang from which all the radical social and political movements of the 1950s and '60s evolved. Perhaps the morning in July 1947 when Jack Kerouac stacked the pages of his then half-written novel *The Town and the City* in a neat pile, said goodbye to his mother, and headed for Route 6 and his first transcontinental adventure. Maybe it would be better to think of Miles Davis cutting class at, and later dropping out of, the Juilliard School of Music to listen to and jam with Charlie Parker, or of Parker's after-hours bebop sessions at Minton's in Harlem with Charlie Christian, Dizzy Gillespie and others; or the day in 1954 when Leo Fender produced his first Stratocaster, the guitar that – even more than the Gibson Les Paul – would later embody the sleek, sexy look associated with Jimi Hendrix and a legion of other guitar heroes of the 1960s and '70s. We could even begin with the marketing man who first dreamed of transforming denim from the uniform of cowboys and Depression-era 'Okies' heading for California in their jalopies into a staple of youth fashion symbolic of a later Westward migration.

Of course, each of the examples cited above exemplifies the differences between the history and the mythology of what later became known as the 'counterculture'. Kerouac's first day on the road famously ended (as fictionalised in *On the Road*) with the would-be author and traveller no nearer to the West than when he started, soaked to the skin, his dream of hitchhiking across America on 'one long red line'[3] shattered by the realities of the post-war road network. Although Davis did drop out of music school, claiming that 'They weren't teaching me nothing and didn't *know* nothing to teach me because they were so prejudiced against all black music',[4] this did not mean that he ever forgot what he *had* learned there, and this knowledge was one factor in his ability to push jazz in new directions for four decades. The birth of bebop did transform jazz, and Parker became immortalised (along with Jackson Pollock, Billie Holiday, Hank Williams and James Dean) as the prototype of the doomed self-destructive artist later manifested by Hendrix, Janis Joplin, Jim Morrison and many others, but bebop's emergence was less revolutionary and less sudden than the mythology suggests. Although the Stratocaster does symbolise '60s musical cool, Fender himself was a conservative accountant and businessman, often uncomfortable with the (ab)uses to which his instrument was subjected, who sold his company to CBS in 1965. Finally, my fantasy of a lone commercial genius reinventing jeans as fashion icon both illustrates the dependency of the counterculture on the very capitalist structures that it often purported to despise and itself mythologises an increasingly sophisticated corporate structure within traditional narratives of individualism.

It is worth, at the outset, explaining what I hope to achieve in this book. In particular, I want to emphasise that many of the artists and texts that I study worked at the intersection of counter- and popular cultures, and that there is a slippery and often uneasy relationship between the 'mainstream' and the 'marginal'. Although I make numerous references to the more revolutionary wings (in a political as well as artistic sense) of the counterculture, especially in Part Two, I am also eager to investigate representations of the counterculture such as those found in Hollywood movies from the 1950s to the early '70s. These representations veer from the trite and hostile to the sophisticated and sympathetic, and indicate both the increasingly high profile of the counterculture and, at times, the presence of some of its members within the corporate Hollywood movie industry.[5]

It should also be stressed that there were more points of contact between popular and oppositional cultures from the 1950s onward than there had been beforehand, and that it is not always possible or desirable to tell the two apart with absolute certainty. Don Henley's ironic reference to the sight of 'a Dead Head sticker on a Cadillac' in his '80s hit, 'Boys of Summer', is a belated instance of the conflation of the symbols of the counterculture and the corporation. Unlike, for example, the anarchist and socialist movements that had emerged from the immigrant working class in the early twentieth century, the post-war counterculture was largely (though by no means exclusively) composed of members of the white middle class, and many of its leading figures – including, most notoriously, former Yippie, Jerry Rubin – returned to corporate America to make fortunes during the Reagan presidency in the 1980s. One reason for this overlap was technological: in the 1950s, large numbers of Americans were purchasing televisions and watching the popular chat shows that featured interviews with and readings by exotic 'Beatniks' with surprising frequency. Developments in print and recording technology also meant that mass-market magazines could include colour reproductions of art by, among others, the Abstract Expressionists, raising their public profile before many of the artists were able to sell their work. The shift from 78-rpm records to 45s and long players, alongside greatly enhanced sound systems (especially with the arrival of stereo long players in 1957), also increased potential sales and meant that artists often moved from the fringe to the mainstream extremely swiftly. Likewise, advances in radio technology (and portability) meant that teenagers could pick up rock and roll in their bedrooms rather than participating in shared familial experience around the radio or, increasingly, the television. At the same time, the reissue of large numbers of recordings from the 1930s, many collected during field projects by the Library of Congress, fuelled the folk and blues booms of the late 1950s and early 1960s. Bob Dylan recalls how, having just signed his first recording contract, listening to the unreleased acetate of Robert Johnson's *King of the Delta Blues* 'left me numb, like I had been hit by a tranquilizer bullet', transfixed by the 'highly sophisticated' songwriting and performing that he heard.[6] Although Johnson had been dead for more than twenty years by the time Dylan heard him, he would have an equally profound impact on Eric Clapton and The Rolling Stones, pivotal figures in the British blues explosion that popularised the genre in America and Europe in the mid-1960s.

Another major reason for this change was demographic. The Baby

Boomer generation reached their teens and twenties during the period covered by this study and many of them had very different tastes and ambitions to those of their parents. The advent of rock and roll accelerated the adoption of African-American musical forms by white youth, a process that had already been set in motion by the popularity of jazz before the war, and contributed to what many official voices referred to as the 'juvenile delinquency' of the mid-1950s, depicted in such movies as *Rebel Without a Cause*, *The Blackboard Jungle* and *The Wild One*. These movies also established a new group of Hollywood stars, most notably James Dean and Marlon Brando, whose rebellious images appealed to the young. A decade or so later, this generation and their younger siblings would constitute the audience at Woodstock and other large musical gatherings, transforming what had started as local, underground scenes into highly profitable global enterprises.

Finally, the permeability of the culture/counterculture divide was facilitated by the prosperity of post-war America: a great deal of the music, literature, art and film that challenged mainstream values was a product of, rather than a reaction against, the material wealth enjoyed by much of the nation in what was widely believed to be a 'post-scarcity' economy. The expansion of the college and university sector resulted in large numbers of relatively highly educated young people living in close proximity to one another on and around campuses, with considerably more freedom than they had experienced at home. Many of these college (and even high school) students had high disposable incomes, which could facilitate record-buying, travel, experimentation with drugs, and other activities not necessarily endorsed by parents. They also had more leisure time than was the case for earlier generations, where a higher percentage of the school-leaving population would move straight into full-time work. The prevalence of families with more than one car also contributed to the sexual revolution of the period, and it is no coincidence that the songs of Eddie Cochran, The Beach Boys and countless other artists of the 1950s and early '60s celebrate the freedom offered by daddy's T-Bird, or lament its confiscation.

That said, it is easy now to forget how threatening the countercultures of the 1950s and '60s seemed then to many Americans, and not just because we may fail fully to remember the deep-rooted conservatism and hostility to otherness that characterised dominant discourse at the time and, in particular, before the 1960s. In part, this amnesia is a product of a corporate capitalist economy adept at appropriating the symbols of youth protest – the leather jacket, the musical soundtrack, images of long-dead figureheads – whilst stripping them of their original cultural significance. The preponderance of commercials and movies that continue to utilise bebop or rock recorded between the 1940s and early 1970s transform what were often moments of genuine cultural dissidence into shorthand evoking the most simplistic clichés about particular times and places in American history. Culture becomes commodity where, as Herbert Marcuse put it in his philosophical critique of Western society, *One-Dimensional Man* (1964), 'The music of the soul is also the music of salesmanship.'[7] In part, it is simply a question of another generation gap, in which many young Americans today will discover that soundtrack outside its historical context by browsing through their parents' record collections. Alongside critical evaluations of individual texts and artists, this book attempts to re-situate movements and events as parts of wider historical processes at a moment when (even during the apparently stagnant and repressive era of the Eisenhower presidency) times were changing and the arts were in the vanguard of cultural protest.

It is also important, however, to reject the idealistic notion that the icons of the counterculture began (as Greil Marcus warns in an analysis of the young Elvis Presley) 'in a context of purity, unsullied by greed or ambition or vulgarity, somehow outside of or in opposition to American life'. Marcus summarises the consensual view of Elvis's career in a manner that could be adapted easily to fit many of the artists who moved from the margins to become mainstays of corporate popular culture (for example, Marlon Brando, Crosby, Stills and Nash, The Rolling Stones), according to which Elvis's 'folk purity, and therefore his talent' was destroyed by:

(a) his transmogrification from naïve country boy into corrupt pop star . . ., (b) Hollywood, (c) the Army, (d) money and soft living, (e) all of the above.

Marcus's point is that it is misleading to attribute this kind of cultural innocence to individual artists, and entirely to blame corporate capitalism for their 'corruption.' Instead, he argues, Elvis was torn between 'contempt' for dominant society's values and the desire to acquire its 'pleasures and status'.[8] In Elvis's case, the fact that he was poor and from the South – 'white trash' in many people's eyes – meant that the transformation was furthered by his move away from the poverty and social marginalisation inherent to his cultural roots, but similar

5

narratives can be applied to other figures. Miles Davis came from a wealthy middle-class family in Saint Louis, but was also shunned by the white élite because of his colour, and manifested similar contempt and desires; Mick Jagger's middle-class English obscurity was overcome by the ambition to live the life of rock and roll rebel as American Dream, even where that meant singing like white trash and mixing with socialites. Whether through the pervasiveness of consumer culture and a class structure that is apparently in direct opposition to democratic American values, or because of ambition fuelled by individual psychological make-up, these artists, and many more, already have the seeds of their 'selling out' in place in their earliest works. As Marcus points out, Sam Phillips of Sun Records (Elvis's first label) 'loved money and he loved the blues . . . pairing a blues and a country tune on Elvis's first record gave him a successful commercial formula, and he stuck to it on every subsequent Presley release'.[9]

The juxtaposition of 'innocent' artist and 'corrupting' corporation also over-simplifies the way in which capitalist culture's relationship with the consumer functions. Although there is no doubt, as Thomas Frank has argued in *The Conquest of Cool* (1997), that 'youth signifiers are appropriated, produced, and even invented by the entertainment industry', that does not mean that corporations retain control over how these signifiers are received by subcultural groups, who will often reassemble or reinterpret them to meet their own needs. Frank goes further, suggesting that the consumer capitalism of the second half of the twentieth century actively encouraged heterogeneous leisure-time behaviour, including actions that rebelled (or appear to rebel) against institutional forces such as 'patriarchy' or 'the State'. For Frank – following cultural historians Warren Susman and Jackson Lears – consumer capitalism 'did not demand conformity or homogeneity; rather, it thrived on the doctrine of liberation and continual transgression that is still familiar today'.[10]

Frank's thesis is persuasive. He charts the transformation of advertising from its devotion to the mass society of the 1950s into a 1960s art form that, at its best, 'constitutes a kind of mass-culture critique in its own right, a statement of alienation and disgust, of longing for authenticity and for selfhood that ranks with books like *Growing Up Absurd* and movies like *The Graduate*'. Whereas, in the 1950s, advertising was characterised by what Jackson Lears has called 'containment of carnival' and (for Frank) 'a stifling vision of managerial order' in which 'the world of consumer goods was a place of divine detachment, a vision of perfection through products'.[11] by the 1960s advertising narratives 'idealised not the repressed account man in gray flannel, but the manic, unrestrained creative person in offbeat clothing'. The new advertising of the 1960s demanded 'perpetual rebellion against whatever is established, accepted, received',[12] constantly bombarding the consumer with new strategies of representation.

It is here that the blurring of the edges of culture/counterculture becomes most evident. What we must remember, of course, is that these advertising strategies were designed specifically to persuade people to consume, unlike many of the professedly anti-capitalist texts of the counterculture. Although the advertising agencies may well have been owned by and employed individuals who did not conform to dominant social values, they were willing to work for large corporations, and those corporations hired them because of their perceived ability to market their products. But the point is slightly more complex when we consider that countercultural calls to expand individual and communal horizons replicate the demands of a successful American consumer capitalist economy – that is, the perpetual generation of new desires, and a refusal to stick with outmoded goods or ideologies. Furthermore, leading representatives of the counterculture were not averse to participating in advertisements, as with Jefferson Airplane's radio commercials for Levi's jeans.[13]

I do not want to suggest that the relationship between big business and the counterculture necessarily and always worked against the possibility of meaningful or successful protest. During the period covered by this book, many groups emerged that were versed in the techniques of the media and understood how to manipulate them to their own advantage. For example, ecological campaigners were adept at utilising the press to promote their campaigns: Rachel Carson's *Silent Spring* (1962) was an exposé of the threat to nature posed by the pesticide DDT, and an early example of the many texts that highlighted the environmental problems created by overuse of chemicals and man-made changes to the landscape. Although *Silent Spring* was meticulous in its attention to scientific detail, it was also accessible to the lay reader and influenced many subsequent books. Greenpeace – founded in Vancouver in 1971 – quickly realised (as had the Diggers and Yippies a few years earlier) that protest would function most effectively if it took place under the spotlight and pitted courageous bands of 'rainbow warriors' against cynical capitalist corporations or baton-wielding police. Alerting the media ahead of protests became an immensely effective means to alter mass consciousness, since the self-evident passion of the protesters could be conveyed to millions of homes on the television news, even where the numbers of protestors were relatively low.

It is also worth noting that the relationships between political activists and the artistic counterculture were complex and unstable. Many of the leaders of the New Left in the 1960s seem to have had little interest in the more obscure and experimental texts that emerged at the time and were concerned that searches for individual enlightenment – through drugs or meditation – were counterproductive in the drive for social transformation. This does not mean, however, that the political 'movement' and the counterculture were entirely discrete, and Fredric Jameson's separation of the 'counterculture' ('drugs and rock') and the 'student New Left and a mass antiwar movement'[14] is rather silly in the light of, for example, the manner in which former Beats such as Allen Ginsberg and Gary Snyder deliberately and persuasively conflated the two, or the cohabitation of leftists and 'freaks' in Berkeley.

There are, however, also dangers in identifying the counterculture too closely with the New Left. While the two were indubitably united first through civil rights and later in anti-Vietnam War protests, many within the hippie community saw politics as a 'drag' while those in the movement appeared to be both fascinated and appalled by the activities of the Diggers, Yippies and other groups who utilised performance and spectacle to draw attention to their demands. While, following the fragmentation of the Students for a Democratic Society (SDS) in the late 1960s, 'revolutionary' groups like Up Against the Wall, Mother-fucker and the Weather Underground drew on both the politics of the New Left – often simplified into trite slogans and chants – as well as the spectacular effects of countercultural performance, their ideology was remote from both the (largely) non-violent SDS and the 'flower power' of the hippies.

The fragmentation of political and aesthetic elements of youth culture around the end of the 1960s has also helped to determine the shape of this book. Politically, the anti-war *movement* effectively started to dismantle by the early 1970s: although there continued to be large marches, such as the November 1969 demonstration in Washington, the combination of Nixon's promises to abolish the draft (and introduction of a draft ballot), the degree to which anti-war protest became mainstream (that is, taking place in Congress, supported increasingly by widespread public opinion) and the recognition (following the fatal shootings of white protestors at Berkeley in 1969 and Kent State in 1970) that there was no longer what Todd Gitlin calls 'white exemption'[15] from the most extreme forms of state repression contributed to this shift. Even more important were the ruptures within the movement that went beyond debates about the war. Both the SDS and the counterculture (of, for example, the Beats in the 1950s and San Francisco's Haight-Ashbury hippies in the mid-'60s) tended to be overtly sexist in their replication of assumptions about traditional gender roles, and the latter, in particular, was overwhelmingly homophobic.[16] The women's movements and gay rights groups that emerged and thrived during the 1970s were both products of (in terms of membership and tactics) and reactions against the dominant anti-Establishment movements of the 1960s. Thus, while Debra Michals is correct to argue that there is a 'vital link' between feminist strategies in the 1970s and countercultural ones in the '60s, and that the two 'overlap greatly,'[17] it would be a distortion of *the* counterculture and a disservice to the women's and gay rights movements to suggest that the latter were merely subsections of the former. In any case, as Alice Echols has suggested, from this angle the 'problem of the counterculture wasn't that it went too far – the typical view – but rather that its libertinism and its elevation of the far-out masked the ways that the hippie subculture mirrored the values of the dominant culture, especially in regard to women and gays'.[18]

For similar reasons, although there are once more many points of contact, I do not offer detailed discussion of the Black Arts Movement. In the Preface to *The Making of a Counter Culture* (1968) – the book that popularised the term, 'counterculture' – Theodore Roszak rightly points out that 'the situation of black youth requires such special treatment as would run to book length in its own right',[19] a point equally applicable to women's and gay rights, or to environmentalist activism. More prosaically, the break-up of The Beatles and the expansion of the '27 Club', with the deaths of Brian Jones, Jimi Hendrix, Janis Joplin and Jim Morrison between 1969 and 1971, marked the end of whatever 'innocence' remained in youth counterculture. These and other factors lead me to conclude this study around 1972: although – given the way in which history is not divided neatly into decade-length segments – there are occasional encroachments into the '70s, I do not follow the lead of recent revisionists such as many of the contributors to Peter Braunstein and Michael William Doyle's *Imagine Nation: The American Counterculture in the 1960s and '70s* (2002), a study that, despite containing several important reconsiderations, too often takes 'reimaginings' and 'overlaps' as invitations further to extend the already-Harlequin countercultural umbrella.

Instead, I trace a narrative that more or less follows that period identified by Roszak as the era of the counterculture, running (for me) from the birth of bebop, Abstract Expressionism and the Beats to Woodstock, Charles Manson and the confused yet sombre meanings of John Boorman's *Deliverance*. Although this period is one of regular and repeated change, it is also one in which the emergence of 'youth' culture forced continual requestioning of hegemonic ideas about 'America' (or, as the New Left came to call it, 'Amerika' or 'Amerikkka'). As much as anything else that it achieved, the counterculture in these decades brought the limits of national doctrines of 'freedom' to the surface. While – at least in the 'management' of the white middle classes – 1950s America could largely be seen as an exemplification of William Burroughs's dictum that 'a functioning police state needs no police', events in Washington in 1967, Chicago in '68, Berkeley in '69 and at Kent State in 1970 (alongside innumerable lesser-known instances) forced the violently oppressive elements of institutional control into the open and demonstrated the lengths to which the State was willing to go to protect its own interests. As Abbie Hoffman put it, explaining the rationale behind the actions of the Yippies, 'It's all in terms of disrupting the image, the image of a democratic society being run very peacefully and orderly and everything according to business.'[20] The quiet despair felt in the 1950s by figures as disparate as Beats and the housewives questioned by Betty Friedan for *The Feminine Mystique* (1963) were replaced by both the global 'happening' of The Beatles' live satellite performance of 'All You Need Is Love' in 1967 and the clamour on the streets of Chicago transmitted to television sets around the world in August 1968. Throughout, however, there was a sense that the 'adult' world had lost touch with cornerstone American values, and that it was the responsibility of the young to recapture the idealism of an America imagined by, for example, the Transcendentalists, or even Fitzgerald's Jay Gatsby gazing at the green light across the bay from his mansion.

Although I stick fairly closely to Roszak's timeframe, my approach to the counterculture runs along rather different lines. *The Making of a Counter Culture* – alongside Philip Slater's *The Pursuit of Loneliness* (1970), Charles Reich's *The Greening of America* and Richard King's *The Party of Eros* (1972) – offered early, significant attempts to understand what had happened to 'youth' (or at least its more radical elements) in America in the quarter-century after the Second World War. Despite their differences, these books focused on the sociological and political 'thinkers' whose ideas inspired the movement, rather than developing lengthy assessments of the artistic productions that emerged from the counterculture. Thus, although Roszak does devote half a chapter to Allen Ginsberg, he is more interested in Herbert Marcuse, Norman Brown and Paul Goodman; likewise, Richard King supplements chapters on these figures with additional attention to Marx and Freud, but is generally sceptical about the worth of, for example, writing by the Beats or the music of the 1960s. In a new introduction, written for the 1995 reissue of *The Making of a Counter Culture*, Roszak suggests that 'if there is one aspect of the period that I now wish had enjoyed more attention in these pages it is the music',[21] and I hope that the current book will do something to redress the balance. Although length demands its own exclusions – most notably, any lengthy discussion of poetry, sculpture, photography, drama and comics (or 'comix'), without each of which the counterculture would be remembered very differently – my gaze here is fixed firmly on how the aesthetics of the counterculture were played out in its music, fiction, film and painting.

The other principal difference in my approach is an adjustment of the balance of group and individual 'influence' on the counterculture. In addition to the sociological and philosophical thinkers listed above, early historians stressed the significance of the Transcendentalist legacy on radical arts after the Second World War. Richard King puts the point most directly, talking of a 'second transcendentalist revolt' coming at the end of the period of Western industrialisation whose beginning was marked by the original Transcendentalists, and noting the shift from a vision of Nature as the 'vehicle, in mediating terms, for the moral and the spiritual' to one where 'Nature, as the sexual and the erotic, becomes the touchstone of individual and collective virtue and health'.[22] I do not wish to downplay the significance of the Transcendentalists, whose legacy is apparent in instances as diverse as Beat fiction and poetry, Abstract Expressionist art and in the communes of the 1960s. Nevertheless, the emphasis on Transcendentalism and European philosophy negates the importance of other sources; most notably, African-American art and culture. While the strategies learned during civil rights struggles in the 1950s and early '60s later helped to shape anti-war protest on and beyond campuses, bop and blues were equally fundamental to the counterculture from the Beats to Woodstock and beyond. As I suggest, their adoption was rarely unproblematic, raising questions of appropriation and of essentialised concepts of race, but this in no way undermines their significance. In the same manner, the presence – and absence – of African-Americans within the counterculture offers many reminders that this was largely a white movement. It is often suggested that Janis Joplin owed her 'overnight' success following her performance at Monterey in 1967 to the absence of singers like Aretha Franklin, whilst Jimi Hendrix's performance at Woodstock can be seen to illustrate the uncomfortable residual racism present at a gathering devoted to 'Three Days of Peace and Music'. Although, as I suggested above, this is not the place for a detailed study of Black Arts, neither is it a site where the role of African-American art in determining the shape of the counterculture is forgotten.

Acknowledgements

Whereas the counterculture was often criticised for its inability to resolve the tensions between its individualistic and collective goals, this project has reminded me how much the 'solo' activities of authorship depend on the personal and professional relationships that surround them. Like many pre-college children growing up in small towns in the 1960s and early '70s, I was fascinated by the exotic spectacle of a counterculture that seemed at once remote and deeply attractive. My father's 'folkie' antipathy to The Beatles' use of electric guitars – 'bastardising a perfectly good instrument' – and my grandfather's self-mocking reflection on how, after working on the door when the band played in Cambridge in 1962, he was convinced that they had no future in entertainment, made me aware, early on, of the gaps between those coming of age pre- and post-Elvis, and also of the kinds of intergenerational countercultural hostility witnessed when Bob Dylan 'went electric' at the Newport Folk Festival in 1965. Nightly games of cricket – the game of the British Empire – with the 'freaks' attending the Isle of Wight Festival in 1969 and 1970, suggested that in many ways their 'otherness' was less extreme, if more exciting, than my (other) grandfather believed rather too passionately. Much later, my teenage daughter Izzy's fascination with Dylan and The Band, and her scepticism about some of my own more far-fetched enthusiasms, provided both confirmation of the on-going interest in the arts of the '60s and a rejoinder to the dangers of becoming too attached to a subject. While I am an unashamed 'fan' of many of the artists covered in this book, I hope that I am also a critic of the tensions and problems within their work.

My 'professional' interest in the counterculture does not go back quite so far as my 'personal' one, but it also depends on the insights and reservations offered by others. In particular, Richard King and Dave

Murray at the University of Nottingham introduced me to the tools with which I could adapt interest into interrogation without losing sight of the aesthetic reasons for tackling the subject in the first place. Although it would be a slight on the camaraderie offered by current and former colleagues to make an absolute distinction between 'social' and 'scholarly' contributors, I owe major debts to academics and students who did not let the etiquette of friendship stand in the way of devotion to professional duty in their scrupulous attention to earlier versions of this project. As ever, a particular debt goes to Scott Lucas for his enthusiastic encouragement and critically informed advice. Other colleagues and postgraduate students in the Department of American and Canadian Studies at the University of Birmingham were unfailing in their support. In particular, Luke Brown, Ian Edwards, Dick Ellis, Andy Green, Liam Kennedy, Paul Woolf and Sara Wood offered invaluable advice in conversation and in their readings of draft chapters. I would also like to thank Ian Bell, Brian Hoyle, Joel Pace, Jay Williams and Lia Yoka for their help in clearing the (metaphorical) smoke that clouded my vision of the counterculture. If a haze remains, it is through no fault of theirs. More than anything else, I express my gratitude to Aliki Varvogli, whose companionship, scholarship and patience all made this book possible. Maybe The Beatles went too far when they claimed that 'Love is all you need', but it certainly goes a long way.

Every effort has been made to trace copyright holders, but if any have been inadvertently overlooked the publisher will be pleased to make the necessary arrangement at the first opportunity.

Notes

1. William Burroughs, *Naked Lunch* (London: Flamingo, 1993), p. 41.
2. Bob Dylan, 'Subterranean Homesick Blues' released as a single and on the album *Bringing It All Back Home* (Columbia, 1965). Copyright © 1965, renewed 1993. Special Rider Music.
3. Jack Kerouac, *On the Road* (London: Penguin, 1976), p. 15.
4. Miles Davis with Quincy Troupe, *Miles: The Autobiography* (London: Picador, 1990), p. 50.
5. See Peter Biskind, *Easy Riders, Raging Bulls: How the Sex 'n' Drugs 'n' Rock 'n' Roll Generation Saved Hollywood* (London: Bloomsbury, 1998).
6. Bob Dylan, *Chronicles: Volume One* (London: Simon and Schuster, 2004), pp. 283–4.
7. Herbert Marcuse, *One-Dimensional Man* (London: Ark paperbacks, 1986),

p. 57. A prime example of this is Wrangler's use of Creedence Clearwater Revival's anti-Vietnam War song, 'Fortunate Son' (1969), in a series of jeans commercials in 2001. Wrangler used only the first two lines – 'Some folks are born, made to wave the flag, Ooh, that red, white and blue' – encouraging a patriotic interpretation entirely at odds with the remainder of the song. The (unused) lines that follow are: 'And when the band plays "Hail to the Chief", Ooh, they're pointin' the cannon at you, Lord.'

8. Greil Marcus, *Mystery Train: Images of America in Rock 'n' Roll Music*, 5th edn (London: Faber and Faber, 2000), pp. 176, 177.

9. Ibid., p. 176.

10. Thomas Frank, *The Conquest of Cool: Business Culture, Counterculture, and the Rise of Hip Consumerism* (Chicago: University of Chicago Press, 1997), p. 18, p. 20.

11. Ibid., p. 55, p. 54, p. 77.

12. Ibid., p. 54, p. 85.

13. See Richie Unterberger, *Eight Miles High: Folk Rock's Flight From Haight-Ashbury to Woodstock* (San Francisco: Backbeat Books, 2003), p. 35.

14. Fredric Jameson, 'Periodizing the 60s,' in Jameson, *The Ideologies of Theory: Essays 1971–1986, Volume 2: The Syntax of History* (Routledge: London: 1988), p. 180.

15. Todd Gitlin, *The Sixties: Years of Hope, Days of Rage* (New York: Bantam, 1987), p. 361.

16. See Robert McRuer, 'Gay Gatherings: Reimagining the Counterculture', in Peter Braunstein and Michael William Doyle (eds), *Imagine Nation: the American Counterculture of the 1960s and '70s* (London: Routledge, 2002), p. 217.

17. Debra Michals, 'From "Consciousness Expansion" to "Consciousness Raising": Feminism and the Countercultural Politics of the Self', in Braunstein and Doyle (eds), *Imagine Nation*, p. 42, p. 45.

18. Alice Echols, *Shaky Ground: The Sixties and Its Aftershocks* (New York: Columbia University Press, 2002), p. 9.

19. Theodore Roszak, *The Making of a Counter Culture: Reflections on the Technocratic Society and Its Youthful Opposition* (Berkeley: University of California Press, 1995), p. xl. A superb book that (indirectly) responds to this call as well as suggesting some of the overlaps between black arts and the counterculture is James Edward Smethurst's, *The Black Arts Movement: Literary Nationalism in the 1960s and 1970s* (Chapel Hill: University of North Carolina Press, 2005).

20. Abbie Hoffman, *Revolution for the Hell of It* (New York: Dial Press, 1968), p. 143.

21. Roszak, *The Making of a Counter Culture*, p. xxxiv.

22. Richard King, *The Party of Eros: Radical Social Thought and the Realm of Freedom* (Chapel Hill: University of North Carolina Press, 1972), p. 174.

Part One
1945–1960

Introduction

Nineteen fifty-five was the apex of the Age of Ike, the year
that President Dwight Eisenhower, in golfing togs, climbed
into an electric cart with the presidents of General Electric
and General Motors and rolled down the fairway. Business
was good and the country was easy, and the French sur-
render to the Vietnamese army at Dien Bien Phu was
happening half a world away. A retired general was running
the country, and that was good, because the United States
and the Soviet Union were in the middle of an arms build-
up, and the Soviets had just raised the ante by developing
their own hydrogen bomb – very likely employing secrets
stolen from the U.S.

Lewis MacAdams, *Birth of the Cool* (2001)[1]

The worlds overlapped in a million ways and places. The art
world, the worlds of jazz, of modern classical music, of
painting and poetry and dance were all interconnected.
There were endless interweavings; they happened slowly,
over several years, and they were the stronger for that slow
growth.

Diane di Prima,
Recollections of My Life as a Woman (2001)[2]

Around this time [1949] . . . Ralph Bunche had just won the
Nobel Prize. Joe Louis had been heavyweight champion of
the world for a long time by then, and he was every black

> person's hero – and a lot of white people's too. Sugar Ray
> Robinson wasn't far behind him in popularity . . . Jackie
> Robinson and Larry Doby were playing baseball in the
> major leagues. Things were beginning to happen for black
> people in this country.
>
> Miles Davis with Quincy Troupe,
> Miles: The Autobiography (1989)[3]

Despite some recent attempts to revisit the 1950s more critically, many conservative Americans continue to look back at the decade as a golden age of ideological consensus. Thus, although movies such as *Quiz Show* (1994), *Pleasantville* and *The Truman Show* (both 1998) peep beneath the veneer of small town or suburban domestic contentment, the era is still celebrated by those on the political right as a time of sexual innocence, cultural accord, and moral and economic stability. For them, the '50s was a period when Americans united against the threat from the Soviet Union and Communism, and benefited from the economic boom that provided high disposable incomes and increased leisure opportunities. Accelerated technological innovation meant that more people than ever before could own automobiles refrigerators, and televisions, but, in an age before cable and satellite technology, viewing options were limited and the moral content of what was broadcast was easier to police. Although the wholesale relocation of the white middle classes to the suburbs could be seen to challenge community spirit, the fact that families were able to watch favourite programmes together and discuss them with school- or workmates the next day established a common bond sufficient to substitute for earlier social activity.

Of course, this picture represents only part of the story, and even that part is more complex than the nostalgic vision would suggest. It is true that the standard of living of many Americans, and not only those from the expanding white middle class, did rise: the post-war years saw a new wave of southern African-Americans move to northern American cities and into comparatively well-paid jobs, even if this employment lacked the relative security of rural work. On the other hand, many African-Americans and women were displaced from the labour market by white servicemen returning from the war, and black soldiers coming home 'having risked their lives for this country' discovered, as LeRoi Jones put it in *Blues People* (1963), 'that they were still treated like subhumans'.[4] For Ralph Ellison, in *Invisible Man* (1952), the confusion his nameless black narrator finds inherent to living in New York City emanates from a situation where whites are generally polite to him, but are unable to see beyond their own preconceptions about race to imagine him as an individual. Ellison suggests that this leads to profound difficulties in defining individual African-American selfhood within – but also beyond – the stereotypes constructed by both white and black Americans.

It was these and similar circumstances that contributed to the emergence of the civil rights movement and (for related reasons) to the stirrings of a new feminism. But prosperity also brought other problems and conflicts: although the advent of the teenager as a phenomenon is often mistakenly located in the 1950s when it seems more appropriate to suggest that the swing era of the mid-1930s witnessed the emergence of the kind of youth culture that resurfaced with rock and roll twenty years later, the teens who danced to Elvis and watched James Dean were perceived as more of a threat to social cohesion than their 1930s counterparts.

Pleasantville is representative of Hollywood's recent attempts to revisit the 1950s, and is a useful illustration of how the period continues to be viewed. Juxtaposing a 1990s America of dysfunctional families, teenage sexual freedom and multiculturalism with a black-and-white '50s soap that foregrounds the strict moral and social codes that governed popular representations at the time, the movie initially suggests that the past offers respite from the complexities of post-modern late-twentieth-century life. The transplantation of sister and brother teens into the soap, however, rapidly unearths the tensions at the heart of the stereotype: the movie indicates that apparent simplicity and conformity are the products of a society that is insular, repressed and intolerant of anything that challenges the comfortably 'pleasant' (white only) community. The freedom of expression and sexual and emotional liberation that stem from the siblings' arrival result in a book-burning, window-smashing mob attempting to restore 'order' with the tacit support of the town elders. The visually effective introduction of colour to Pleasantville reminds us of how grey the town's 1950s world really is, and allows the film to enact a series of puns on the racial dimensions of 'color'. The movie suggests that contemporary society can learn from the past – both siblings mature as a result of the experience and examine the shallowness of their own lives – but that the past would also have been better if it had been willing to embrace aesthetic and sexual freedoms, even when these could be disturbing.

As such, *Pleasantville* offers an astute commentary on hegemonic attitudes from the 1950s, and also on the way in which our culture still draws on what Fredric Jameson calls the 1950s' 'own representation of itself' in its popular television programmes as source for our reconstructions of the decade. As Jameson points out, 'high' art (and, we could add, much countercultural art) was unwilling or unable to engage with the 'stifling Eisenhower realities of the happy family in the small town, of normalcy and nondeviant everyday life'. Instead, these representations came in the form of a mass culture recording the very kind of ' "false" happiness . . . that has no way of telling itself apart from genuine satisfaction and fulfilment since it has presumably never encountered this last',[5] precisely the genre that is parodied so cleverly in the early stages of *Pleasantville*.

Despite this knowingness about its use of representation, however, there are also limits to *Pleasantville*'s critique. In particular, it does little to investigate the roots of suburban bigotry and pays scant attention to genuine historical detail. Thus, whereas the kind of imagined community represented in the movie would have been forced, in the 1960s, to confront apparently irreconcilable attitudes to race, freedom of sexual expression and the Vietnam War, *Pleasantville* seems to pretend that – bar its limited allusions to the sexual revolution – the '60s never happened, and offers a cosy resolution in which the town becomes interested in life beyond its boundaries, and where the exploration of an emotional intensity that transcends the 'pleasant' is embraced by everyone. Unsurprisingly, given Hollywood's need for upbeat endings, the film closes with Pleasantville accepting individual freedom, and with the suggestion that all can be made well in both past and contemporary America.

Although *Pleasantville*'s tidy resolution fails fully to address the consequences of 1950s suburban isolationism, the movie does deal with the themes that preoccupied many of the pre-eminent sociologists of the time. Strikingly, although the post-war period was marked by the emergence of the civil rights movement, by the Korean War, by the onset of the Cold War, by the FBI's J. Edgar Hoover-led paranoia about 'Beatniks' and by McCarthyism, much of the academic discourse that was produced at the time avoided these issues, or tackled them in uncontroversial fashion. In one way, this is unsurprising: given the climate of fear that stemmed from McCarthy's investigations, many academics chose to steer clear of overtly 'political' topics. The study of English literature, for example, was marked by the New Critics' interest in the work of art *itself*, usually stripped of any political or historical context. The emergence of American Studies as an academic discipline in the 1950s resulted in books by critics such as R. W. B. Lewis, Richard

Chase and Harry Levin that used classic American literature to illustrate United States exceptionalism and to justify the nation's resistance to the 'totalitarian' Soviet Union. Although a few critics did put forward narratives counter to this kind of celebration of nationhood – see, for example, C. L. R. James's *Mariners, Renegades, and Castaways* (1953) and C. Wright Mills's *The Power Elite* (1956) – their views were largely ignored in narratives of white America's triumph.[6]

The critiques of American society that did emerge tended to focus on problems associated with a culture of consumption, marked by material abundance, rather than on questions of race or poverty, and were clear in their distinction between these issues and the much more serious flaws they identified (either explicitly or implicitly) in the totalitarian Soviet Union. Thus, although a writer such as Michael Harrington could produce a series of studies of poverty in the United States (most notably, *The Other America*, 1962), the vast majority of 'major' texts at the time focused on the suburbs and the middle classes. Books like David Riesman's *The Lonely Crowd* (1950) and William H. Whyte's *The Organization Man* (1956)[7] are more concerned with white-collar employees in corporate middle management than with factory workers. For Riesman and Whyte, the figure of the 'inner-directed' man – that is, the hard-working, self-made American epitomised in Benjamin Franklin's *Autobiography* (1793) – is replaced by the 'other-directed' character whose sense of self and relations with the outside world are largely shaped by consumption and by the mass media.

Riesman and Whyte both explore the dangers associated with other-directedness. On the one hand, they highlight the perils of what Whyte calls the 'soothing' powers of the organisation, which has become so powerful that it risks the destruction of individual 'intellectual armour'.[8] On the other, there is the individual's fear of shallow conformity in a world defined largely by economic success. It is the latter point that is adopted more fully by two other critics, whose work points directly to the alienation felt by many young people within affluent suburban America in the 1950s.

Paul Goodman and Betty Friedan

In some ways, Paul Goodman's *Growing Up Absurd* (1960) and Betty Friedan's *The Feminine Mystique* (1963) may seem like strange books to examine in a study of the counterculture. Although Goodman is sensitive to the causes of youth discontent, he is generally unsympathetic to the alternatives put forward by, in particular, the Beats. Likewise, though Friedan's work has assumed retrospective status as a pioneering example of the feminism that would emerge in more radical forms later in the 1960s, its subject is almost exclusively the middle-class American housewife whose routine of cooking, cleaning, coffee mornings and school-runs represents everything that the counterculture sought to reject. And yet, both texts point to the problems ignored by the mass cultural shows parodied in *Pleasantville* yet inherent to the suburban culture of consumption, and both highlight the sense of alienation felt by many individuals within this society in ways that echo or anticipate statements made by countercultural artists.

Goodman's thesis is relatively straightforward and – unusually for a sociological study – depends upon the author's candid confession that the book stems from his own 'tears of frank dismay for the waste of our humanity' in the estrangement of young males from dominant American culture.[9] For Goodman, issues such as juvenile delinquency and Beat ennui are the products of corporate America's cynical indifference to any needs of the individual that transcend the economic. Likewise, events like the quiz show fraud of 1959 or the payola scandal that destroyed the career of top rock and roll disc jockey Alan Freed in 1960 are exemplifications of a corrupt American culture, 'doomed to nausea and barbarism',[10] and offering no meaningful guidance to the nation's youth. The problem with American life, as Goodman sees it, is the absence of 'real opportunities for worthwhile experience'[11] in a society where men are allocated to jobs wherever they are required in the productive system, and persuaded to consume worthless goods through incessant advertising and peer pressure. Goodman dismisses what he sees as the dominant belief that people can be adapted to do anything and argues that problems in growing up are the consequences of a social structure that is 'against human nature, or not worthy of human nature'. Thus, in a summary that rejects almost all hegemonic ideas about the United States, he suggests that:

Our abundant society is at present simply deficient in many of the most elementary objective opportunities and worth-while goals that could make growing up possible. It is lacking in enough man's work. It is lacking in honest public speech, and people are not taken seriously. It is lacking in the opportunity to be useful. It thwarts aptitude and creates stupidity. It corrupts ingenuous patriotism. It corrupts the fine arts. It shackles science. It dampens animal ardour. It discourages the religious convictions of Justification and Vocation and it dims the sense that there is a creation. It has no Honor. It has no Community.[12]

Goodman's critique stems from a perspective based closely upon the earlier 'inner-directed' model of American selfhood, in which personal fulfilment comes from meaningful, satisfying employment, rather than from consumption. As such, it rejects the replacement of production-based capitalism with the culture of consumption and manifests nostalgia for an earlier American society. The qualities valued by Goodman – such as personal freedom, utility, 'genuine culture' – are perceived as dangerous in an economy that places 'maximum profits and full employment' above true individual fulfilment.[13] Although Goodman does not recognise it, this aspect of *Growing Up Absurd* is similar to the ethos of many Beat artists, who likewise sought meaning in work – for them, usually writing or painting – rather than in the acquisition of material things. It also implicitly shares the Beat interest in nineteenth-century 'countercultural' opposition to the onset of the American industrial revolution, when Transcendentalist writers such as Ralph Waldo Emerson in 'Self-Reliance' (1841) and Henry David Thoreau in *Walden* (1854) warned of the dangers facing American manhood in the face of new economic realities. This kind of resistance to modernity, grounded in Transcendentalist anti-materialism, became one of the defining features of the counterculture of the 1950s and '60s, although it was often ironically juxtaposed with a fondness for the material comforts provided by the corporate economy that the counterculture purported to oppose.

Goodman's concern – like Emerson and Thoreau's a century before – is with the crisis facing American masculinity, since he claims that 'a girl' is 'not expected to "make something" of herself . . . for she will have children, which is absolutely self-justifying, like any other natural or creative act'. And yet, when he suggests that a society obsessed with a 'so-called high standard of living of mediocre value'[14] is bound to generate individual emotional and intellectual discontent, he inadvertently addresses many of the problems associated with white suburban womanhood by Betty Friedan in *The Feminine Mystique*. Thus, although Goodman focuses on young males and Friedan on wives and mothers, they share a strikingly similar perspective in their critiques of dominant structures that make it hard for individuals to articulate their discontents.

In Friedan's case, this difficulty provides the title of the opening chapter of *The Feminine Mystique*, 'The Problem That Has No Name'. For Friedan, middle-class women have been afraid even silently to ask the question, 'Is this all?', since the combination of abundant consumer comforts and (largely male) 'experts' telling them that they have all they could desire results in any kind of discontent being internalised as personal deficiency. Within an unashamedly patriarchal society, all women have to do is 'devote their lives from earliest girlhood to finding a husband and bearing children', since to desire a career, political rights, or higher education is 'unfeminine'.[15] The difficulty for any woman not content with such a constrictive role is the sheer weight of 'expertise' pitted against her: in the 1950s, advertisers promoted hair products and diets to condition appearance, and bombarded women with information about the ideal kitchen, now 'once again the center of [their] lives'. In this world, there is no apparent difference between individual liberty and the ability to consume – 'She was free to choose automobiles, clothes, appliances, supermarkets; she had everything that women ever dreamed of.' Doctors and psychoanalysts supplemented the message, all seeming to endorse the same image of ideal womanhood, while media culture sexualised girls at ever-younger ages.[16]

Echoing Thoreau's assessment of American (male) life a century before, Friedan observes the 'quiet desperation' surrounding women's 'problem that has no name'. These women feel 'empty' and 'incomplete' and discover that redecorating the house or resorting to tranquillisers does little to help.[17] Although the media were becoming aware of the issue by the late 1950s, the expert remedies published in mass magazines – offering classes in adjusting to domestic life, tips to improve sexual satisfaction, advice to have more children – all fail to address what Friedan sees as the real causes of discontent. In part, this appears to be the result of the newness of a problem not related to poverty or sickness, and not (directly, at least) related to sex. Friedan's response is similar to Goodman's analysis of the alienation felt by young American males: the women she discusses share the sense that not only do their domestic routines not satisfy deeper human needs, they also mitigate against this satisfaction, since they attack the power to concentrate on reading anything more demanding than a magazine.

Friedan ends her opening chapter on a positive note, suggesting that women are starting to listen to their inner voice and seeking a truth that has 'been puzzling their [male] doctors and educators for years . . . "I want something more than my husband and my children and my home." '[18] Much of her work depends on case studies, and, importantly, on the realisation that the sharing of experience offers women the best chance of addressing problems that are not tackled effectively within patriarchal society. Although the issues discussed in *The Feminine Mystique* hardly seem radical when contrasted with the feminism of the later 1960s, this is one important aspect of the book that anticipates the kinds of collective action advocated by later feminists as an alternative to the culture of individualism that did so much to silence women's voices.

The Feminine Mystique illustrates the difficulties faced by women when they attempted to articulate their discontents in 1950s America. In addition, it indicates how hard it was for middle-class women to abandon the kind of life that consumer capitalism promised, since rejection of the path to husband, suburban home and children tended to lead to accusations of being 'unfeminine'. As such, it also points to several issues that directly relate to the emergence of the counterculture. First, it is important to note that both Goodman and Friedan's books claim that there were large numbers of white middle-class Americans feeling alienated within a culture of material abundance. Although, of course, only a small proportion would abandon this life for the impoverished bohemianism of Greenwich Village described by Diane di Prima in her autobiography, *Recollections of My Life as a Woman* (2001), or in John Clellon Holmes's Beat Generation novel, *Go* (1952), this does illustrate the fact that widespread discontent with suburban values was not a new phenomenon in the 1960s. As di Prima and other countercultural women in the 1950s and '60s discovered, however, the rejection of a culture of consumption by male Beats tended not to be accompanied by similar rejection of that culture's patriarchal values.

Friedan's study is rooted in 1950s American suburban culture, but does inadvertently point to at least two other factors relating to the countercultural explosion of the 1960s. The sexualisation of girls – with 'brassieres with false bosoms of foam rubber for little girls of ten' – and the startling drop in the average marriage age of women to twenty by the end of the 1950s probably had the unintended consequence of raising knowledge of and curiosity about sex in ways that did not necessarily involve engagement or marriage. The ten-year-olds of the late '50s were the late-teenagers of 1967's 'Summer of Love', and many were involved in the sexual liberation of that time. Likewise, the post-war culture's focus on encouraging women to find fulfilment through motherhood led to a situation where women 'who had once

25

wanted careers were now making careers out of having babies',[19] and to a baby boom that would have a profound impact on the demographic spread of the 1960s. As a result of the same economic optimism that fuelled the move to the suburbs in the 1950s, the unprecedented numbers of Americans reaching adulthood in the early 1960s would be able to congregate on university campuses and have the economic security to enjoy both the leisure and political dimensions of a youth culture that would reject many hegemonic values.

The Emergence of a Counterculture

The most significant obstacle facing the subjects of Goodman and Friedan's studies was the difficulty inherent in finding a discourse of protest that could counter the many voices championing the benefits of 'American' life. As *The Feminine Mystique* makes clear, it is hard to articulate alienation or unhappiness as anything other than a personal problem, rooted in personal or familial failings, when every authority tells you that you are living the American Dream. Given the political climate of the Cold War, it is also evident that the leftist politics of the 1930s would not attract widespread support, and, as we shall see, it is notable that the Beats and associated countercultural movements of the 1950s seemed (with a few notable exceptions) largely uninterested in major political campaigns. Instead, they tended to appeal to what they identified as genuine 'American' values, such as individual freedom of choice, as alternatives to a corporate capitalism that they perceived to be corrupting American ideals.

Significantly, however, the language used to express these views often attempted to mimic the voices of an urban African-American culture largely denied both the freedoms that the Beats saw as epitomising true American individualism and the spoils of American national prosperity. There is an irony in this appropriation that appears to have been lost on many of the Beats themselves, since their focus on certain forms of African-American cultural production was not paired with much understanding of the historical factors that had helped to shape black art. Although there was only minor interest in civil rights on the part of most of the Beat Generation, for example, the attention that they paid to jazz and urban black vernacular is evident in their writings and lifestyles. Likewise, the emergence of rock and roll as soundtrack to the new teenage generation represented an engagement with African-American musical forms by white teenagers based – at least in part – on rather simplistically identifying their own feelings of alienation with the very different conditions experienced by the music's African-American originators, a point ironically undermined by the fact that most of the biggest stars were white.

Although many of what later became known as the 'Beat Generation' had met in New York in the early 1940s, their profile only started to assume national significance as an alternative to white American orthodoxies after the publication of Allen Ginsberg's *Howl and Other Poems* in 1956. Drawing on a combination of Walt Whitman's free verse and black bebop jazz idioms, Ginsberg offers a hyperbolic indictment of 'respectable' American culture, highlighting many of the dissatisfactions pointed to by Goodman and Friedan, but voicing his own oppositional stance more dramatically. The title poem itself opens with probably the best-known countercultural assault on the damaging effects to the individual of authoritarian surveillance and control, with Ginsberg witnessing the 'best minds of my generation destroyed by madness, starving hysterical naked, / dragging themselves through the negro streets at dawn looking for an angry fix',[20] in a lengthy passage chronicling his own and his friends' mental instability and turn to drugs, jazz, alcohol and (homosexual) sex as alternatives to the stifling worlds of the university and the workplace.

Following the highly personal narratives of part one, part two of 'Howl' constitutes an attack on a patriarchal society willing to sacrifice its children to an obsession with profit. Using imagery reminiscent of the closing chapters of Herman Melville's *Pierre* (1852), Ginsberg berates a culture so obsessed with wealth that it is blind to beauty and condemns emotion. This society – named 'Moloch' in the poem after the Canaanite fire god for whom parents burned their children in sacrifice – is seen as a machine, a prison, a 'cannibal dynamo' and as the home of 'granite cocks! monstrous bombs!', and Ginsberg expresses anxiety about the difficulties inherent in avoiding complicity with its systems. Therefore, the final section, with its repeated refrain, 'I'm with you in Rockland', also appears to look back to the Transcendentalists, in this case to find a place from which to critique society. In 'Resistance to Civil Government' (1849), Thoreau suggested that, 'Under a government which imprisons any unjustly, the true place for a just man is also a prison.'[21] In an age where analysis was often seen as little more than the chance to re-tune 'malfunctioning' individuals (such as homosexuals) and adjust them in anticipation of a return to 'normal' life, for Ginsberg – as later for Ken Kesey in *One Flew Over the Cuckoo's Nest* (1962) – the jailhouse is replaced by the asylum as the only place to find any kind of salvation and personal integrity.

Although 'Howl' often veers towards the melodramatic in its representations of a generation driven to insanity, it is important to historicise the poem within the crisis-strewn culture in which it was produced. Lewis MacAdams has suggested that the 'dizzying inconsistencies of prosperity and the Cold War made 1955 the nadir of American paranoia',[22] an argument that is borne out by the plethora of political and popular cultural responses to the fear of nuclear annihilation. The Civil Defense Administration distributed sixteen million copies of its pamphlet *Survival Under Atomic Attack* in an effort to reassure citizens and on 15 June 1955 Operation Alert simulated a Russian nuclear attack on the nation, with everyone being required to take cover for fifteen minutes. The release of *Godzilla*, the low-budget Hollywood movie *Them* (both 1954) and *The Invasion of the Body Snatchers* (1956), with their respective casts of dinosaur, giant mutant killer ants and seed pods, provided allegorical portrayals of the fears felt by much of the population.[23]

Nevertheless, 'Howl' is also representative of a trend in counter-cultural art at the time that is as much to do with form as with content. The poem was first presented at the Six Gallery in San Francisco on 13 October 1955 as part of a reading by five poets (the others were Michael McClure, Gary Snyder, Philip Whalen and Philip Lamantia), in an event that is often celebrated as one of the founding moments of countercultural artistic expression. As Preston Whaley has noted, there are few certainties about the details of the night, which was most famously recalled in Kerouac's novel *The Dharma Bums* (1958), a work of the imagination rather than a claim to historical fact. Whaley points out that the 'multiple versions of the story reflect its oral basis . . . this story slants toward myth in the sense that its facts are variant and its presence ubiquitous, both in oral and later in literary-cultural histories'. This multiple, oral telling – which runs counter to ordered, written 'official' versions of history – coupled with the 'decidedly antibourgeois' content and tone of the event, has served to establish the countercultural significance of the Six Gallery reading as birthplace of both the San Francisco Renaissance and the Beat Generation.[24]

The fact that 'Howl' was delivered in this manner before it was published is significant: Ginsberg's dramatic readings of his work stressed the physicality of his verse in a way that matches Jackson Pollock's style of painting or the early performances of Elvis Presley, and self-consciously draws on the breathing techniques of bop musicians. In each case, the emphasis on the body functions as a rejection of a puritanical legacy in which physicality is repressed and, additionally for Ginsberg, offers a way to move outside the then dominant New Critical celebration of poetry that, as Michael Davidson puts it, 'valued detachment and ironic distance'. For Davidson, such physicality is inherent to a poetry that emerged in the 1950s 'through a return to speech rhythms, through the disordering of conventional syntax, through a lineation based on the breath', and is characteristic of the poetry of Charles Olsen, Robert Creeley and others, as well as Ginsberg.[25]

The overlaps between various forms of countercultural artistic production at this time are no coincidence. In the America of 'Howl' and *Growing Up Absurd*, where the pressure to conform and to prosper financially was so overwhelming, it is unsurprising that artists working in different genres should construct communities like that in Manhattan's Greenwich Village. Although there were indubitably tensions between, for example, black musicians and Beat poets, or even white and black Beats – as well as clear differences between choosing to drop out of hegemonic white society or being marginalised by that society's racism – the social ties inherent in a community encouraged individual formal experimentation within a collective environment marked by rejection of artistic as well as political conventions. Thus, when art critic Harold Rosenberg begins his seminal essay 'The American Action Painters' (1952) with observations on the spontaneity of painters like Pollock, and on how the canvas 'began to appear to one American painter after another as an arena in which to act . . . not a picture but an event', he could also be describing the Beat approach to poetry or prose.[26]

Rosenberg's observation that the typical Action Painter 'is not a young painter but a re-born one. The man may be over forty, the painter around seven' also relates to the radical rejection of traditional form and content inherent to Beat writing and bop jazz. Where Pollock and others had begun their artistic careers as participants in the social realist movement of the 1930s, Ginsberg's early poetry is also more formal than his much better known later verse, and Jack Kerouac's first published novel, *The Town and the City* (1950), adheres to the conventional crafted realism that he would later abandon. Likewise, although its emergence as an alternative to the big-band swing and jazz of the late 1930s has been overly mythologised, bebop is another example of an art form that deploys the mastery of dominant structures in the creation of a radically different aesthetic encouraging the visionary rather than the representational.

It would, however, be overstating the case to argue that McCarthyism managed to silence all the leftist artists of the pre-war era, or to turn them from social realists into 'apolitical' experimentalists. Small communities of activists did survive, and subsequently also proved influential in shaping the counterculture of the 1960s. For example, the actor Will Geer, who had starred in films such as *Broken Arrow* and *Winchester 73* (both 1950) before falling foul of the House UnAmerican Activities Committee and losing his home and most of his money, bought a house and land in the then virtually deserted Topanga Canyon north-west of Los Angeles. Geer established his Theatricum Botanicum, an open-air summer theatre performing the works of (among others) Shakespeare and Tennessee Williams for anyone who happened to be passing. The group was successful in itself, but is also significant in the way that it established Topanga – later the home of Neil Young and other countercultural icons – as a site for communal artistic experimentation close enough to LA to enable easy access, but also remote and (at the time) inexpensive enough to sustain non-mainstream artists living what was generally a simple, communal existence. The presence of folksinger Woody Guthrie, who stayed on Geer's land for periods during the 1950s, is a further indicator of the ongoing significance of such leftist projects, with Guthrie, of course, becoming the most important formative influence on Bob Dylan.

Rock and Roll Rebels Without a Cause: The Emergence of the Teenager

In an important reconsideration of post-Second World War America, Alice Echols has suggested that many critics 'mistake the fissures of the fifties for the outright rebellion of the sixties'.[27] Her point is that the sites of cultural and political resistance identified by recent historians in, for example, magazines directed at African-American women were localised instances of defiance of dominant culture rather than the harbingers of fully-fledged revolution. Echols is talking here about the place of women in the United States at the time, but her argument is also applicable more widely: despite occasional media or political hysteria such as the widespread attack on 'Beatniks', the 'countercultural' (retrospectively to apply a term not widely used until the following decade) arts of the 1950s were a sideshow when contrasted with the mass movements that fused a rock soundtrack with anti-war protest a decade later.

There is no doubt, however, that the seeds of '60s activism *were* nurtured by the very different but connected civil rights protests in the South and the emergence of a national teenage culture – increasingly enacted to a soundtrack of rock and roll – in the mid-1950s, as well as through the Beats. Although Beat interest in African-American culture was largely confined to a fascination with the bebop of young urban blacks in the North and Midwest, the legacy of civil rights was to become vital to the development of the '60s counterculture. Thus, despite the overwhelmingly white nature of most of that decade's counterculture, from the Students for a Democratic Society to Woodstock, tactics developed during the civil rights struggles in the South were repeatedly adopted in, for example, campus sit-ins and anti-war demonstrations.

The civil rights protests that had been brewing since the end of the Second World War and that exploded into the national consciousness with the commencement of the Montgomery bus boycott in December 1955, had consequences that transcended the race question for a combination of political and technological reasons. First, the fact that many Americans now had televisions meant that what could previously have been contained or suppressed as a story of only local interest was transmitted into homes (both black and white) across the nation. Police brutality and the atrocities of the Jim Crow system were screened almost daily in an obvious illustration of the limits to the Cold War rhetoric of 'freedom' and 'democracy'. As Echols has pointed out, the Government 'finally moved against segregation in large measure because the necessities of the Cold War required it. If the U.S. was going to prove the virtues of democracy and capitalism over Communism . . . it was going to have to dismantle segregation and close the credibility gap with regard to America's commitment to freedom and democracy.'[28] Before this occurred, many young white Americans had already journeyed to the South to help in the struggle and also to learn strategies that would resurface in protests in the later 1960s.

Although it is virtually impossible to overstate the significance of civil rights to the ongoing effort to dismantle America's unequal social systems, its impact on the emergent counterculture only became apparent several years later. Thus, especially before the arrival of rock and roll itself, the panics about the rise of the 'juvenile delinquent' were enacted in sociological and journalistic treatises as well as in movies such as *The Wild One* (1953) and *Rebel Without a Cause* (1955) that (while often directly or indirectly linked to fears about race) regarded youth rebellion as representative of a general alienation from hegemonic culture rather than as the product of particular political desires. Although some of the leading figures from the Beat movement would join this younger generation in the '60s – most notably, Ginsberg, Neal Cassady and Diane di Prima – the teen culture of the '50s was shaped by very different factors from those that underlay the Beats, many of whom were already well into their thirties by this time.

Attitudes to young people were curiously mixed in the 1950s. On the one hand, members of the old left and the liberal intelligentsia despaired at what they regarded as the political apathy of a generation of students more concerned with careers than with protest. On the other, novels such as J. D. Salinger's *Catcher in the Rye* (1951) were widely believed to articulate a significant generation gap.[29] Likewise, fears of teen gangs and juvenile delinquency abounded, inspired by texts such as Frederic Wertham's *Seduction of the Innocent* (1954), a study that rather simplistically suggested a link between crime comics and youth misdemeanours.

It was the advent of rock and roll, however, that generated the greatest hysteria about teenage culture in the mid-1950s. To a large degree, this was the predictable reaction of a white community already deeply suspicious of the integration of African-American culture into the 'mainstream'. After the 1954 *Brown* v. *Board of Education* ruling outlawing separate schooling for whites and blacks, many affluent whites sent their children to private schools and/or relocated to suburbia. Integration was gradually becoming legally enshrined, but this did not generally result in dramatic demographic transformation. In this context, it is unsurprising that the presence of African-American musicians performing for white teens resulted in numerous local and nationwide illustrations of residual racism. For example, in 1957 CBS television cancelled Alan Freed's *Rock 'n' Roll Dance Party* after Frankie Lymon (leader of the doo wop group Frankie Lymon and The Teenagers) was filmed dancing with a young white woman. In the same year, the Juvenile Delinquency and Crime Commission in Houston banned over thirty songs – almost all by black musicians – that it considered to be obscene. Although not all the attacks on rock and roll were overtly motivated by racism – Elvis Presley was warned that he would be arrested on obscenity charges if he moved at all during performances in San Diego and Florida in 1955, and in 1959 Link Wray's single, 'Rumble', was banned by most radio stations nationally, despite having no lyrics, because its title was believed to condone teen violence – the perception that the music was infused with African-American idioms likely to subvert white youth underlay much of the hostility directed at it.[30] Radio stations attempted (with considerable success) to promote sanitised versions of rock and roll songs by white artists such as Pat Boone, but throughout the 1950s there were innumerable attempts to confiscate jukeboxes, ban the music from the radio or limit the places where it could be played. Ultimately, however, such efforts probably only served to fuel the sense of rebellion amongst teenagers: much of the so-called 'rioting' that adults identified with rock and roll was actually dancing, and interventions by police and parents in efforts to prevent such behaviour had the effect of creating a greater gulf between adults and teens as well as furthering the sense of age-based community that would develop more fully in the 1960s.

The success of rock and roll points to one further significant difference between the Beats and the teens who would also go on to participate in the counterculture of the following decade. Where figures like Ginsberg, di Prima and Kerouac tended to renounce materialism in their work and their lifestyles, rock and roll was often a celebration of the culture of abundance, especially in its eulogies to fast cars that could be borrowed from parents for dating rather than thumbed-down as the cheapest way to cross the continent. It is important to remember that the music was very much a product of national prosperity: George Lipsitz has pointed out that the arrival of large numbers of Southerners (both white and black) in northern and western cities during and after the Second World War encouraged cultural exchange across colour lines. Greater purchasing power in both the black and white communities led to the formation of hundreds of new record companies and the release of large numbers of records.[31] Although these records were originally directed largely at working-class consumers, they increasingly appealed to middle-class white youth with relatively high disposable incomes. Unsurprisingly, the major protests against rock and roll only developed after it was adopted as teenage music in the mid-1950s. This disparity between Beat anti-materialism and teenage consumption would contribute to tensions and contradictions within the ideology of the counterculture in the following decade.

The divided nature of the antecedents to '60s counterculture has determined the shape of the first half of this volume. The book is not intended to be a survey and I focus on particular case studies in each chapter, rather than rushing through a catalogue of texts and artists. Nevertheless, I do attempt to account for the different strands of countercultural production between the end of the Second World War and (approximately) the election of John F. Kennedy through focusing on different groups – as well as genres – in the following four chapters. This has ramifications both within the individual chapters and across their entirety. The chapter on fiction focuses on the Beats, drawing on pivotal figures such as Jack Kerouac and John Clellon Holmes, but also juxtaposing them with writers like Diane di Prima and James Baldwin, whose sexual and racial identities placed them away from the centre of what was very much a white male clique. Although the chapter on painting necessarily and rightly pays close attention to Jackson Pollock's role as iconic Abstract Expressionist, it also investigates how and why non-white artists such as Norman Lewis became excluded from the artistic canon, and looks at countercultural art produced away from New York. Abstract Expressionism occupies a strange, borderline position in the politics of the Cold War: figures like Pollock were clearly not men in 'gray flannel suits', yet their work was used by Government organisations to promote 'American' values as well as by jazz record labels to adorn the covers of bop records. In the chapter on music, I divide my focus between jazz – the soundtrack to the Beat Generation – and rock and roll, which appealed to a younger and very different audience, as well as taking a brief detour into the world of the Chicago blues that would be so influential on much of the rock of the '60s. Once more, the chapter highlights not only the fissures within the nascent counterculture but also the sites of resistance and complicity in the relationship between hegemonic and counterhegemonic groups. Finally, in the chapter on film, I look at popular cultural representations of youthful rebellion that, though hardly countercultural in themselves, provide insights into how Hollywood sought to depict and attract young people. I do this here because, unlike the writers, painters and musicians who made national and international impressions with their work, most independent filmmakers were restricted to local audiences. The costs inherent to shooting and distributing a movie meant that even Robert Frank's *Pull My Daisy* (1959), narrated by Kerouac and featuring many of the leading Beats, received little exposure whereas actors perceived as being associated with the counterculture, such as Marlon Brando, were moving from the New York stage to Hollywood stardom.

Notes

1. Lewis MacAdams, *Birth of the Cool: Beat, Bebop and the American Avant-Garde* (London: Scribner, 2002), p. 185.
2. Diane di Prima, *Recollections of My Life as a Woman: The New York Years* (New York: Viking Penguin, 2001), pp. 186–7.
3. Miles Davis with Quincy Troupe, *Miles: The Autobiography* (London: Picador, 1990), pp. 118–19.
4. LeRoi Jones, *Blues People: The Negro Experience in White America and the Music That Developed From It* (New York: William Morrow, 1963), p. 178.
5. Fredric Jameson, *Postmodernism, or the Cultural Logic of Late Capitalism* (London: Verso, 1991), p. 281, p. 280.
6. R. W. B. Lewis, *The American Adam: Innocence, Tragedy and Tradition in the Nineteenth Century* (Chicago: University of Chicago Press, 1955); Richard Chase, *The American Novel and Its Tradition* (New York: Doubleday, 1957); Harry Levin, *The Power of Blackness: Hawthorne, Poe, Melville* (New York: Alfred A. Knopf, 1958); C. L. R. James, *Mariners, Renegades, and Castaways: The Story of Herman Melville and the World We Live In* (New York: James (self-published), 1953); C. Wright Mills, *The Power Elite* (New York: Oxford University Press, 1956).
7. David Riesman, with Nathan Glazer and Ruel Denney, *The Lonely Crowd: A Study of the Changing American Character* (New Haven, CT: Yale University Press, 1950); William H. Whyte, *The Organization Man* (New York: Simon and Schuster, 1956).
8. Whyte, *The Organization Man* (Harmondsworth: Penguin, 1960), p. 17.
9. Paul Goodman, *Growing Up Absurd: Problems of Youth in the Organized Society* (New York: Vintage Books, 1960), p. 35.
10. Ibid., pp. 27–8.
11. Ibid., p. 12.
12. Ibid., p. 11, p. 12.
13. Ibid., p. 15.
14. Ibid., p. 13, p. 30.
15. Betty Friedan, *The Feminine Mystique* (London: Penguin, 1992), p. 13, p. 14.
16. Ibid., p. 15, p. 16.
17. Ibid., p. 17, p. 18.
18. Ibid., p. 29.
19. Ibid., p. 14.
20. Allen Ginsberg, 'Howl', in Ginsberg *Howl and Other Poems* (San Francisco: City Lights, 1956), p. 9.
21. Henry David Thoreau, 'Resistance to Civil Government' ('Civil Disobedience'), in Thoreau, *Walden and Civil Disobedience* (Harmondsworth: Penguin, 1983), p. 398.

22. MacAdams, *Birth of the Cool*, p. 185.

23. See MacAdams, *Birth of the Cool*, pp. 185–8.

24. Preston Whaley, Jr., *Blows Like a Horn: Beat Writing, Jazz, Style, and Markets in the Transformation of U.S. Culture* (Cambridge, MA and London: Harvard University Press, 2004), p. 17.

25. Michael Davidson, *The San Francisco Renaissance: Poetics and Community at Mid-century* (Cambridge: Cambridge University Press, 1989), p. 80.

26. Harold Rosenberg, 'The American Action Painters', *Art News*, 51.8 (December 1952). Reprinted in *The Tradition of the New* (London: Thames and Hudson, 1962), p. 25.

27. Alice Echols, 'The Ike Age: Rethinking the 1950s', in Echols, *Shaky Ground: The Sixties and Its Aftershocks* (New York: Columbia University Press, 2002), p. 56.

28. Ibid., p. 60.

29. See Richard King, *The Party of Eros: Radical Social Thought and the Realm of Freedom* (Chapel Hill: University of North Carolina Press, 1972), pp. 100–1.

30. See Eric Nuzum's detailed chronology of censorship incidents at http://ericnuzum.com/banned/incidents/50s.html. The chronology makes clear that censorship and protest were not confined to the 1950s: as late as 1968, sponsors of a programme showing interracial 'touching' (when the white Petula Clark put her hand on the black Harry Belafonte's arm) threatened to withdraw support; and in 2001, Ani DiFranco's performance on the David Letterman show was cancelled because she refused to drop the song 'Subdivision', an examination of racism and white relocation to the suburbs.

31. See Echols, *Shaky Ground*, p. 58; George Lipsitz, *Time Passages* (Minneapolis: University of Minnesota Press, 1990), p. 123.

CHAPTER ONE

Fiction

The Beat Generation, that was a vision that we had, John Clellon Holmes and I, and Allen Ginsberg in an even wilder way, in the late Forties, of a generation of crazy, illuminated hipsters suddenly rising and roaming America, serious, curious, bumming and hitchhiking everywhere, ragged, beatific, beautiful in an ugly graceful new way – a vision gleaned from the way we had heard the word 'beat' spoken on streetcorners in Times Square and in the Village, in other cities in the downtown city night of postwar America – beat, meaning down and out but full of intense conviction . . . It never meant juvenile delinquents, it meant characters of a special spirituality who didn't gang up but were solitary Bartlebies staring out the dead wall window of our civilization.

Jack Kerouac, 'About the Beat Generation' (1957)[1]

What I do know is that choosing to be an artist: writer, dancer, painter, musician, actor, photographer, sculptor, you name it, choosing to be any of these things in the world I grew up in, the world of the 40s and early 50s, was choosing as completely as possible for those times the life of the renunciant. Life of the wandering sadhu, itinerant saint, outside the confines and laws of that particular and peculiar culture.

Diane di Prima,
Recollections of My Life as a Woman (2001)[2]

Asked once to define the Transcendentalists, James Freeman Clark replied that they were 'a club of the likeminded, I suppose, because no two of us thought alike'.[3] Much the same could be said of the 'Beat Generation', whose leading writers each worked from a very different agenda and composed highly distinctive literature. Like the Transcendentalists a century before, the Beats shared an emphasis on self-reliance and on efforts to create their work spontaneously – Jack Kerouac developed a writing habit that he labelled 'spontaneous prose' and most of the Beats preached (even if they did not practise) Allen Ginsberg's mantra of 'first thought, best thought' – but it is not easy to identify obvious formal or thematic similarities between, say, Ginsberg's free verse confessional poetry of revelation and Gary Snyder's more intellectual use of Native American and Oriental influences in his work, or between Kerouac's and William Burroughs's novels. Indeed, the reasons why a small group of artists on the East and West coasts of the United States should be called a 'generation' at all stem more from a combination of biographical overlap, the mistaken assumption that the characters in Kerouac's novels are unmediated representations of real people, the pivotal role of Neal Cassady as muse to Kerouac, Ginsberg and others, and Ginsberg's tireless efforts to promote his own and his friends' writings than from a coherent collective artistic or political manifesto. Moreover, Ginsberg's campaigning and the early critical studies of the Beats constructed what now seems like an unnecessarily narrow and distorted canon that frequently treated work by writers other than Kerouac, Ginsberg, Burroughs and, to a lesser extent, Snyder, Gregory Corso, and the poet/publisher Lawrence Ferlinghetti as minor.

Of course, this does not mean that there were no similarities. Many of the group were born in small towns in the 1910s and '20s, were raised during the Depression before moving to New York, meeting and coming to maturity around the time of the Second World War; most started to think seriously of themselves as 'writers' in the 1940s. Many also later relocated to San Francisco, either permanently or temporarily, and were present as either performers or audience at the famous Six Gallery reading in October 1955, reconstructed in Kerouac's *The Dharma Bums* (1958) and remembered best for Ginsberg's performance of 'Howl'. As such, they were shaped by a combination of similar forces: a fascination with the metropolis that was less cynical than was common amongst people born there; formative education during the Depression and war years; exposure to and embrace of a combination of 'high' and popular cultures (combining Byron, Blake,

Gertrude Stein and Ezra Pound with jazz and the movies, identifying particularly with figures such as Charlie Parker, Marlon Brando and Jackson Pollock); and despair at the growing authoritarianism and standardisation of the post-war United States. The poet and novelist Diane di Prima is typical in her account of how becoming a part of the Beat community in New York felt like a renunciation of 'the wars, the cruelty, murder, oppression' carried out in the name of the nation, and in her association of 'sliding glass doors looking out on decorous gardens' and 'the narrow and cruel judgments in the name of decency' that fuelled the persecution of anyone who did not conform to acceptable social standards.[4] Although the Beats represented a wide range of ideological perspectives – Kerouac, for example, considered himself a Republican; Ginsberg moved gradually further towards the political left – their writing either obliquely (Kerouac), allegorically (Burroughs) or directly (Ginsberg) questions an ever more authoritarian America, increasingly shaped by what Eisenhower would later call the military-industrial complex.

Di Prima is typical in her attacks on the repressive nature of hegemonic American society in the 1940s and '50s. In her autobiography, she recollects that:

> The laws of the land were a hodgepodge of prejudice, fear, and bigotry. That much was clear. Homosexuality was illegal. It was illegal in many states to experiment in your own bed with your own 'legal' partner: your own willing husband or wife. Married couples were being arrested for sodomy. Kids were (mostly still are) owned outright by parents. The dance we had all performed to keep parents and the law from ganging up on us when we were teenagers had not been lost on us. Nor had we forgotten the many friends who had disappeared: madhouses, deportation.[5]

As di Prima's memoir suggests, the Beats are perhaps the exemplary instance of the dissatisfaction within 1950s white America that would act as a precursor to what Japhy Ryder in *The Dharma Bums* correctly prophesises as a forthcoming 'rucksack revolution'[6] a decade later. It would, however, be a mistake to see them as an entirely isolated group, whose interests and concerns bore no relationship to the sense of alienation felt elsewhere in the United States at the time. Although Godfrey Hodgson is just one of many historians to claim that 'it is impossible not to be struck by the degree to which the majority of Americans in [the 1950s] accepted the same system of assumptions', and that 'confidence and satisfaction would remain the prevailing mood in a prosperous, developed country',[7] the escalation of civil rights, the publication of a series of sociological texts analysing white middle-class discontent in a world of bureaucratisation, corporate consolidation and suburban relocation, and the first signs of a new feminism, illustrate the degree to which a range of Americans – from Southern blacks to suburban housewives – were not at ease within what Robert Lowell termed the 'tranquillized Fifties', and Norman Mailer in his influential essay 'The White Negro' (1957) labelled 'the years of conformity and depression'.[8]

This was not, however, how the Beats were perceived once their profile had been raised by the success of *On the Road* and 'Howl' in the late 1950s, either by themselves or by mainstream media and literary cultures keen to find what Michael Davidson has called a 'scapegoat for the anxieties facing mass society'. Davidson illustrates the ways in which the 'Beatnik' (a hostile term coined by *San Francisco Chronicle* columnist Herb Caen, following the high-profile launch of the Soviet Sputnik satellite in October 1957) 'could be associated in the public mind not only with antisocial behaviour but with things subversive and anti-American'. Thus, *Life* magazine could sum up the Beats as 'talkers, loafers, passive little con men, lonely eccentrics, mom-haters, cophaters, exhibitionists with abused smiles and mortgages on a bongo drum – writers who cannot write, painters who cannot paint, dancers with unfortunate malfunction of the fetlocks'. Even critics from the left, writing in magazines such as the *Partisan Review* and the *Nation*, were critical of the anti-intellectualism, 'primitivism' and lack of activism that they contrasted with the bohemianism of the 1920s.[9]

Within this culture, the decision to become an artist could be regarded as countercultural in itself and, given the suspicion and hostility felt by much of American society toward the arts, it is not surprising that alienation is the dominant theme in so much of the work produced at the time. As LeRoi Jones (later Amiri Baraka) pointed out in *Blues People* (1963), the 'complete domination of American society by what Brook Adams called the economic sensibility, discouraging completely any significant participation of the imaginative sensibility in the social, political, and economic affairs of society . . . has promoted . . . hatred of the artist by the "average American"'.[10] Although this attitude was hardly new in the 1950s – it had been identified by Herman Melville and Nathaniel Hawthorne a century before, and by many others after them – the combination of Cold War hysteria, the ascendance of a standardised popular cultural and the association of a corporate work ethic with patriotism, alongside the Beats' adoption of urban African-American and junkie vernacular as signifiers of their own alienation, ensured that artistic otherness was accepted by both sides.

Kerouac and Beat

On the Road is often seen as the exemplification of the 1950s counter-culture, but it is largely set in the 1940s and had gone through numerous revisions in the decade before its publication in 1957. The America that it represents, in terms of Sal Paradise and Dean Moriarty *and* of the society they encounter, is very different from both the dominant culture of the later 1950s and the Beat*nik* community that was treated near-hysterically by the mass media, and that was despised by Kerouac. A consequence of the lengthy and complicated pre-publication history of *On the Road* was that it appeared several years after Kerouac's first novel, *The Town and the City* (1950), and also the 'first' Beat Generation novel, John Clellon Holmes's *Go* (1952), thereby creating misconceptions about Kerouac and Neal Cassady (as they were in 1957) in the minds of both critics and public. The novel's belated publication also meant that Kerouac had completed the majority of his other novels (though not *The Dharma Bums*, which he wrote largely to cash in on the success of *On the Road*) before he had a second book in print.

Although there seems to be little doubt that Kerouac invented the term 'Beat Generation', this history also meant that the phrase first appeared in *Go*. But whereas Kerouac's Sal Paradise is very much a part of the underground community that he describes – even if he does make regular trips home to his aunt's and spends much of the novel observing Dean – Paul Hobbes, the protagonist of *Go*, is an outsider to that world. As a self-styled alienated intellectual, trapped in a marriage that gives little satisfaction to Hobbes or his wife, Kathryn, he is fascinated by the antics of a group of acquaintances that includes fictional representations of Kerouac (Gene Pasternak) and Ginsberg (David Stofsky). Nevertheless, Hobbes is too much of a 'square' to behave like they do, and feels that they

lacked any caution . . . They made none of the moral or political judgements that he thought essential; they did not seem compelled

to fit everything into the pigeon holes of a system . . .; they seemed
to have an almost calculated contempt for logical argument. They
operated on feelings, sudden reactions, expanding these far out of
perspective to see in them profundities which Hobbes was certain
they could not define if put to it.[11]

Where Pasternak can travel around the country, Hobbes lies about a
plan to go to Mexico; while he professes the desire for an open
marriage, he finds it hard to accept Kathryn's relationship with
Pasternak, and (in a moment symbolic of his more general impotence)
loses his erection just before he can consummate his relationship with
another woman. Thus, while Hobbes's comments about Pasternak and
Stofsky do offer a valid critique of some aspects of Beat behaviour, and
while Holmes constructs an ironic gap between Hobbes and a more
knowing narrator, *Go* does not offer a representation of the early Beat
community from the inside.

In contrast, one of the reasons for Kerouac's ongoing status as 'King
of the Beats' is that his novels do claim to show that world from the
perspective of a central figure.[12] Of course, *On the Road* is now one
of the best-known American novels of the twentieth century, while
Go and its author are largely forgotten outside the circle of Beat
aficionados. Yet, in some ways, the enduring (and growing) legacy
of the book is strange. First, it tends to be read as a stand-alone piece,
rather than how Kerouac intended as one piece of the 'Legend of
Duluoz', the multi-volume fictional recreation of his life. Although
many of Kerouac's other books have been republished, their readership
remains comparatively small, especially in the case of the novels about
his childhood and youth in Lowell, Massachusetts. Second, the novel
is actually rather traditional: the lengthy editorial process removed
many of Kerouac's stylistic idiosyncrasies, and the form – participant
narrator follows and observes another, more interesting character –
replicates the 'classic' American literary pattern of the relationship
between, for example, Ishmael and Ahab, or Nick Carraway and Jay
Gatsby. Third, Sal displays a startling naivety about the position of
other racial groups in America, associating his personal sense of
alienation in a white world that offers him 'not enough ecstasy
. . . not enough life, joy, kicks, darkness, music, not enough night'
with a desire to be a 'Negro . . . a Denver Mexican, or even a poor
overworked Jap'.[13] As I indicate later in this chapter, many writers
have objected to Kerouac's representations of race, which, for contemporary African-American novelists such as James Baldwin, are

indicative of the limits to Beat repudiation of dominant American values.

When the 'Legend of Duluoz' is read in its entirety, it becomes clear that Kerouac was capable of writing in many different ways, from the sentimentality of *Visions of Gerard* (1958) to the 'bop' prosody of *The Subterraneans* (1960) or the avant-garde experimentalism of sections of *Visions of Cody*, the 'alternative' version of *On the Road* that was not published in full until 1973. Some of these styles – as well as the subject matter of the Lowell novels – appear to have little to do with the Beat Generation, and others, such as *Visions of Cody*'s transcripts of tape-recorded conversations between Kerouac and Cassady (or Duluoz and Cody Pomeray), feel interminable and highlight the gulf between spoken and written prose. But the legend does provide a personal chronicle of the rapid transformation of the United States between the 1920s and 1960s, and illustrates the manner in which Sal and Dean's adventures from the 1940s would have been impossible in the changed world of the late '50s to early '60s, which perceived the Beats to be such a threat. Writing in *Big Sur* (1962) of an attempt to hitchhike after a gap of several years, Kerouac represents a public attitude very different from that of a decade before. In addition to the police's abuse of their power over impoverished travellers (which was already apparent to him in *On the Road*), he witnesses the gridlocking of American highways and the refusal of the people – as opposed to the law – to sanction his lifestyle. Although he always maintained that he hated hitchhiking (a point generally forgotten by his legions of imitators), by 1960 he cannot even get a ride.

> This is the first time I've hitch hiked in years and I soon begin to see things have changed in America, you can't get a ride any more . . . – sleek long stationwagon after wagon comes sleering by smoothly . . . husband is in the driver's seat with a long ridiculous vacationist hat with a long baseball visor making him look witless and idiotic – Beside him sits wifey, the boss of America, wearing dark glasses and sneering, even if he wanted to pick me up or anybody up she wouldn't let him – But in the two deep backseats are children . . . – There's no room anymore anyway for a hitch hiker, tho conceivably the poor bastard might be allowed to ride like a meek gunman or a silent murderer in the very back platform of the wagon, but here no, alas! here is ten thousand racks of drycleaned and perfectly pressed suits and dresses of all sizes for the family to look like millionaires everytime they stop at a

roadside dive for bacon and eggs . . . – 1960's, it's no time for [the father] to yearn for Big Two Hearted River and the old sloppy pants and string of fish in the tent, or the woodfire with Bourbon at night – it's time for motels, roadside driveins, bringing napkins to the gang in the car.[14]

Big Sur charts the extension of the standardised citizen's domain far beyond anything imagined by Kerouac in *On the Road*. The narrator feels that he and Cody (the Dean Moriarty figure of *On the Road*) have been 'hemmed in' and 'outnumbered', with Cody recently released from two years' imprisonment for possession of marijuana. More significantly still, Cody has been tempted into his 'crime' by the inducements of an undercover policeman. Kerouac represents an America afraid of idiosyncrasies and attempts at individualism, and Barry Gifford points out that the success of *On the Road* and the subsequent arrest of Neal Cassady (Cody) were not coincidental.[15]

Women in the Beat Generation

The first generation of critics to write about the Beats tended to accept the canonical hierarchy established by its most famous exponents. Because Kerouac's novels feature thinly disguised versions of his male acquaintances as major characters who reappear throughout the 'Legend', but tend (with a few exceptions) to relegate women other than his mother to minor roles in single books, readers interested in following up on his references have tended to seek out writing by these male figures. As Michael Davidson summarises, 'the Beat ethos relegated women to the role of sexual surrogate, muse, or mom; it did not raise them to a position of artistic equality. Literary friendships throughout the period were marked by a kind of boys' club mentality in which women were excluded.' Much of this crude sexism was the product of 1950s society more generally, and many critics have noted the manner in which women were returned to more 'traditional' tasks such as child-rearing and housekeeping once their services in the marketplace were no longer required for the war effort. For the Beats, as Davidson sums up, the kind of male bonding found in Kerouac's novels such as *On the Road* and *The Dharma Bums* 'offers a healthy release from the obligations of suburban, heterosexual family life'.[16] Even a novel like John Clellon Holmes's *Go*, staged entirely in New

York City, has a protagonist who dreams of the freedom symbolised by a trip to Mexico, but feels trapped in his urban world by his marriage and contrasts his lot with that of Gene Pasternak, the roaming figure closely based on Kerouac.

In addition, many of the most prominent Beats were homosexual, one of the factors underlying their migration to San Francisco, which, according to the writer Kenneth Rexroth, was 'the only city in the US which was not settled overland by the westward-spreading puritan tradition, or by the Walter Scott fake-cavalier tradition of the South.'[17] The city had sustained a large homosexual community since before the Second World War and, as Davidson points out, 'Allen Ginsberg's "Howl" censorship trial, publications by Robert Duncan, Jack Spicer, James Broughton, and Robert Blaser, and even Jack Kerouac's novels brought national attention to a city where variant sexual modes were possible.'[18] This artistic community tended to be suspicious of women, or even openly hostile toward them. In 'Howl', Ginsberg sees 'the best minds of my generation'

> who lost their loveboys to the three old shrews of fate the one eyed shrew of the heterosexual dollar the one eyed shrew that winks out of the womb and the one eyed shrew that does nothing but sit on her ass and snip the intellectual golden threads of the craftsman's loom[19]

For Ginsberg, capitalism is heterosexual and anti-intellectual, and it is women who stifle or destroy male creativity. As such, it is unsurprising that his construction of a Beat canon is almost entirely male. It is also evident that to succeed as a female artist necessitated overcoming many obstacles. Diane di Prima looks back on a 'determinedly male community of writers around me in the 50s . . . There truly was this male cabal: self-satisfied, competitive, glorying in small acclaims', and suggests that 'there was inevitable guilt in being woman and artist . . . and that this guilt would bring one down eventually. At any rate make one sick. I knew no older women artists who were not ill. Not in the 1950s.'[20]

More recently, some critics have started to challenge the dominant narrative and to highlight the presence of women as artists within the artistic community in the 1950s: although James Campbell's *This is the Beat Generation* (1999) continues to see the Beat Generation revolving around the Kerouac, Ginsberg, Burroughs 'troika',[21] many other critics have illustrated the participation of women as much more than housekeepers and lovers. The essays collected in *Girls Who Wore Black* (2002), edited by Roanna C. Johnson and Nancy M. Grace, for example, highlight the participation of three generations of women in Beat writing, and stress the impact of their work on the feminism of the 1960s and beyond. Although Johnson and Grace oversimplify the world of male writers – it seems reductive, for example, unproblematically to situate Allen Ginsberg within the 'white male hegemonic norm' – and artificially extend the notion of Beat culture into the 1960s and '70s in order to claim later women artists as 'Beats', there is no doubt that figures such as Jane Bowles, Denise Levertov, Helen Adams and di Prima utilised the self-reliant Beat attitude to artistic and social individuality in their 'antiestablishment critique of women's assigned place and value in patriarchy'.[22]

Beat and African-American Cultures

Although the Beats drew upon numerous sources ranging from Transcendentalism and Modernism to the junkie and petty criminal subculture of Times Square, recent assessments of their legacy have focused primarily on their attitudes to (and appropriation of) African-American culture. In particular, scholars such as Jon Panish and Peter Townsend have noted the importance of bebop – and above all of Charlie Parker – as inspiration to what Kerouac in *The Subterraneans* (1958) called the 'bop generation'.[23] Both Panish and Townsend are uncomfortable with the manner in which white writers sought to identify with African-American jazz, with Panish being especially judgemental of Kerouac's novels. For Panish, Kerouac's version of Parker is a 'white fantasy of a black self . . . Kerouac uses jazz not only for its ideal of improvisation but also for its status as a music and subculture that is outside what is traditional and accepted.'[24] The argument is hardly original: LeRoi Jones had made much the same point in *Blues People* in 1963, when he noted that 'the white bebopper of the forties was as removed from society as the Negroes, but as a matter of choice . . . [The] Negro himself had no choice.'[25] But Panish goes further: discussing Kerouac's 'Essentials of Spontaneous Prose', he argues that Kerouac's writing philosophy depends on equating black consciousness (in the form of the jazz musician) with 'emotions, and life experience' rather than study.[26] Panish points out that, of course, improvising 'cannot be characterized accurately without referring to the kinds of modification of existing material that reflect dedication and rumination rather than pure spontaneous inspiration'. He is also sceptical about Kerouac's claims to be mimicking bop in his prose, pointing out that when Kerouac released recordings of himself reading from his novels to a jazz accompaniment, they contained more or less verbatim reproductions of the written texts.[27]

Although these criticisms do contain much validity, they are also problematic. First, as both Kerouac's own novels and other people's recollections of him make clear, he did not believe that his own (or others') improvisational designs could be created without training. Kerouac's method of 'sketching' what he witnessed was developed over many years, and noted by others, as when, in *Go*, Paul Hobbes observes Gene Pasternak (Kerouac) 'sitting at a table by the window with cooling coffee and a notebook before him, in which he was writing leisurely'.[28] Although, at times, it could suit Kerouac to conceal the labour involved in the writing process, his 'spontaneity' – like that of the jazz musician – came from years of practise. In addition, it was not merely the result of identification with jazz, since, as Peter Townsend has noted, the Beats 'were the inheritors of an American philosophy of composition that descended from Emerson, Whitman and William Carlos Williams . . . Williams spoke of the usefulness of "headlong composition."' Likewise, the interest in Zen and Surrealism, and the use of hallucinatory drugs, all contributed to the Beat emphasis on spontaneity.[29] Finally, Kerouac's prose also developed from his study of the techniques of the wandering con-man/artist figure of Neal Cassady/Dean Moriarty, who provides the inspiration for the formal construction of *On the Road* and *Visions of Cody*. Dean is used to travelling without money and, as the opening paragraph of Kerouac's novel informs us, 'is the perfect guy for the road because he actually was born on the road'.[30] Most importantly, he is also the perfect spontaneous storyteller, adept at acquiring food, sex or cash in exchange for his inspired stream-of-consciousness spiel. Dean is able to adjust his narratives to almost any situation, whether it is captivating Sal Paradise (Kerouac), charming Sal's aunt or seducing women from a range of social backgrounds. Kerouac's prose is a transformation of such exchange into a *literary* medium, a written rather than an oral tradition, suited to the communications revolutions of the twentieth century.

Panish's criticism of the limits of Kerouac's improvisation when performing his work aloud also depends on a simplistic notion of the relationship between the written and spoken word. When reading aloud, it is possible to stress the same words in many different ways and – in the same way that the bop soloist's playing interacts with the rest of the group – Kerouac's performance depends upon rhythmic communication with his backing musicians. In addition, Panish seems unaware of the improvised (in terms of phrasing and rhythm) nature of some of Kerouac's other recordings, such as his commentary to the film *Pull My Daisy* (1959), taped in a single session after he had watched the film twice, or (understandably, given that it was released in the same year in which his book was published) of the way that the poet-musician Patti Smith used Kerouac's words as a springboard into her own improvisations on the tribute CD, *Kerouac – Kicks Joy Darkness* (1997). The latter is proof that a subsequent generation of countercultural icons were willing to take Kerouac at his word – and jam on it.[31]

Of even more significance is the fact that many leading radical black thinkers of the time did not see Kerouac and the other Beats in this way. For example, both LeRoi Jones and Eldridge Cleaver are much more sympathetic to the reasons for and effects of Beat identification with African-American culture than Panish's retrospective analysis would suggest. In *Blues People*, Jones highlights the 'aesthetic analogies, persistent similarities of stance that . . . create identifiable relationships' between 'young Negro musicians' and the Beats and other white artists (especially painters like Jackson Pollock), and observes that the relationship between jazz, art and fiction resulted in 'predicable hostility' to all three from traditionalists. Jones stresses the 'cross-fertilization' between genres, noting that the free jazz of the late 1950s feels a rapport with other forms of artistic production at the time.[32]

For Jones, this is important since it is a rare example of positive interaction between black and white cultures. Earlier in *Blues People* he suggests that in the 1940s the 'only assimilation that society provided was toward the disappearance of the most important things the black man possessed, without even the political and economic reimbursement afforded the white American'; at that time, the 'individuality of local [black] cultural reference only reinforced separation from the [dominant white] society'.[33] This leads Jones to assess the American culture of the 1950s in a particularly noteworthy manner:

> What seem most in need of emphasis here are the *double* forms of assimilation or synthesis taking place between black and white American cultures. On one hand, the largely artificial 'upward' social move, demanded by the white mainstream of all minorities, and the psychological address to that demand made by the black

bourgeoisie, whereby all consideration of local culture is abandoned for the social and psychological security of the 'main.' On the other hand, the *lateral* (exchanging) form of synthesis, whereby difference is used to enrich and broaden, and the value of any form lies in its eventual use. It is this latter form of synthesis . . . that became so important after World War II, and even more magnified after the Korean War. The point is that where one form of synthesis, which was actually assimilation, tended to wipe out one culture and make the other even less vital, the other kind of synthesis gave a local form to a general kind of nonconformity that began to exist in American (Western) society after World War II.[34]

For Jones, the artistic scene around Greenwich Village is the prime example of a new culture of race relations. In place of old melting-pot ideologies, he argues that the fusion of black and white cultures is not only advantageous to both individually, but also beneficial to the emergence of a multi-racial artistic counterculture structured around opposition to a dominant national narrative stressing conformity and economic individualism.

In a way, Eldridge Cleaver's observations in *Soul On Ice* (1968) are even more striking, given that, unlike Jones, who (at least at this stage in his life) was closely aligned with the Beats, he was writing as one of the best-known militant African-American spokesmen of the late 1960s. For Cleaver, the Beat interest in African-American culture is part of a much wider, generational shift in attitudes that culminates in the widespread countercultural protests of the 1960s. Cleaver sees a rejection of white history by the young, who recognise that figures such as Washington and Jefferson were 'heroes whose careers rested on a system of foreign and domestic exploitation'. Although the Beat position in his argument is modest when contrasted with what follows, it is significant as the first stage of four in a process leading to the creation of a 'generation of white youth that is truly worthy of a black man's respect'.[35] Thus, the Beat 'rejection of the conformity which America expected' shows a discovery that 'America, far from helping the underdog, was up to its ears in the mud trying to hold the dog down'. From this recognition, non- and post-Beat white youth would go on to see the need for 'positive action' before joining black protests in 'large numbers'. The final stage, for Cleaver, sees white youth 'taking the initiative, using techniques learned in the Negro struggle to attack problems in the general society,' as exemplified by student demonstrations at Berkeley or the anti-Vietnam War movement.[36] As with Jones's model, Cleaver identifies a form of lateral synthesis in the adoption of African-American behaviour by one part of the white community, but whereas Jones limits this aspect of his argument in *Blues People* to a discussion of contemporary arts, Cleaver suggests that it can result in more widespread political and cultural revolution.

Of course, this was not a position shared by all black writers at the time, and Cleaver's celebration of what he calls the 'remarkable' 'wishing I were a Negro' passage in *On the Road*[37] suggests a degree of blindness to Kerouac's naïve and patronising view of non-white American culture. In contrast, the African-American writer to be most critical of the artistic community living in and around Greenwich Village in the 1950s was James Baldwin, who had abandoned the Village for Paris in the late 1940s as a result of the 'violent, anarchic, hostility breeding' racism that he detected there.[38] Baldwin's *Another Country* (1962) is largely staged around the same areas of Manhattan as those represented in John Clellon Holmes's *Go* a decade before, but the kinds of alienation experienced by Baldwin's characters ultimately have less to do with narrowly personal experience than with an inability to escape the forces of American racial history.

Whereas *Go* and *On the Road* are intensely individual narratives focalised through a single character and based upon recollections of actual events, *Another Country* represents the lives of several people, both white and black, male and female, American and French, through their relationship to the African-American jazz drummer Rufus Scott, who commits suicide at the end of chapter one. Thus, although the other books convey a sense of the alienation from mainstream culture that is experienced by their (white) protagonists, this can, to varying degrees, be compensated for through engagement with the like-minded. Baldwin's novel, in contrast, examines the historical, racial and linguistic barriers that seem to preclude almost any kind of meaningful, unmediated relationship, even between those on or beyond the margins of the dominant culture. Some of his targets are soft – the Italians who 'merely wished to be accepted as decent Americans', 'hating . . . all the [white and black, countercultural Greenwich] Villagers, who gave their streets a bad name'; or Richard Silenski, the author who has sold out and who barely masks his hatred of 'Little black bastards' behind a veneer of liberal openness[39] – but others are less immediately apparent. Rufus's white Southern girlfriend is driven insane by their relationship, in part because of the impossibility of transcending the historical memories attached to words. When she comments on the reaction of an Italian-American youth who 'looked at [Rufus] with hatred; his glance flickered over Leona as though she were a whore', she is 'startled' by Rufus's reaction to her use of 'I'm telling you, boy, I know' to conclude her statement. For Rufus, who longs for a place where 'a man could be treated like a man',[40] 'boy' carries the connotations of centuries of racial oppression, especially when uttered by a white Southern woman.

Baldwin's appreciation of language's control over subjectivity is even more evident in a longer passage describing Richard's wife Cass's efforts to buy a hat in Harlem to wear at Rufus's funeral. When Cass enters the store,

> The girl was smiling, the same smile – as Cass insisted to herself – that all salesgirls, everywhere, have always worn. This smile made Cass feel poor and shabby indeed. But now she felt it more vehemently than she had ever felt it before. And though she was beginning to shake with a thoroughly mysterious anger, she knew that her dry, aristocratic sharpness, however well it had always worked downtown, would fail of its usual effect here.
> 'I want,' she stammered, 'to see a hat.'
> Then she remembered that she hated hats and never wore them. The girl, whose smile had clearly been taught her by masters, looked as though she sold at least one hat, every Saturday morning, to a strange, breathless, white woman.
> . . . Cass tried to smile; she wanted to run. Silence had fallen over the shop. 'I think I'd just like to get a scarf. Black' – and how the word seemed to roll through the shop! – 'for my head,' she added, and felt that in another moment they would call the police. And that she had no way of identifying herself.[41]

On one level, the scene offers a kind of cultural inversion, in which the racial norms of Cass's lower-Manhattan world are upended in order to make her aware of the sense of otherness felt by the African-American outside Harlem. In this reading, the sales girl's use of 'lady' to describe Cass serves as an ironic reminder of the latter's heightened visibility here, and Cass's fear that the police will be called echoes black experience in affluent white environments. But this interpretation of the encounter overlooks the subtleties of Baldwin's narrative: it is clear that much of what occurs is focalised through Cass and, unlike the instance of, for example, a black male in white America who could very well be arrested simply for being there, it is evident that the police will not be summoned to apprehend a white woman in Harlem. It does not matter that she has 'no way of identifying herself' since the colour of her skin already confirms her social position. In a later passage, Cass's lack of cultural knowledge here is contrasted with Rufus's sister Ida's awareness of how the same process works to different ends for the African-American in 'the way the world treated girls with bad reputations and every coloured girl had been born with one'.[42] Baldwin further develops the imbalance with a reference to the sales girl's smile, 'clearly taught her by masters', the ambiguity of the final word moving beyond the obvious allusion to her expertise to incorporate connotations of racial oppression and its links to consumer capitalism. Finally, it is clear that Cass cannot even utter the word 'black' without a sense that the word's links to the nation's racial history resonate throughout the shop and highlight her own complicity in that history.

Vivaldo, the ethnic Italian would-be Beat author, understands this situation more fully than does Cass, but his attitude to Harlem seems uncomfortably close to that of Sal Paradise. Vivaldo is aware of some – though by no means all – of the difficulties inherent to being black in America, although he tends to turn this awareness inward, feeling that it is 'very painful for him to despise a coloured girl, it increased his self-contempt'. Likewise, he enjoys being in 'those dark streets uptown precisely because the history written in the colour of his skin contested his right to be there . . .; uptown, his alienation had been made visible and therefore almost bearable.' Like Sal, Vivaldo chooses to express his alienation through a relation to blackness, albeit a slightly different one, but the ability to choose instantly marks his experience as beyond that available to the African-American. Nothing more than the 'banal indeed'[43] befalls him in Harlem, and he is free to resume his Village life as a writer without having to confront the historical forces that have driven Rufus to suicide. As Ida tells Cass near the end of the novel, 'Vivaldo didn't want to know my brother was dying because he doesn't want to know that he would still be alive if he hadn't been born black . . . There's no way in the world for you to know what Rufus went through, not in this world, not as long as you're white.'[44]

The inability to communicate pervades Baldwin's New York like a 'kind of plague', to the extent that when Eric (a white Southern-born actor) returns from France he feels that people have become accustomed to 'brutality and indifference'.[45] Ultimately, this results in a rather startling correspondence between *Another Country* and books that would appear to be very different, like *On the Road*, since both must depend upon something beyond words to generate shared experience. For Dean Moriarty, this something is 'IT', a concept that always appears to be frustratingly out of reach for Sal, but which Dean recognises in jazz, sex and fast cars, even if he is unable to explain what he means. For Dean, 'IT' is the tautological moment when 'Time stops. [The jazz musician] is filling empty space with the substance of our lives . . . He has to blow . . . with such infinite feeling soul-exploratory for the tune of the moment that everybody knows that it's not the tune that counts but IT.'[46] When Ida sings in a bar in Greenwich Village, she compensates for her lack of training with

> a quality so mysteriously and implacably egocentric that no one has ever been able to name it. This quality involves a sense of the self so profound and so powerful that it does not so much leap barriers as reduce them to atoms – while still leaving them standing mightily, where they were; and this awful sense is private, unknowable, not to be articulated, having, literally, to do with something else; it transforms and lays waste and gives life, and kills.[47]

The blues enable Ida to transmit emotions that appear, as with Dean's explanation, to transcend words – a process that is powerful, but also potentially dangerous since it can expose an 'uneasy' mixed race audience to 'her private fears and pain'.[48] And although Ida's subsequent decision to sell out illustrates the ease with which such power can be appropriated by a dominant popular culture, it does here provide one of the very few moments in Baldwin's novel where unmediated emotion can be conveyed. Although there is a difference between Dean's ecstatic reception of jazz's 'meaning' and the uncomfortable, guilty understanding afforded to Ida's white audience, Baldwin and Kerouac share the belief that black music (or music of black origin) is more powerful than words as a bridge between both individuals and groups kept apart by memories of conflict or oppression. In order to investigate this possibility more fully, the next chapter will focus more directly on the role of music (and musicians) in the emergence of the counterculture in the 1940s and '50s.

Notes

1. Jack Kerouac, 'About the Beat Generation', in *The Portable Jack Kerouac*, edited by Ann Charters (New York: Penguin, 1996), p. 559.
2. Diane di Prima, *Recollections of My Life as a Woman: The New York Years* (New York: Viking Penguin, 2001), p. 101.

3. Quoted by Michael Meyer in his introduction to Henry David Thoreau, *Walden and Civil Disobedience* (Harmondsworth: Penguin, 1983), p. 9.
4. Di Prima, *Recollections of My Life as a Woman*, p. 102.
5. Ibid., p. 203.
6. Jack Kerouac, *The Dharma Bums* (St Albans: Granada, 1982), p. 72.
7. Godfrey Hodgson, *America in Our Time* (New York: Vintage Books, 1976), p. 68, p. 69.
8. Robert Lowell, 'Memories of West Street and Lepke', in *Life Studies and For the Union Dead* (New York: Noonday Press, 1967), p. 85; Norman Mailer, 'The White Negro', in *Advertisements for Myself* (London: Panther, 1961), p. 271.
9. See Michael Davidson, *The San Francisco Renaissance: Poetics and Community at Mid-century* (Cambridge: Cambridge University Press, 1989), p. 62, p. 61. For a particularly scathing example of anti-Beat sentiment, see Norman Podhoretz, 'The Know-Nothing Bohemians', in Podhoretz, *Doings and Undoings* (London: Rupert Hart-Davis, 1965), pp. 143–58. A slightly more sympathetic review of *On the Road* is Paul Goodman's 1958 *Midstream* essay, republished in *Growing Up Absurd: Problems of Youth in the Organized Society* (New York: Vintage Books, 1960), pp. 279–84.
10. LeRoi Jones, *Blues People: The Negro Experience in White America and the Music That Developed From It* (New York: William Morrow, 1963), p. 230.
11. John Clellon Holmes, *Go* (New York: Thunder's Mouth Press, 1988), p. 35.
12. One of the best biographies of Kerouac draws on this description for its title. See Barry Miles, *Jack Kerouac: King of the Beats: A Portrait* (London: Virgin, 1998). The definitive Kerouac biography, at least in terms of detail, is Gerald Nicosia's *Memory Babe: A Critical Biography of Jack Kerouac* (New York: Grove, 1983).
13. Jack Kerouac, *On the Road* (London: Penguin, 1972), p. 169.
14. Jack Kerouac, *Big Sur* (London: Panther, 1980), p. 42.
15. See Barry Gifford and Laurence Lee, *Jack's Book* (London: Hamish Hamilton, 1979), p. 269.
16. Davidson, *The San Francisco Renaissance*, p. 176.
17. Quoted in James Campbell, *This is the Beat Generation: New York, San Francisco, Paris* (London: Secker and Warburg, 1999), p. 159.
18. Davidson, *The San Francisco Renaissance*, p. 193.
19. Allen Ginsberg, *Collected Poems, 1947–1980* (London: Penguin, 1987), p. 128.
20. Di Prima, *Recollections of My Life as a Woman*, p. 107, p. 198.
21. Campbell, *This is the Beat Generation*, p. ix.
22. Roanna C. Johnson and Nancy M. Grace (eds), *Girls Who Wore Black: Women Writing the Beat Generation* (New Brunswick, NJ and London:

Rutgers University Press, 2002), p. 4, p. 12. I return to di Prima in the fiction chapter in Part Two.

23. Jack Kerouac, *The Subterraneans* (New York: Grove Press, 1971), p. 19.
24. Jon Panish, *The Color of Jazz: Race and Representation in Postwar American Culture* (Jackson: University Press of Mississippi, 1997), p. 57.
25. Jones, *Blues People*, p. 188.
26. Panish, *The Color of Jazz*, p. 110.
27. Ibid., p. 125, pp. 137–8.
28. Holmes, *Go*, p. 250. The one exception to this can be found in Kerouac's repeated encouragement of Neal Cassady, who showed little aptitude for writing despite his ability to entertain and surprise with his spoken monologues.
29. Peter Townsend, *Jazz in American Culture* (Edinburgh: Edinburgh University Press, 2000), p. 148.
30. Kerouac, *On the Road*, p. 140.
31. Campbell discusses Kerouac's performance in *This is the Beat Generation*, p. 259; *Kerouac – Kicks Joy Darkness* was released by Rykodisc.
32. Jones, *Blues People*, pp. 233–4.
33. Ibid., p. 186.
34. Ibid., p. 191.
35. Eldridge Cleaver, *Soul on Ice* (London: Panther, 1970), p. 71, p. 83.
36. Ibid., pp. 74–6.
37. Ibid., p. 74.
38. Campbell, *This is the Beat Generation*, p. 147.
39. James Baldwin, *Another Country* (London: Black Swan, 1984), p. 292, p. 241.
40. Ibid., pp. 38–9, p. 75.
41. Ibid., p. 121.
42. Ibid., p. 146.
43. Ibid., p. 135.
44. Ibid., p. 344.
45. Ibid., pp. 228–9.
46. Kerouac, *On the Road*, p. 194.
47. Baldwin, *Another Country*, p. 250.
48. Ibid., p. 253.

CHAPTER TWO

Music

Each true jazz moment . . . springs from a contest in which each artist challenges all the rest, each solo flight or improvisation, represents . . . a definition of his identity: as individual, as a member of a collectivity and as link in the chain of tradition. Thus, because jazz finds its very life in an endless improvisation upon traditional materials, the jazzman must lose his identity even as he finds it.

Ralph Ellison, *Shadow and Act* (1967)[1]

The breakthrough year was 1955, when the airwaves rocked with Fats Domino's 'Ain't That a Shame,' Bill Haley and his Comets' 'Rock Around the Clock,' Chuck Berry's 'Maybelline,' and Little Richard's 'Tutti Frutti.' That same year, *The Blackboard Jungle* linked the boiled-down 'Rock Around the Clock' with the dread juvenile delinquency.

Todd Gitlin,
The Sixties: Years of Hope, Days of Rage (1987)[2]

Protest is an element of all art, though it does not necessarily take the form of speaking for a political or social program.

Ralph Ellison, 'The World and the Jug' (1963–4)[3]

Broadly speaking, it is possible to summarise the Beat aesthetic under a small range of influences and interests. In literature, the poetic tradition of Blake and Whitman, alongside a wider indebtedness to the American Renaissance, and twentieth-century poets such as William Carlos

Williams and Hart Crane, contributed to the emphasis on personal, often confessional, texts such as 'Howl' and *On the Road*. Like Whitman, the Beats were happy to collapse the divide between high and popular culture, being as willing to celebrate *The Shadow* (Kerouac, Amiri Baraka) or Lana Turner (Frank O'Hara) as to cite Melville or Pound. This concern is extended in the practice of incorporating American idioms and vernacular into almost all Beat novels and poems. Likewise, as we have seen in the previous chapter, Beat writers regularly explored African-American and other 'ethnic' cultures as alternatives to the monochrome lifestyle they identified in white America. Although there were dangers in their approach to otherness, with the risk of what James Edward Smethurst has called 'Romantic-inflected primitivist notions of race and ethnicity . . . that we might well consider essentialist or racist', Smethurst asserts that Beat approaches were 'frequently far more nuanced and provisional' than is generally argued, a point largely supported by the readings I have offered in the previous chapter.[4]

Within this more general interest in African-American art and culture, of course, the Beats displayed an almost obsessive fascination with bebop and its star performers, most notably Charlie Parker. In part, this was a result of a shared desire to explore new possibilities in art, drawing on years of training – as musician, writer, painter, actor, and so on – in order to generate an immediate, improvised and apparently 'spontaneous' product. In addition, there was a recognition by writers such as Kerouac and Ginsberg that bebop was a music of non-conformity, 'weird' – as LeRoi Jones puts it – to middle-class white and black Americans alike.[5] If the Beats had removed themselves from the mainstays of dominant ideology, then the same could also be said of the beboppers who, from the early 1940s, challenged the norms of jazz and swing. As Jones continues, bebop was 'a feast to the rhythm-starved young white intellectuals as well as to those young Negroes . . . who were still capable of accepting emotion that came from outside the shabby cornucopia of popular American culture . . . The music, bebop, defined the term of a deeply felt nonconformity among many young Americans, black and white. And for many young Negroes the irony of being thought "weird" or "deep" by white Americans was as satisfying as it was amusing.'[6]

It is important to remember, however, that jazz was far from the only musical form to offer alternatives to more official versions of popular culture: the migration of African-Americans from the rural South to Northern cities such as New York and Chicago also resulted in the emergence of an urban electric blues led by figures such as Muddy Waters (McKinley Morganfield), Elmore James and Howlin' Wolf (Chester Burnett) that provided an alternative to bebop (and one that could more easily be danced to) and would come to serve as a major influence for the rock music of the 1960s; the country singer-song-writer Hank Williams would provide a model of the self-destructive genius to rival Parker; and the political folk tradition of Woody Guthrie would be perpetuated by artists like Pete Seeger, and would subsequently help to shape the folk boom and protest movements of the '60s. Most significant of all, the 'arrival' of rock and roll in the mid-'50s would introduce a much wider audience of young white Americans to a black-led musical form than had been the case with bebop. The perceived threat to the nation's moral well-being posed by a hip-swivelling Elvis Presley is not easy to understand without appreciating quite how tightly self-appointed guardians of public decency attempted to control youth culture. Whereas bebop largely appealed to urban African-Americans and to slightly older white artists later easily parodied – and thus marginalised – as 'Beatniks', rock and roll seemed to strike at the heart and soul of middle-class white America, threatening to fortify the gulf between Baby Boom teens and their parents that many adults feared had been developing even before the music arrived.

Jazz

There are two instances in Chester Himes's novel, *Cotton Comes to Harlem* (1965), when the detective protagonists, Coffin Ed Johnson and Grave Digger Jones, momentarily interrupt their investigations of a tangled case involving fraud, murder, robbery and a host of other standards of the thriller genre in order to debate the meaning of jazz. In each example, the music assumes a racial significance, conveying – or attempting to convey – a message that cannot be spoken in English. Thus, in the first:

> The horns were talking and the saxes talking back.
> 'Listen to that,' Grave Digger said when the horns took eight on a frenetic solo. 'Talking under their clothes, ain't it?'
> Then the two saxes started swapping fours with the rhythm always in the back. 'Somewhere in that jungle is the solution to the world,' Coffin Ed said. 'If only we could find it.'

'Yeah, it's like the sidewalks trying to speak in a language never heard. But they can't spell it either.'

'Naw,' Coffin Ed said. 'Unless there's an alphabet for emotion.'

'The emotion that comes out of experience. If we could read that language, man, we would solve all the crimes in the world.'

'Let's split,' Coffin Ed said. 'Jazz talks too much to me.'

'It ain't so much what it says,' Grave Digger agreed. 'It's what you can't do about it.'[7]

What commences as an examination of the sexual overtones of the music – in this case, in a bar 'filled with the flashily dressed people of many colors' representing the one genuine site of equal inter-racial activity in the novel – quickly develops into a suggestion that jazz expresses both the history of and, potentially, the solution to the problems of African-American urban experience. For Coffin Ed and Grave Digger, jazz provides both the utopian hope of 'solv[ing] all the crimes in the world' and an example of the indecipherability of the complex modern city in which their inability to arrive at satisfactory solutions is a constant source of anxiety.

The second example occurs when the detectives visit Mammy Louise's 'fancy all-night barbecue joint':

Suddenly they were listening.

'Pres,' Grave Digger recognized, cocking his ear. 'And Sweets.'

'Roy Eldridge too,' Coffin Ed added. 'Who's on the bass?'

'I don't know him or the guitar either,' Grave Digger confessed. 'I guess I'm an old pappy.'

'What's the platter?' Coffin Ed asked the youth standing by the jukebox who had played the number.

His girl looked at them through wide dark eyes, as though they'd escaped from the zoo, but the boy replied self-consciously,

'"Laughing to Keep from Crying." It's foreign.'

'No, it ain't,' Coffin Ed said.

No one contradicted him.[8]

In some ways, this exchange echoes the first: once more, the detectives appear to hear some kind of deep, collective meaning in the track which, for them, represents both a telling of racial history and an instance of recognisable, distinctive voices within that history. And yet, this sense is clearly undermined by the revelation that the record is 'foreign', and by the silence that follows Coffin Ed's denial of this fact.

The suggestion of foreignness transforms the music into a kind of aural simulacrum, threatening to reduce it to a standardised example of popular culture, and it is only the terrifying appearance of Coffin Ed and Grave Digger that precludes debate on the matter. Where they insist on jazz being a distinctively urban African-American cultural form, involving conversation between individual voices collectively exploring black racial identity, the implication is that their view of bebop as jazz's modernist moment is out of touch with an urban environment in which the music is international and its audience is multiracial.

The position of the two black detectives in the novel hints at Himes's challenge to the notion of a racially 'pure' art form. As African-Americans, Coffin Ed and Grave Digger identify with the people of Harlem; as cops, they are separated from this community, even where they use their power to help fight white injustice and oppression. As jazz aficionados, they seem to be able to identify the idiosyncrasies of pre-eminent instrumentalists, but cannot recognise the extent to which individual style can be mastered and reproduced by others. More importantly, however, the two passages cited above point to key negotiations about the 'meaning' of jazz in American culture: is it a black art form shaped and defined by African-Americans, and used to express a sense of racial alienation and resistance to hegemonic white America, but which has been appropriated by others with more cultural weight? Or is it a genre that transcends race in a manner absent from other sites of exchange? If it is the former, then Coffin Ed's silencing of the debate about the music's source can be read as a localised reversal of the dominant power relations that either negated the African-American jazz narrative or reduced it to a form of 'primitive' culture; if the latter, then how does this relate to the identification of bebop – a genre that slightly post-dates the heyday of Coffin Ed and Grave Digger's favourite musicians such as Roy Eldridge and Lester Young – as soundtrack to the Beat Generation in the 1940s and '50s?

Of course, Himes's reference to jazz in *Cotton Comes to Harlem* is by no means unique: in addition to the representations of bebop in the fiction discussed in chapter one, the use of the jazz of the mid-twentieth century has become something of a cliché as the accompaniment to literary and cinematic representations of a seedy urban underworld of drunks, drug dealers, junkies and whores, as epitomised by Elmer Bernstein's score for *The Man With the Golden Arm* (1955) or Charles Mingus's music for the John Cassavetes film, *Shadows* (1959). For many, rather than seeing jazz as the chronological extension of African-American 'traditional materials' (to use Ralph Ellison's term), the genre is understood as a synchronistic feature of this environment, and it has become almost indivisible from the black-and-white noir movies shot at the time in characterisations of a subcultural inversion of the idealised white America portrayed in mainstream television and in the popular domestic comedy films starring the likes of Rock Hudson and Doris Day. The embrace of bebop and cool jazz by Kerouac and other writers as soundtrack to the 'Beat Generation' – and especially the links between the early New York Beat scene and Times Square's junkies and small-time crooks as represented in John Clellon Holmes's *Go* as well as Kerouac's fiction – has blended Greenwich Village bohemia into this association, both at the time and subsequently, as have the links between jazz and other counter-cultural heroes like Jackson Pollock. For many, bebop is *the* countercultural music of the period.

Attempts to sustain an absolute distinction between self and other – here, in Coffin Ed and Grave Digger's efforts to protect their 'own black people' and to provide racialised definitions of jazz – thus fail to account for what Henry Louis Gates has called the 'complex social dynamism of marginalized cultures' and 'the relation between margin-ality and centrality'.[9] In the case of bebop and the forms of jazz that followed it during the 1950s, the issue is further problematised by the presence of mixed-race bands. As early as 1939, Doug Ramsay and Charles Edward Smith's *Jazzmen* had charted the racial mix of the origins of jazz and in the 1930s Benny Goodman – the pre-eminent swing band leader of the time – had recorded with African-American performers such as Billie Holiday, Ethel Waters and Coleman Haw-kins, as well as hiring arrangers including Fletcher Henderson and Jimmy Mundy.[10] A further complication is the interplay between jazz and the counterculture revolving around the Beats in Greenwich Village.

The lives of many leading musicians of the time have reinforced the countercultural connection: Charlie Parker's legendary appetite for drugs and alcohol, along with his early death, have cemented his status as cultural icon (alongside James Dean and Pollock) for people born much too late to hear him play. Unlike Dean and Pollock, whose work survives in their movies and paintings, Parker's genius is not fully realised in his studio recordings, most of which were made on equip-ment that could only be used to cut short tracks that were unlike his live performances.[11] During Parker's best years in the mid-1940s, when, with Dizzy Gillespie and others, he was shaping bebop, very few recordings were made because of a wartime ban, further limiting direct access to what he was playing but doing nothing to harm the mythologising process that has surrounded him since his arrival in New York already playing in a style resembling what would become bebop. Virtually all jazz musicians and critics agree that Parker revolutionised the way the saxophone was played, drawing upon Lester Young's earlier innovations in the development of complex rhythmic patterns for his soloing and – with Gillespie, Thelonious Monk, Charlie Christian and others[12] – creating a small group sound based upon original chord changes and harmonic arrangements.[13] Unlike some other musicians, Parker was celebrated by both black and white audiences. Ross Russell has written that Parker was a 'genuine culture hero' for urban African-Americans, admired because the 'revolutionary nature of his music was explicit. Implicit in his lifestyle was defiance of the white establishment.'[14] Miles Davis – despite being highly critical of Bird's 'greed' for drugs, alcohol and women, and destruction of his own talent – also recognised him as the greatest saxophone player that he ever heard,[15] and Kerouac is just one of the white Beats to see Parker as a spiritual figurehead.

Innumerable other players were also junkies, in part (according to Davis) because they associated Parker's drug use with his genius and in part because of the sheer demands of playing several lengthy sets per night or travelling long distances between engagements. Davis himself was another of the many leading musicians of the period to experience a lengthy period of heroin addiction, and his autobiography makes clear that in the early 1950s he was acting as a pimp to fuel his habit. Although the association has led to distortions surrounding what being a professional jazz musician involved – and Davis repeatedly points to the discipline necessary to master complex and innovative forms – there is no doubt that, from the mid-1940s, shared interest in drug culture contributed to the significant overlap between the worlds of black and white musicians, painters and writers (especially in New York) who constituted the principal cultural opposition to hegemonic American ideology. But what is most significant about these associations and overlaps is not comparisons of lifestyles of alcohol and narcotic use, although these are essential aspects of the counterculture of the time. Instead, it is the extent to which each artistic community was responsible for major advances in their field, rejecting what had become tired generic structures and replacing them with startling modern compositions that generated conflicting responses in hegemonic America.

Bebop's position on the margins of black and white culture is symbolised by its presence in two very different areas of New York: Harlem and 52nd Street, or simply 'The Street'. In the former, although figures like Kerouac did attend, the audience was predominantly black and contained large numbers of musicians; in the latter, the crowd contained many more whites, including music critics and Beats. Miles Davis – alongside Allen Ginsberg and (almost) John Coltrane – was one of the few artists to remain at the vanguard of the counterculture throughout the period covered by this book, and offers pertinent insights into the differences between playing in the two areas. As the story of a trumpeter whose career extended from the mid-1940s to the 1980s and included a lengthy spell with Charlie Parker, plans to work with Jimi Hendrix, and a band that, in the 1950s, featured at various times many of the most significant jazz musicians of the post-war era, Davis's autobiography is a particularly rich memoir of what it was like to be a successful African-American musician in an era when race relations in the United States were marked by a state of almost constant crisis. In it, he suggests contrasts between playing Minton's and 52nd Street in a manner that is useful in understanding the place of jazz at the time. Talking of Minton's as the 'black jazz capital of the world', he suggests that it was '*the* ass-kicker back in those days [the 1940s] for aspiring jazz musicians . . . It was Minton's where a musician really cut his teeth and *then* went downtown to the Street. Fifty-Second Street was easy compared to what was happening up at Minton's.'[16] Davis goes on to state that being permitted to play and receiving acclaim from other African-American musicians at Minton's was what mattered, rather than the reception from white audiences downtown:

> If you got up on the bandstand at Minton's and couldn't play, you were not only going to get embarrassed by people ignoring you or booing you, you might get your ass kicked. One night this guy who couldn't play worth shit got up to try and do his thing – bullshit – and style himself off to get some bitches, playing anything. A regular street guy who just loved to listen to all the music was in the audience when this dumb motherfucker got up on the stage to play, so the man just got up quietly from his table and snatched this no-playing cat off the stage, dragged him outside and into the alcove between the Cecil Hotel and Minton's, and just kicked this motherfucker's ass. I mean *real* good . . . That was Minton's. You had to put up or shut up, there was no in between.[17]

Although Davis also suggests that The Street was 'unbelievable' and 'something else when it was happening', he recalls that some of the clubs there were 'real racist'[18] and makes clear that playing Minton's was a more significant gig. In part, this seems to be the result of an awareness of the history of race relations on Davis's part that he believes is not shared by all other musicians. Thus, he is critical of the way in which Louis Armstrong and Dizzy Gillespie would 'laugh and grin for the [white] audience', and refuses to 'sell out [his] principles' in the same way.[19] Jon Panish has argued that, for all his musical virtuosity, Gillespie 'good-naturedly obliged the mainstream press's desire for a cartoon image of the bebopper with his beret, horn-rimmed glasses and ostrich leather shoes',[20] an act that was clearly anathema to Davis. Nevertheless, Davis's (and Panish's) stance also overlooks not only the impact of French Existentialist style on Gillespie's dress and goatee beard, but also, more importantly, why Gillespie acted in this manner: at a time when bebop was seen by many white critics as emblematic of a dangerously aggressive black culture, Gillespie's conduct helped to popularise the music and to counter the more outlandish behaviour of musicians such as Parker and Thelonious Monk.

There is no doubt that attempts to regulate jazz clubs in the 1940s and '50s continued to be governed by forms of institutional hostility to the music that sought to drive 'awkward' performers out of business. In 1940, the police in New York began fingerprinting every performer at licenced cabarets, issuing identity cards that were denied to 'people they thought were not of good character', a policy that resulted in many musicians, including Thelonious Monk, Miles Davis and Billie Holiday, being unable to work for lengthy periods. Although these regulations were implemented as part of a more general attack on the 'deviance' associated with the world surrounding jazz clubs, there is no doubt that they were underpinned by a racism that would not tolerate individuals who openly resisted conventional taste.[21] Bebop seemed to represent a particular threat, with its 'disjunctive melodies, polyrhythmic accents . . . and relentless speed' providing – as Preston Whaley sums up – a sonic register of the 'social instability' generated by the double standard of African-Americans being expected to fight for 'their' country while being discriminated against at home. The term 'bebop' itself was coined (according to Whaley) 'as a "fighting" word for a "fighting" music', and there is no doubt that the combination of the music with 'nonmusical elements' such as the 'argot, the zoot suits, the smack, the goatees, the berets, the green-tinted, horn-rimmed glasses' represented a combination of the intellectual and the worldly that offered a 'hip' – and thus, invariably, threatening – challenge to the hegemonic conventions of mid-century America.[22]

Blues

Bebop received acclaim both from black critics such as LeRoi Jones (Amiri Baraka), who saw it as a return to African-American tradition in what James Edward Smethurst summarises as 'an expression of modern, urban, African American militancy in the politically difficult moment of the Cold War',[23] and from the Beats, who believed that it echoed their own emphasis on spontaneity. For the former, bebop could be celebrated, as Smethurst continues, for its 'self-conscious stylistic internationalism', in which it drew upon European composers such as Igor Stravinsky as an equal partner and 'promoted a new sense of the status of the black artistic tradition as equal or superior to European art music', through the 'prominent appropriation and assimilation' of European compositions. As such, it served to reverse a lengthy tradition of classical composers borrowing from jazz and helped to modernise and empower black vernacular discourse.[24]

In contrast, the urban blues concentrated in Chicago and other Northern cities tended to be looked upon as an unfortunate throwback to an era when suffering was an accepted part of African-American existence. Thus, although the Chicago Black Arts movement that emerged in the 1960s was willing to celebrate earlier, acoustic blues singers such as Leadbelly (Huddie Leadbetter), they rarely saw contemporary electric artists like Muddy Waters, Howlin' Wolf and Buddy Guy as participating in their notion of a 'Black Aesthetic'.[25] Likewise, until the British blues invasion of the mid-1960s, few white Americans were aware of urban blues: although artists like Josh White and Big Bill Broonzy were championed by the Old Left folk movement, and Waters and John Lee Hooker did play at the Newport Folk Festival (and were able to use electric instruments without comment, unlike white artists), their world rarely overlapped with that of, for example, the Beats, in the manner of bop musicians'. Nevertheless – and although this marginality indicates a distance from the counterculture that only began to be narrowed by the folk revival that developed from the late 1950s – it is important to say something about the blues here, given the significance that blues numbers recorded in the 1940s and '50s subsequently acquired as rock standards.

Like rock and roll, the blues does, of course, stem from a Southern tradition. Almost all of the pre-eminent Chicago bluesmen had been born and raised in the South, before heading to the city in the 1940s. Muddy Waters' career is typical in this respect, even if his subsequent fame transcended that of other electric blues artists, with the possible exception of John Lee Hooker and B. B. King. Born in Mississippi, Waters had been 'discovered' and recorded by folk anthropologists Alan Lomax and John Work in 1941, as they travelled through the South looking for Robert Johnson, unaware (as had been John Hammond on a similar quest in 1939) that he had died in 1938. This encounter, alongside a more general sense that the future of the blues lay in the North, was probably one of the factors that precipitated Waters' move to Chicago in 1943. After various manual jobs, Waters established himself as the pre-eminent artist on the independent Chess record label (founded by Polish immigrant brothers Len and Phil Chess, and responsible for issuing many classic blues records) and released a catalogue of songs – including 'Hoochie Coochie Man', 'I Got My Mojo Working' and 'Mannish Boy' – that would become staples of the white rock repertoire in the 1960s and beyond. Drawing on the tradition of Southern acoustic blues exemplified by Johnson and Son House, Waters helped to reinvent a genre best known for its solo musicians as a newly citified ensemble style whose arrangements established the format for much '60s rock. In particular, the line-up of Waters' band – comprising a lead guitarist, pianist, harmonica player, drummer and, at times, saxophone, in addition to Waters on slide guitar and vocals – served as blueprint for the white rock bands that followed.

As significant as the composition of Chicago blues bands was the way in which they adopted the opportunities made possible by electrification. While Charlie Christian and the pioneering electric blues guitarist T-Bone Walker had turned the guitar from a rhythm instrument into one capable of soloing like a saxophone over a backing band, their style tended to be 'pure' – using amplification to make the pre-existing sound louder, rather than changing it. In contrast, bands like Muddy Waters' were unafraid to experiment with a harder, distorted tone that could be seen to represent the grittiness of metropolitan life as well as supporting a rhythm more conducive to dancing than bebop's esoteric variations. Although there is no doubting the virtuosity of musicians such as Buddy Guy, Otis Spann and James Cotton – all of whom played with Waters at some point – their soloing was based around the relatively straightforward blues scale rather than the complex chromatics deployed in bop, and was usually set against an uncomplicated and rhythmically steady twelve-bar blues chord sequence that 'regularized' – as Carlo Rotella has put it – the 'often irregular country beat' of acoustic Southern performers.[26] Of course, the twelve-bar progression is also integral to the rock and roll of the 1950s, and musicians including the important bassist-songwriter Willie Dixon, whose songs were widely covered by white acts in the '60s, moved freely between the two genres. The twelve-bar structure remained fundamental to the blues rock of the 1960s and blues-scale based soloing continued to dominate white rock throughout the decade, even when song structures moved away from traditional blues patterns. Musicians at the heart of the '60s counterculture, such as The Rolling Stones, Janis Joplin, Cream, Jimi Hendrix, The Grateful Dead and Bob Dylan, drew heavily upon the blues (generally acknowledging sources, if not always paying composer royalties), although the extent to which Chicago's tourist trade now depends upon the music illustrates the manner in which a once-marginal art form can be appropriated and stripped of its original significance to be incorporated within dominant culture.[27]

Chicago blues developed alongside and initially appealed to the expanding class of African-American urban industrial workers whose lives had been shaped by segregation in the South and the effects of migration North. As Rotella suggests, in a lengthy assessment of legendary guitarist and club-owner Buddy Guy, Chicago blues was 'singularly expressive of the encounter with industrial urbanism: expressive in lyrics, theme, and the juxtaposition of strong, southern-accented feeling with mechanized, routinized mass-produced – that is, industrialized – sound and experience'.[28] Such origins explain why the (largely white) folk purists of the 1950s were less interested in urban than rural blues: the latter were taken to represent 'authentic' folk culture, providing an alternative to standardised mass culture; the former were too much a product of that standardisation, their rhythms a constant reminder of the monotony of daily life. This does not, however, account for the extraordinary degree to which the 1960s counterculture drew upon the musical style of figures like Waters and the songbooks of composers like Willie Dixon, alongside a twin fascination with Robert Johnson's 1930s recordings.

The reasons for this transformation – at the very moment that the emergence of Black Power led to widespread African-American rejection of blues in favour of more militant soul and funk artists – are complex and somewhat contradictory. On the one hand, they do indicate the legacy of the folk boom being recreated by a younger audience already accustomed to electric arrangements through their familiarity with rock and roll, and with white artists (in particular, Bob Dylan) switching from solo acoustic to amplified band performances. The arrival of British blues enthusiasts such as The Rolling Stones and The Animals, who actively sought out Waters and other Chicago blues players, also generated interest within the white American youth community. In this context, the blues appealed because its energy and overt sexuality provided an invigorating contrast to the sterile pop broadcast by most white radio stations at a time when many of the first-generation rock and roll stars had either died (Buddy Holly, Eddie Cochran) or were forced away from the spotlight by personal problems (Chuck Berry, Jerry Lee Lewis). The blues was also – unlike bebop and the forms of jazz that followed it – a relatively easy form to play, if not to master. Thus, although musicians such as Eric Clapton, Johnny Winter, Mike Bloomfield and Ry Cooder adopted an almost professorial approach to their study of acoustic and electric blues guitar, it was also possible to perform a passable imitation of the music with the knowledge of a few chords and a single scale.

The '60s counterculture tended not to look too deeply at the lyrical content of the songs they were covering. While black blues vernacular provided an attractive counter to 'standard' American English, just as the hip language of bop players had appealed to the Beats, white reconstructions of Robert Johnson's pact with the devil or Waters' sexual potency seemed, at best, ill conceived. Predictably, the kind of technical virtuosity (and self-indulgence) that characterises the blues 'supergroups' of the late 1960s, such as Electric Flag, Blind Faith and even Cream, suggests performers whose mastery of musical form cannot disguise their lack of empathy with lyrics representative of Southern or migratory black experience. Although there is no doubt that early blues aficionados such as Alexis Korner, John Mayall and Long John Baldry in Britain, and Paul Butterfield in the United States, not only had genuine appreciation for the music they adopted but also aided the original blues musicians in finding a new and wide audience, the latter phase of white blues mentioned above is indicative of the problematic relationship between the counterculture and African-American cultures in the '60s and – alongside the political reasons why many young blacks were, by this time, uninterested in blues – helps to explain the small presence of African-Americans at major festivals such as Woodstock and the Monterey Pop Festival.

Rock and Roll

One of the songs on Muddy Waters' *Hard Again* (1977) is titled 'The Blues had a Baby and They Named It Rock and Roll.'[29] Although the verses detail pregnancy and delivery, the song fails to mention the child's father. In one way, this is unsurprising, given the scandalous – within the cultures of both the 'respectable' Northern *and* Southern United States of the 1950s – encounter between blues and country music that led to a Southern hybrid becoming the soundtrack to rebellious youth in the late 1950s. In another way, however, the co-parenting of rock and roll by blues and country music was inevitable, given the cross-fertilisation of white and black working-class musical traditions in the South throughout the first half of the twentieth century. Thus, alongside the heavy country emphasis of early white rock and rollers such as Buddy Holly – a presence that now seems almost inescapable given Holly's roots in Lubbock, Texas – there is an equally significant country influence in the songs and guitar-playing of Chuck Berry, the rock and roll performer whose legacy was most pronounced in the 1960s. Likewise, there is a heavy blues – and rhythm and blues – presence in the work of even the most country-oriented early rockers, such as Jerry Lee Lewis and Johnny Cash, and many of the early recordings of artists such as Fats Domino and even Berry himself are, in essence, blues songs.

The term 'rock and roll' was probably coined by the disc jockey and promoter Alan Freed, whose radio shows in the 1950s were the first to attract significant numbers of white listeners. Despite his subsequent disgrace in the payola scandal that precipitated his alcoholism and early death in 1965, Freed is an immensely important figure, in that he was instrumental in the promotion of touring shows featuring a mix of black and white performers. His television programme represented a major breakthrough in terms of inter-racial broadcasting, and its demise after Frankie Lyman danced with a young white woman was a widely documented instance of the residual power of racist Southern corporations that helped to precipitate the alliance between young whites and the civil rights movement. It is possible that Freed was singled out for punishment over payola – which was common practice at the time – because of his determination to promote black, as well as white, artists; what is certain is that his defence of the right to stage rock and roll events, in the face of enormous pressure from police and local government (especially after an alleged 'riot' in Boston in 1958), was essential to the spread of live rock and roll.

For all Freed's efforts, however, there is no doubt that, despite his rapid transformation form rockabilly rebel into movie star and Las Vegas regular, Elvis Presley remains not only the greatest rock and roller of all time, but also (probably much against his own will) a pivotal participant in the emergence of the counterculture and, as Greil Marcus has suggested, a 'supreme figure in American life'.[30] In part, this is because of his combination of voice, looks, ability to fuse African-American blues and white country music into a dynamic new form during his brief period with Sun Records in the mid-1950s, and the good fortune to be in the right place at the right time. In addition, it involved willingness, almost from the start of his career, actively to assist in what Marcus calls the 'assimilation of a revolutionary musical style into the mainstream of American culture'.[31]

The young Elvis both epitomises and transcends the fusion of blues and country that I outlined above. He drew on the poor white tradition of country music chronicling not only poverty, but also a sense of dispossession and nostalgia for the old South. This music – as exemplified in the early 1950s by Hank Williams – represented the situation of figures like Elvis's father, himself a failed sharecropper. But, as Marcus points out, Elvis responded to much more than this:

> On the radio, he listened with his family to the old music of the Carter family and Jimmie Rodgers . . . and to white gospel groups like the Blackwood Brothers. Elvis touched the soft center of American music when he heard and imitated Dean Martin and the operatics of Mario Lanza; he picked up Mississippi blues singers like Big Bill Broonzy, Big Boy Crudup, Lonnie Johnson, and the new Memphis music of Rufus Thomas and Johnny Ace, mostly when no one else was around, because that music was naturally frowned upon.[32]

Of course, Elvis was not the only white musician to be making these connections in the South at the time: Jerry Lee Lewis and Carl Perkins, for example, were developing similar syntheses, and creating a music that, as Marcus continues, 'proved white boys could do it all – that they could be as strange, as exciting, as scary, and as free as the black men who were suddenly walking America's airwaves as if they owned them'.[33] Marcus' point is that the early white Southern rockers took a line diametrically opposed to the corporate strategies developed to profit from black rock and roll by cashing in on it through soft cover versions performed by white artists like Pat Boone – a strategy that was commercially successful, but unlikely to attract long-term interest from rebellious teenagers. In contrast, the energy of rockabilly, coupled with the charismatic sex appeal of Elvis and the sheer menace of Jerry Lee 'brought home' – as Marcus puts it in his account of the reactions to Elvis's version of 'That's All Right' – 'the racial fears of a lot of people', and 'touched the secret dreams of others'.[34]

Rockabilly provides a pivotal moment in the emergence of the counterculture, but one that, like Chicago blues, is by no means a straightforward antecedent to '60s rock. It did appear to demonstrate that 'race' music's energy, sexuality and, at times, aggression could be replicated by white musicians, a significant achievement that in some ways contains parallels with Marlon Brando's early stage and screen performances a few years before. On the other hand, there were aspects of white Southern culture that were unlikely ever to appeal to the middle-class core of the '60s counterculture. Elvis's swift embrace of the fruits of the American Dream seemed like a crass rejection of the rebel posture, even if its promise was what had driven him in the first place. Worse was the sheer otherness of Jerry Lee Lewis, who, as Marcus rightly suggests, 'came to represent all the mythical strangeness of the redneck South: lynch-mob blood lust, populist frenzies, even incest'.[35]

Rockabilly did offer a model for white artists such as the early Beatles, The Rolling Stones and The Animals, and for the rock music of the later '60s – and it is notable that blues rock players such as Johnny Winter regularly included covers of Elvis and Jerry Lee songs in their live performances. Nevertheless, by the time The Beatles arrived in America for the first time in 1964, its influence was hard to detect amidst their Buddy Holly, Chuck Berry and Everly Brothers references. Indeed, despite his death in a plane crash in February 1959, Holly is another pivotal figure: although his songs lack both the sex appeal and the menace of rockabilly, they share its fusion of country and blues, and demonstrate Holly's pioneering and influential use of multi-track-ing and string arrangements, techniques that would be developed by The Beatles in their more avant-garde experimentations in the late 1960s. Of course, The Beetles/Beatles also chose their name with Holly's backing band, The Crickets, in mind.

Although Elvis provides the supreme example of the rebel rocker becoming a mainstream star, it would be a mistake to imagine a sharp divide between 'outsider' musicians and mass culture in the late 1950s.

Unlike the Beats and many of the bop musicians of a decade earlier, early rock and rollers were willing and able to draw upon relatively sophisticated marketing techniques to promote their music. Holly enjoyed a 'double' career through the simple strategy of releasing some songs under his own name and others under the moniker 'The Crickets', although the same band played on much of the 'solo' material; Gene Vincent's leather-jacked rebel look was dreamed up to make him more appealing to the youth market. Ironically, the early deaths of many of the first-generation rock and roll stars – including Holly, Vincent and Eddie Cochran – contributed further to the mythologising of their role and probably stopped them drifting back into country music and alienating '60s youth.

The rock and roller whose career overlaps with the '60s counterculture more regularly than any other is unquestionably Chuck Berry. While Elvis had moved to Hollywood, and Holly and Cochran were dead, Berry managed to combine appearances on the rock and roll nostalgia tours that sprung up from the 1960s with performances alongside bands like the Stones. To some extent, this ability to move between vastly different musical arenas can be attributed to Berry's shrewdness as a businessman and his resentfulness at the sense that managers and disc jockeys had cheated him early in his career. For example, his first hit, 'Maybelline' (1955), is co-credited to Alan Freed, whose extensive playing of the record boosted sales, but who is unlikely to have contributed much to the song itself. In addition, Berry appears to have become more driven by financial concerns after having served a jail sentence in the early 1960s on charges related to the Mann Act, but stemming from white resentment at the wealth and fame of an African-American in the vanguard of youth rebellion.[36]

Infinitely more important than these biographical details, however, is the quality of Berry's song writing, playing and performing, each of which was a decisive influence on not only the Stones, but also Jimi Hendrix, The Beach Boys and many other leading figures in 1960s rock. Although many of his songs – including 'Johnny B. Goode', 'Roll Over Beethoven', and 'Carol' – are built around the twelve-bar blues format, they challenge the norms of blues composition both musically and lyrically. First, as outlined above, Berry's guitar style draws as heavily from country and swing as it does from the blues. His riffs and solos tend to revolve around playing two strings together – unlike, say, B. B. King's blues style – and are mostly based on a major, as opposed to blues, scale. The style was later lifted, virtually note for note, by The Beach Boys for 'Surfin' U.S.A.', and also served as the prototype for countercultural icons like Keith Richards and Jimi Hendrix. Coupled with this, Berry's songs have a lyrical sophistication unlike anything else produced by early rock and rollers. Whereas most rock and roll is based around three or four verses with straightforward, often repeated, lines, Berry's songs construct lengthy narratives and depend upon unexpected and witty rhymes, delivered with clear diction. While Bob Dylan's 'story' – and, later, stream-of-consciousness – songs obviously draw on a narrative tradition revolving around Woody Guthrie, they also apply this tradition to electric ensemble arrangements in the manner pioneered by Berry. Finally, Berry's famous 'duck walk', performed during his guitar solos in live performances, has been imitated by innumerable rock musicians. While Jerry Lee Lewis's antics at the piano were certainly influential, the fact that the guitar was the instrument of choice for the majority of the major rock acts of the '60s means that Berry's stage moves were more significant in a genealogy featuring Hendrix's playing of his guitar with his teeth and behind his neck and, in a gesture that transported the sexuality of the blues in a manner that scandalised much of white America, using it to simulate masturbation.[37]

It is important to remember that almost all of the styles – and musicians – described above had either tangential or highly problematic relations to the Beat community at the core of the counterculture of the 1940s and '50s. Bebop, despite providing the 'soundtrack' to the Beat Generation, was a genre whose leading musicians were mostly African-American and lived in Harlem – rather than Greenwich Village – and whose sources and ideology did not always correspond comfortably with Beat interpretations of their work. Urban blues and rock and roll largely assumed retrospective countercultural significance in the 1960s, and represented other forms of marginality or alienation in the 1950s. The former was a genre with little contact with either the Beats or other forms of African-American art; the latter became indelibly associated with a white teenage discontent that only acquired a clear ideological focus with the move from high school to university campus, the emergence of the New Left, and growing interest in civil rights and the anti-war movement in the 1960s. In the chapter that follows, I examine similar tensions surrounding Abstract Expressionist art, a form whose relationship to mid-twentieth-century hegemonic and countercultural America remains contested in the twenty-first century.

Notes

1. Ralph Ellison, *Shadow and Act* (London: Secker and Warburg, 1967), p. 234.
2. Todd Gitlin, *The Sixties: Years of Hope, Days of Rage* (New York: Bantam, 1987), p. 39.
3. Ralph Ellison, *Collected Essays* (New York: Modern Library, 1995), p. 158.
4. James Edward Smethurst, *The Black Arts Movement: Literary Nationalism in the 1960s and 1970s* (Chapel Hill: University of North Carolina Press, 2005), p. 37.
5. LeRoi Jones, *Blues People: The Negro Experience in White America and the Music That Developed From It* (New York: William Morrow, 1963), p. 199.
6. Ibid., p. 200.
7. Chester Himes, *Cotton Comes to Harlem* (London: Allison and Busby, 1988), pp. 33–4.
8. Ibid., p. 101.
9. Henry Louis Gates, Jr., 'African American Criticism', in *Redrawing the Boundaries: The Transformation of English and American Literary Studies*, ed. Stephen Greenblatt and Giles Gunn (New York: The Modern Language Association of America, 1992), p. 310.
10. See Preston Whaley, Jr., *Blows Like a Horn: Beat Writing, Jazz, Style, and Markets in the Transformation of U.S. Culture* (Cambridge, MA and London: Harvard University Press, 2004), p. 97.
11. Miles Davis discusses the new opportunities provided by the introduction of 'microgroove' in 1951: 'We could stretch out our solos like we played them live in clubs . . . and I was excited about the freedom this new technology would give me. I had gotten tired of that three-minute lockstep that the 78s had put musicians in. There wasn't any room for really free improvisation: you had to get in your solo real quick and then get out.' Miles Davis with Quincy Troupe, *Miles: The Autobiography* (London: Picador, 1990), p. 137.
12. Although Christian is generally less well remembered than bebop contemporaries Parker, Gillespie and Monk (in part because of his death from tuberculosis at age 26 in 1942), his impact was almost as significant. As a featured soloist with the immensely popular Benny Goodman band, Christian – who thus had an unusually high profile for an African-American musician at the time – pioneered the use of the electric guitar, at once virtually eliminating the banjo from all but the most traditional jazz bands and demonstrating the possibilities of the instrument to a wide audience. Although there were clearly limits to what Christian could play with Goodman's band, he could be more experimental in the after-hours

sessions at Minton's, where his soloing was one of the main attractions of the early bebop jams. Along with early electric blues guitar players such as T-Bone Walker, Christian would later serve as a major model for the blues and rock guitarists of the 1960s. A good idea of Christian's versatility and of his bluesy soloing can be gleaned from the compilation CD *Charlie Christian: Swing to Bop* (Disques Dreyfus, 2000).

13. This is not to deny the power of what does survive: Jon Panish argues that listening to Parker, even now, 'one understands, almost instantly, why his playing affected listeners so powerfully. Fast and dynamic but also bluesy and melodic, Parker's alto solos are continually amazing, surprising, and inspiring. Even in groups filled with other supremely talented musicians . . . Parker's playing stands out.' Jon Panish, *The Color of Jazz: Race and Representation in Postwar American Culture* (Jackson: University Press of Mississippi, 1997), p. 44.

14. Quoted in Lewis MacAdams, *Birth of the Cool: Beat, Bebop and the American Avant-Garde* (London: Scribner, 2002), p. 56.

15. See Davis, *Miles*, pp. 178–9.

16. Ibid., pp. 43–4.

17. Ibid., p. 44.

18. Ibid., p. 88.

19. Ibid., p. 73.

20. Panish, *The Color of Jazz*, p. 9.

21. See Hazel V. Carby, *Race Men* (Cambridge, MA: Harvard University Press, 1998), p. 147.

22. Whaley, *Blows Like a Horn*, p. 40.

23. Whaley, *Blows Like a Horn*, p. 40.

24. Ibid., pp. 273–4.

25. See Smethurst, *The Black Arts Movement*, p. 244.

26. Carlo Rotella, *Good With Their Hands: Boxers, Bluesmen, and Other Characters From the Rust Belt* (Berkeley: University of California Press, 2002), p. 64.

27. See Rotella, *Good With Their Hands*, pp. 51–103. Rotella points out that, 'Black people do [still] listen to Chicago blues, but the local, national, and international CD-buying and festival-going audience is overwhelmingly white, and for two decades most of Chicago's clubs have been on the North Side and filled with white people' (p. 70).

28. Ibid., p. 64.

29. Muddy Waters, 'The Blues had a Baby and They Named it Rock and Roll', *Hard Again* (Sony, 1977).

30. Greil Marcus, *Mystery Train: Images of America in Rock 'n' Roll Music*, 5th edn (London: Faber and Faber, 2000), p. 132.

31. Ibid., pp. 134–5.

32. Ibid., p. 153.

33. Ibid., p. 157.

34. Ibid., p. 163.
35. Ibid., p. 189.
36. Ironically, Berry was in his mid-thirties by this time, an uncanny echo of Jack Kerouac's situation when *On the Road* was published
37. This element of Hendrix's performance was the subject of particular attack during his (bizarrely ill-conceived) tour with The Monkees, then at the height of their teenybopper success.

CHAPTER THREE

Painting

A painting is not a picture *of* an experience, it *is* an experience.

Mark Rothko (1959)[1]

This is not painting! Only in America could it happen.

Constantine Nivola[2]

The canonisation of Jackson Pollock as the tortured genius of post-war American art has tended to reinvent him as a soul brother to other iconic countercultural figures such as Jack Kerouac, Charlie Parker, Lenny Bruce and James Dean. In this narrative, Pollock exemplifies the alienated artist struggling to produce original work within a culture of consumption defined by its obsession with mass-produced objects. Pollock's painterly techniques – especially the dripping that led to *Time* magazine dubbing him 'Jack the Dripper' – have encouraged many critics to draw comparisons across genres; with bop improvisation, with the spontaneous prose associated with Kerouac and other Beats, and with Bruce's stream-of-consciousness stand-up comedy. Pollock's death in an automobile accident in 1956 has done nothing to dispel such mythologising, further linking him with Dean and with Parker, who had both died the previous year.

There is much to be said in defence of this account: alongside the social ties between writers, artists, musicians and painters that were developed in places such as Greenwich Village's Cedar Tavern and Waldorf Cafeteria, there are indubitably compositional, ideological and formal links. David Anfam has suggested that Kerouac's spontaneous prose was developed, in part, as a result of Pollock's work, and has pointed out that in the late 1940s, when Pollock had largely abandoned the use of an easel and was drip painting onto large canvases stretched out on the floor, it was 'commonplace in New York artistic circles . . . to assume that direct gesturing was more powerful than verbal expression'.[3] The illustrated article about Pollock published in *Life* magazine in August 1949 and the famous photographs and film shot by Hans Namuth in 1950 consolidated the image of the artist in precisely these terms, drawing parallels with Method acting and, in particular, with Marlon Brando's portrayal of Stanley Kowalski in the 1947 Broadway staging of Tennessee Williams' *A Streetcar Named Desire*.[4] Moreover, the nature of Pollock's work at this time invited viewers to respond emotionally to the painting as object – or what fellow Abstract Expressionist Mark Rothko terms 'experience' – in itself, rather than attempt to read it as a representation of something else, a marked contrast with much of the art that predates it, including the Social Realism of the 1930s. Again, this conviction that language is secondary and distractive echoes both bebop and (to a lesser extent) much Beat poetry, where rhythms and sounds are celebrated on their own terms rather than as things to be interpreted.

There are, however, significant hazards in accepting this story too readily. In the first place, such readings risk elevating Pollock himself at the expense of his art. Louis MacAdams suggests that the *Life* article created a new type, the 'art star', but that '*Life*'s readers weren't as interested in Pollock's work as in Pollock himself',[5] and Pollock did become a favourite of the gossip columns. Although *Life* was hardly a staple of avant-garde reading at the time, the same process has occurred in re-tellings of countercultural history that construct narratives of individualism – again, featuring Parker, Dean, Kerouac and others – at the expense of the collective experiences that differentiated much of the counterculture. Pollock – or Parker, or Kerouac – becomes the exemplar of a 'movement' – in this case, Abstract Expressionism – in a process that tends to flatten out the differences between artists and subsume diversity beneath stereotype.

In addition, the congregation of Pollock and other painters under the banner 'Abstract Expressionism' leads to other questions. To what extent was the spiritual alienation claimed by many of the group's preeminent figures an invention, and how does their relationship with hegemonic American culture during the Cold War function? As with the Beats, it is clear that the hierarchies established within Abstract

Expressionism produced some awkward paradoxes: if the artists were (as they and their defenders often claimed) illuminating universal truths about the human condition, why were women and non-white painters excluded not only from what became known as the 'essential eight' – Adolph Gottlieb, Willem de Kooning, Robert Motherwell, Barnett Newman, Pollock, Ad Reinhardt, Rothko and Clyfford Still – but also largely from the sub-canon surrounding them and including artists such as Philip Guston, William Baziotes and Fritz Cline?[6] How have the histories of American art of the 1940s and '50s marginalised artists not considered to be Abstract Expressionists, or not based in New York, and how does this relate to the emergent counterculture?

I do not wish to suggest that Pollock is not a central and important figure, as well as a cult hero for much of the counterculture, and I will return to him and to his work repeatedly throughout the following pages. Nevertheless, his emergence as iconic representative of the alienated American artist during the Truman and Eisenhower presidencies is emblematic of a wider complicity between counter- and hegemonic cultures at the time. In this chapter, I will examine the highly complex relationship between Abstract Expressionism and the Cold War culture industry, assessing not only the difficulties conservative America had in accommodating it as politically acceptable, but also the manner in which the State and wealthy individuals and museums deployed Abstract Expressionist art as an ideological tool. I will go on to look at the effects of this relationship on artists excluded from the processes of institutionalisation because of race, and then to offer a brief look at some of the more overtly anti-Establishment art being produced elsewhere in the United States during this period.

Abstract Expressionism and the Cold War

Although attempts to identify a distinctively 'American' school of painting had been made since at least the final quarter of the nineteenth century, there was a general sense that before the Second World War the United States had played a marginal role in visual art. In an influential essay first published in 1973, Max Kozloff argued that even distinguished pre-war painters such as Georgia O'Keefe and Edward Hopper were 'considered too parochial in coloration, and thus too "unmodern" to provide models for mainstream work'. It was only at mid-century – uncoincidentally, just as the United States was being recognised as the dominant power in the world – that the 'complete transformation of this state of affairs' occurred, with the 'switching of the art capital of the West from Paris to New York'.[7] This shift was marked by the emergence of Abstract Expressionism as the most recognisable – and 'American' – form of painting.

In part, this move came about because the onset of war resulted in some of the leading painters of the time relocating to the United States. Most significantly, André Breton, Max Ernst and other Surrealists introduced Pollock and Motherwell to the practice of 'automatism', in which rapid, spontaneous work was believed to result in artistic expressions of the unconscious.[8] In addition, the increased accessibility to the Cubism of Picasso and Georges Braque made possible by the wealth pouring into New York museums and galleries alerted the artists of Pollock's generation to what Francis Frascina has called the 'establishment of a new paradigm in art *practice*' (original italics), in which illusionism was superseded by abstraction.[9] The timing was propitious since it coincided with a shift away from Social Realism and towards forms less overtly (if at all) critical of capitalism on the part of many of the artists who would become Abstract Expressionists. Pollock, for example, was by this time a student of Native American art and had witnessed Navajo artists making sand paintings on the floor at the Museum of Modern Art (MoMA) in New York in 1941. Rothko, too, cited the presence of 'eternal symbols . . . of man's primitive fears and motivations' in 'archaic art and mythology',[10] and suggested that such symbols were an effective way of conveying the horrors associated with the atomic age without actually representing them, a key point given the belief that turning nuclear destruction, for example, into a spectacle would be akin to accepting it.

It should also be noted that most of the best-known Abstract Expressionists came from backgrounds that were similar to one another but different from those of many of the pre-eminent Beats and jazz musicians of the time. First, they tended to be a few years older, having entered adulthood during the early years of the Depression. They were also mostly from working-class, geographically mobile families – Pollock's migratory childhood and interrupted education is more Dean Moriarty than Sal Paradise – and served apprenticeships in Regionalism and Social Realism before moving to New York and Abstract Expressionism. In contrast, most of the leading first-generation Beats, as well as musicians like Miles Davis, had come from middle-class families and had attended prestigious institutions such as Columbia (Kerouac and Ginsberg) and the Juilliard School (Davis).

In addition, many of the artists had been members of the Communist Party and groups like the John Reed Clubs and the American Artists Congress in the 1930s, adhering to Marxist assertions that art should always serve to educate the working classes.

As a result, it is unsurprising that Abstract Expressionists were the subject of much criticism during the McCarthy era, despite the fact that they had abandoned the overtly leftist styles of the 1930s. In 1949, Michigan Congressman George A. Dondero delivered a speech with the title 'Modern Art Shackled to Communism', in which he claimed that Cubism was anti-American in its desire to 'destroy by designed disorder'.[11] Dondero's career as the pre-eminent political opponent of many American artists progressed through three distinct phases. As Jane de Hart Mathews has explained,

> The initial stage, opposition to social commentary in predominantly representational art, involved at first little more than an objection to the particular message conveyed by artists who used their work to communicate what they perceived to be social injustice. The second stage, objection to the political affiliations of the artist . . . attempted to link ideology and art in the person of the artist irrespective of the content of specific works. The objection to modern art as Communist conspiracy, the final stage, involved . . . the assumption . . . that rejection of traditional ways of seeing form and space inherent in vanguard style of painting implied rejection of traditional world views.[12]

The final point is useful in illustrating why large numbers of conservative Americans were disturbed by art – for example, Abstract Expressionism, bebop, Kerouac's fiction – that even the most ardent McCarthyite would have trouble identifying as *explicitly* un-American. It was enough for these works to depart from traditional forms for them to be labelled 'subversive' since, as Mathews continues, abstraction 'seemed to impart to [conservative America's] highly structured world the quality of chaos and the demonic that they so easily identified with communism'.[13] Ideologies integral to the American experience appeared to be subverted in other ways: a 'difficult' art form that could only be understood by experts was a challenge to the equality of taste implicit in a democracy; it was impossible to fit artists like Pollock within conventional accounts of the work ethic and, therefore, to determine whether they 'deserved' the success that came with hard work; the self-control fundamental to Puritan conservatism was undermined by the lack of closure to the paintings and – even more threateningly – by the sexualised Freudian significance often ascribed to Abstract Expressionism.[14] The narrative of post-war American artistic hegemony was rewritten by Dondero as a 'horde of foreign art manglers' and 'international art thugs' arriving in the United States and indoctrinating artists such as Pollock and Motherwell. 'Red' universities trained a new generation of museum directors hostile to more traditional art and determined to feed the public a diet of modern art, in a 'sinister conspiracy conceived at the black heart of Russia'.[15]

Dondero's attacks on Abstract Expressionism were popular in the early 1950s but – as I discuss later in this chapter – were soon superseded by an institutional recognition that not only was the Soviet Union extremely hostile towards modern art, but also that the avant-garde could be deployed as an exemplary illustration of the freedoms equated with America. Nevertheless, they were a contributory factor in many artists' perception of their lifestyles and work as challenges to dominant ideologies. In addition, despite the hysterical tone of Dondero's approach, he did recognise something that many of the painters and their defenders denied – that is, that art is not autonomous and that it cannot be understood outside the political and economic conditions of its production.

The principal theorist of Abstract Expressionism, Clement Greenberg, formulated an argument depending upon a non-partisan position, hostile to dominant American and Soviet ideologies alike and based, increasingly, on what Leonhard Emmerling has called a 'unique symbiosis between artist and theoretician' in his relationship with Pollock.[16] In 'Avant-Garde and Kitsch' (1939) – which was later to assume the status of a virtual manifesto for Abstract Expressionism – Greenberg suggests that the 'avant-garde poet or artist tries to imitate God by creating something valid solely on its own terms in the way nature itself is valid, in the way a landscape – not a picture – is aesthetically valid; something *given*, increate, independent of meanings, similars, or originals. Content is to be dissolved so completely into form that the work of art or literature cannot be reduced in whole or part to anything not itself' (italics in original). In this process, for Greenberg, 'expression [matters] more than what is being expressed'. Many of Pollock's most famous works, such as *Mural* (1943–4), *Cathedral* (1947) and *Lavender Mist: Number 1* (1950) can be seen in these terms. The paintings signify Pollock's abandonment of representational art and a turn to linear complexity, stunning coloration and exuberant gestural abstraction. Their sheer size – *Mural*, for example, is 247×605 cm – contributes further to the sense of 'excitement' invoked by Greenberg in the artist's 'preoccupation with the invention and arrangement of spaces, surfaces, shapes, colors, etc.', and to the impression that painterly inspiration stems from immersion in the medium rather than from 'other preoccupations'.[17]

It would be a mistake to suggest that this emphasis on the medium rather than the message meant that Greenberg did not recognise the political dimensions of abstract art. Marx heavily influenced Greenberg's early writings, such as 'Avant-Garde and Kitsch', which was published in the then Trotskyist (and, by that time, anti-Communist Party) journal, *Partisan Review*, in 1939. As David and Cecile Shapiro have noted, the essay contains an implicit attack on Social Realism and other forms of representational painting, calling instead for a difficult or elitist art that is hard to understand and is perpetually new, offering a constantly evolving avant-garde culture that opposes the debased, synthetic 'kitsch' representations to be found in Social Realism in both the United States and the Soviet Union. Thus, as the Shapiros point out, Greenberg highlights a correspondence between avant-garde culture – here, abstract art – and Trotsky's 'theory of permanent revolution'.[18] Abstract art represents an inherently anti-Establishment position, since it provides 'true culture' in a world dominated by cheap reproduction. Clearly – and contrary to what Dondero would later claim – this is an ideology opposed to the mass culture of both sides in the Cold War, rather than the product of a devious Soviet conspiracy. The hostility to the horrors of the modern world leads the artist to turn away entirely from representing that world and instead to create a work of art as a world of its own.

'Avant-Garde and Kitsch' is not solely an essay about painting, and Greenberg also discusses poetry and prose in similar terms and in a manner that anticipates many of the practices associated with other countercultural arts. His description of 'kitsch' – or 'ersatz culture' – 'destined for those who, insensible to the values of genuine culture, are hungry nevertheless for the diversion that only culture of some sort can provide' targets precisely the kind of 'faked sensation' of quiz shows and soap operas rejected by the Beats.[19] For the Abstract Expressionists and the Beats, as well as the musicians creating bebop at the same moment that Pollock was turning to abstract art, 'kitsch' is the enemy, even if poetry and fiction must enter some sort of compromise with the representational in so far as they must use words to communicate.

Greenberg's subsequent involvement with the development of Abstract Expressionism does, however, point to one key difference between painting and other, contemporaneous, art forms, since the latter generally lacked the kind of theoretical expertise and weight that he could provide. Beat writing, for instance, received little support either from the New Critical hegemony or from *Partisan Review*, despite the fact that Kerouac and Ginsberg had both studied at Columbia with Lionel Trilling, a chief proponent of the journal's cultural manifesto. Likewise, bebop found virtually no institutional approval either from leftist critics such as Theodor Adorno or from music schools like the Juilliard, who (for reasons often associated with racism) saw jazz as merely another example of a debased – or 'kitsch' – mass culture.[20]

Alongside warning of the perpetual danger of the avant-garde being tempted by the financial rewards available to those who modify their work and are drawn toward kitsch, Greenberg also calls attention to the historic relationship between 'true culture' and the 'rich and the cultivated',[21] in a manner that (inadvertently) highlights both a further difference between painters and other artists, and one reason why hostile attitudes to Abstract Expressionism as exemplified by George Dondero's speeches and articles were superseded by an embrace of abstract art by the mid-1950s. There has been a long tradition of wealthy patronage for the arts in the United States, sometimes as a result of genuine interest in what is being produced, though more often because of the social kudos that could be accrued from association with 'exotic' bohemians. This has been the case with musicians and writers, as well as painters, and is evident in the 1940s and '50s in, for example, the social life of 'Jazz Baroness' Nica de Koenigswarter, in whose suite Charlie Parker died of liver failure in March 1955. Nevertheless, there is a key difference with art: a painting is a unique object whose value depends on this fact. Although it can be reproduced, a poster or print will not share the qualities – for example, evidence of brush stroke and texture – that characterise the original. In contrast, although the original manuscript of a poem or novel, or the master of a recording, may well accrue value, this tends to be as a result of the success of the work in mass-produced format such as a book or record.

The consequences in terms of the relationship between artist, marketplace and – as the respective receptions of Abstract Expressionism, bop and Beat literature make clear in the 1950s – dominant nationalist ideology are significant. In the first instance, a number of wealthy patrons, including, most notably, Peggy Guggenheim, were willing to support artists who, in the mid-1940s, had very little money. Although it could be argued that Guggenheim's long-term motives were shaped by self-interest, since she acquired many works very cheaply that were later worth enormous sums, her New York gallery, Art of This Century, which opened in 1941, provided the first opportunity for many of the Abstract Expressionists to exhibit their work to a wide audience. The gallery gave Pollock one-man shows in 1943, 1945 and 1947, and also had one-man shows for others, including Robert Motherwell (1944) and Mark Rothko (1945). In addition, the money that Guggenheim loaned to Pollock (offset against future sales) helped him to purchase the Long Island house and barn that provided the space and environment that facilitated the creation of his most famous works.

Guggenheim's role points to a wider process through which Abstract Expressionism was made part of 'official' culture. The Museum of Modern Art was instrumental in creating a canon of 'great works' illustrating the emergence of American painting on the global stage. Its steady acquisition of these paintings, and policy of exhibiting them around the world, created an environment in which Abstract Expressionism became accepted as the exemplary artistic example of Americanism, championed in galleries, museums and universities. Other museums and galleries, including the Betty Parsons and the Charles Egan, also staged numerous exhibitions, with Pollock having seven one-man shows, Rothko and Hofmann six, Motherwell five, and de Kooning three.[22] Although, aesthetically, there is no doubt that Pollock, Motherwell, Rothko, de Kooning and others *were* revolutionary, the speed with which their work was incorporated and deployed by private and state organisations (most notably, the Rockefeller family and, covertly, the CIA) eager to champion American freedom in the Cold War is suggestive of ideological overlaps with dominant political nationalism. In this light, the claims of neglect by an 'uncultured' society seem disingenuous, and David and Cecile Shapiro suggest that the 'most surprising fact about American art in the 1950s is the dearth of well-written published material critical of or hostile to Abstract Expressionism'.[23]

The real and apparent disparities between the values espoused by particular artists and the deployment of their work in the service of hegemonic Americanism illuminate many of the complexities of the relationship between culture and counterculture. Greenberg's belief that art should be the bastion of true culture in an increasingly debased modern world echoes the views of the Transcendentalist counterculture that marked the onset of the American industrial revolution, but which was later incorporated within a canon of national artistic achievement.

Barnett Newman was a long-time anarchist and many of the other leading Abstract Expressionists (including Rothko and Clyfford Still) adopted anarchist ideals. Willem de Kooning was a prototypical Beat, being one of the first artists illegally to occupy and transform a New York factory loft into a studio and living space.[24] In these respects – and others – the artists demonstrated a profound lack of regard for 'American' values and yet their work was redefined as archetypally American even more swiftly than their Transcendentalist ancestors' had been.

Abstract Expressionism can be read as a challenge to the norms of social life in post-war America. The emphasis on originality and hand-crafted products went counter to a society dominated by reproduction and standardisation; the wilful resistance to interpretation evident in the paintings rejected the obsession with communication – even when there is nothing to say – illustrated by the rise of television; claims to 'spontaneity', and the dismissal of what Motherwell called the 'precision' of machines,[25] were antithetical to a culture obsessed with scientific 'progress'. In this context, the interest in non-Western artistic traditions and techniques also functions as a refutation of dominant discourse.

Nevertheless, there are several aspects of Abstract Expressionism that highlight why it could be appropriated so easily. First, it was not Social Realism, a comparative point that made it seem acceptable because of the absence of overtly left-wing content. More importantly, the art and artists were considered to embody national ideals of masculine vigour – a contention reinforced by the *Life* magazine feature on Pollock and by Hans Namuth's photographs and film. Likewise, Government and private institutions keen to promote American freedom were quick to note that the presence of an avant-garde depends upon a combination of personal freedom and private patronage that they suggested existed only in the United States. Although this argument is by no means irrefutable, it was adopted both widely and rapidly. Jane de Hart Mathews notes that 'this new generation of New York painters ultimately came to be regarded as the embodiment of the kind of freedom denied their colleagues behind the iron curtain, their works celebrated as quintessentially American'.[26] Even when works of art could not be fitted into watertight national narratives, they could still be deployed in the name of 'freedom': their ambiguity seemed to invite a host of different responses, and their presence in America demonstrated the nation's ability to tolerate controversial materials; the sweeping gestures of Pollock's painting were indicative of lack of restraint; Abstract Expressionism served, as Serge Guilbaut has noted, 'to present the internal struggle to those outside as proof of the inherent liberty of the American system . . . Expressionism became the expression of the difference between a free society and totalitarianism; it represented an essential aspect of liberal society: its aggressiveness and ability to generate controversy that in the final analysis posed no threat.'[27]

Ironically, the infusion of nationalist narrative into Expressionist art was increasingly apparent in theoretical accounts of it. American Modernism had deployed an interest in Native American artefacts as a sign of the emergence of nationalistic literary genealogies in the 1920s, with novels such as Willa Cather's *The Professor's House* (1925) chronicling archaeological excavation of Indian ruins as a form of ancestor identification. Pollock's interest in Native American painting could be seen in similar terms, as an important ideological tool in the construction of a 'national' genealogy to differentiate Abstract Expressionism from European Surrealism. Greenberg used his weekly articles in the *Nation* to differentiate between American art (especially Pollock's) and its European equivalent. For Greenberg, the features used to identify quality in French art – what Guilbaut summarises as 'grace, craft, finish' – were replaced by American ones such as 'violence, spontaneity, incompleteness',[28] a point made easier for the public to understand by the images of Pollock as an artist using his whole body rather than merely the wrist and hand. In 'The American Action Painters' (1952), an essay as influential as Greenberg's 'Avant-Garde and Kitsch', Harold Rosenberg also identified what was 'American' about modern art, although his categorisation is less nationalistic than Greenberg's. As the title suggests, the act of creation is, for Rosenberg, even more important than the work of art itself, with the canvas beginning 'to appear to one American painter after another as an arena in which to act – rather than as a space in which to reproduce, re-design, analyze, or "express" an object, actual or imagined. What was to go on the canvas was not a picture but an event.'[29] For Rosenberg, the artist acts as a kind of pioneer, imposing a new world onto a blank canvas, although this narrative is tempered by Rosenberg's desire to portray Pollock as gripped by what David Anfam describes as 'an almost mindless spontaneity'.[30]

One of the most disappointing legacies of the incorporation of Abstract Expressionism within Cold War narratives of American freedom is that it has resulted in the stereotyping – at least, outside the community of art historians and theorists – of many disparate artists under a generic banner that erases difference. It is an obvious – though often overlooked – point that Abstract Expressionism did not suddenly emerge, fully formed, as artists simultaneously abandoned Social Realism and turned to non-representational painting. Likewise, even a cursory glance at the work of the movement's most famous painters illustrates the manifold stages in their careers and diversity of their output. Pollock, for example, despite the 'Jack the Dripper' moniker, only used his dripping and spilling techniques extensively between 1947 and 1950.

Even more significant are the differences between various painters, and their respective relation to the 'abstract'. Most of Pollock's best-known art, for example, does not 'look' like things and many of his titles were suggested by other people, calling into question even the *apparently* figurative elements of paintings such as *Autumn Rhythm: Number 30* (1950). In contrast, Willem de Kooning's works often not only represent people and things – albeit in a non-mimetic fashion – but also contain clearly indicated inter-textual allusions to earlier paintings. *Pink Angels* (c. 1945), for example, appears to be an investigation of the act of representation itself in its reference to Titian's *Diana Surprised by Actaeon* (1556–9).[31] Although Barnett Newman's 'zip' paintings can be seen as *purer* in their abstraction, they are also very different from Pollock's work in almost every respect bar size. Where Pollock's art can be bright, with lines and patterns that suggest spontaneity and accident, a painting like *Onement 1* (1948) or *Cathedra* (1951) looks more deliberate, with the zip itself dividing the smooth single-coloured surface that dominates the canvas in a manner that suggests a rupture in the conformity ascribed to post-war America.[32]

Abstract Expressionism: Other Voices

Despite these differences, the rapid acceptance of Abstract Expressionism as exemplary American art form almost certainly also reflected and reaffirmed the white heterosexual male nucleus of the group of best-known artists. As Ann Eden Gibson has noted, the 'rebellious' image associated with Pollock, de Kooning, Motherwell and other white artists, alongside their own claims for 'marginality', led to a revolution in American painting, but did little to challenge gender and ethnic inequalities. For Gibson, Abstract Expressionism's 'redefinition of styles and themes . . . neatly invalidated the products of those who were not among America's most powerful persons: white heterosexual males'.[33]

It is possible that the process was fuelled by elements of racism in the artists themselves, but the contribution of the African-American painter Norman Lewis, for example, at key moments in the development of the movement seems to challenge (at least in part) this suggestion. Lewis was an active participant in de Kooning and Franz Kline's Studio 35 meetings and the Studio Artists' sessions in 1950, as well as featuring in major exhibitions of abstract art and having his own shows. Although several recent studies have focussed on the residual racism manifested by the iconic white figures of 1940s and '50s New York counterculture,[34] Lewis's own writings do not suggest that this was the reason for his relative obscurity.

Instead, the problem seems to have been caused by a combination of factors that made it harder for African-Americans to succeed as artists than as writers or musicians. One reason was the sense that black fiction, poetry and music had already been recognised as fields of significant achievement. The painter Melvin Edwards has explained that he 'understood . . . that to be somebody I would have to make aesthetic advances on a par with those made by African-American jazz musicians',[35] and apart from work identified with Primitivism there was little tradition of Black art reaching mainstream American culture. Another was the resistance within some parts of the Black arts community to abstraction. The fact that 'meaning' and overt social commentary were rarely welcome in Abstract Expressionism created particular problems for artists from socially disadvantaged groups, who would often be expected to represent the struggle against prejudice in their work. In this context, as the art historian Richard Powell has pointed out, African-American Abstract Expressionists could be seen 'to subordinate blackness – and all that was associated with it – and to place themselves and their work in a larger, wider and, ultimately, whiter art world that provided more opportunities to exhibit, sell and enter into artistic dialogue with others'.[36]

The most significant obstacle to African-American artists selling their work, however, was the fact that they rarely moved in the same circles as art dealers and buyers. In 1957, Lewis was obliged to apply for a taxi driver's licence because he was making no money from painting, despite having a critically acclaimed solo show at the Willard Gallery the previous year. Explaining the disparity between critical and commercial success, he noted:

> This was a good gallery. For the white artists there it was financially successful, but not for me. There is a hell of a lot of discrimination because black artists don't have this intercourse of meeting people. I don't enjoy half the success of people like de Kooning. I've been in shows with Picasso, but I don't have that intercourse.[37]

Ultimately, Lewis's work – like that of other African-American artists identified with Abstract Expressionism, such as Rose Piper and Thelma Johnson Streat – could be marginalised because it contained social commentary and figuration deemed antithetical to the core values identified by Greenberg and other leading art critics. Many of Lewis's paintings deal with representations of jazz and of Harlem; Piper's work draws on black work-songs to illustrate social issues.[38] But, as I have suggested above, figuration is present in the work of de Kooning and others of the 'essential eight'. Likewise, as Gibson has pointed out, Piper's themes – the idea of the 'primitive,' images of women – are also integral to the work of Pollock, de Kooning and Newman. As such, it is hard to disagree with Gibson's assertion that it is in the relations between Piper's and Streat's 'social identities and their subject matter' that they are 'least "like"' Abstract Expressionists, and that this is the reason for their exclusion from the history of the movement that has emerged. By emphasising their status as Black artists, they immediately position themselves as 'other' than the white male norms that ironically define an art making claim to universal human truths.[39]

Beyond New York: Other Countercultural Art

In addition to the New York-based artists marginalised by a white heterosexual male artistic 'élite', many other painters outside the city – and especially on the West Coast – also lived and worked in ways that challenged cultural orthodoxies. It is a mark of the success of Abstract Expressionism and its theorists that these artists are often forgotten in narratives of the emergence of American art that champion one 'movement' in a single city to the exclusion of other significant figures. As Michael Kimmelman has observed, even the exhibitions sent overseas by MoMA stressed 'diversity in twentieth-century American art', with rooms dedicated to folk art, prints and sculpture,[40] yet they tend to be remembered for their use of the work of a very few artists.

Although there is insufficient space here for a detailed discussion of the San Francisco art scene of the late 1940s and 1950s, a brief look at some of its key components illustrates a very different culture to that surrounding Abstract Expressionism. While New York painters did meet both socially and to discuss art, the West Coast featured a more collaborative approach than was apparent in the East, where attempts to suggest a group atmosphere, such as the well-known photograph 'The Irascibles' (featuring Pollock, de Kooning, Newman and other leading Abstract Expressionists and first published in *Life*, January 1951), could not disguise the absence of collective identity. San Francisco's Six Gallery, for instance, where Ginsberg gave his first reading of 'Howl', was so-named because it was set up by poet Jack Spicer and five artists (Wally Hedrick, Deborah Remington, John Allen Ryan, Hayward King and David Simpson). Even before Ginsberg's reading, the Gallery had been characterised by its eagerness to blend art, poetry and drama, in anticipation of the 'happenings' that helped to define the San Francisco counterculture of the 1960s.

The careers of two pairs of married artists – one in the East, the other in San Francisco – also suggest differences. Although Pollock's wife, Lee Krasner, has recently received considerable attention, highlighting her status as a significant artist, this was not the case at mid-century, when sexist attitudes to women were as evident among Abstract Expressionists as they were in society more generally. Krasner remembered women being treated 'like cattle' at the Cedar Tavern, and the domination of women is a recurring theme in work by de Kooning, Rothko, Pollock and others.[41] It seems clear, too, that Krasner made sacrifices in her own career in order to assist Pollock's. In contrast, the relationship between Wally Hedrick and Jay DeFeo – though troubled and ending in divorce in the mid-'60s – is illustrative of a more equal dynamic.

Hedrick's career, in particular, reads like a lifelong challenge to the American Dream. Having turned his Model A Ford into a studio – in itself, a subversive act involving appropriating an icon of conformity and transforming it into the site of countercultural creativity – Hedrick also became an active participant in Progressive Art Workers, a co-operative established by the founders of the Six Gallery and other local artists and designed to facilitate the exhibition of local art. Although he was conscripted to fight in Korea, Hedrick subsequently used his enforced army experience as background to a series of anti-Vietnam and Gulf War protests that continued until his death in 2003. Most notable are a series of variations on the American flag – *Flag* (1953) anticipates the countercultural iconography of 1967 by replacing the stars with flowers; another painting in the series has 'Peace' painted across it; a 1990 re-working has 'Burn Me' written across the flag – and the act of blacking-over his works during the Vietnam War as a symbolic withdrawal of his labour from the cultural production of the United States. Although Hedrick did paint abstract works, his most significant paintings, such as the flag series, are both representational and political to a degree largely absent from Abstract Expressionism.

In a way, Hedrick is as significant for his lifestyle as he is for his work. Despite critical acclaim, most conspicuously his inclusion in MoMA's 'Sixteen Americans' show in 1959, his career is marked by both anti-consumerism and a rejection of the 'art star' culture. But what makes him particularly noteworthy as a precursor of the art forms that would emerge in the 1960s is the degree to which lifestyle and art become inseparable as political commentary in a manner absent from Abstract Expressionism. In addition to painting, Hedrick was also a pioneer of California Assemblage sculpture, collecting other people's discarded 'junk' and reshaping it into representations of consumer goods as a commentary on American obsessions.[42] More than anything, Hedrick's 'career' – if such a term is appropriate for such a non-conformist approach to life – resembles an extended re-working of Thoreau's experiment at Walden Pond a century before, albeit one in which a commitment to collectivism within the community replaces individual retreat from it.

The difficulty in categorising Jay DeFeo indicates the degree to which she embodied the multi-disciplinary approach to art characteristic of the West Coast counterculture of the 1950s and '60s. She is best known for her monumental painting, *The Rose* (1958–66), a work weighing over a ton and measuring 330×240 cm. *The Rose* is a piece that defies classification: DeFeo worked on it obsessively for several years, building layer upon layer of paint to a depth of almost 30 cm in places, and challenging the distinction between painting and sculpture. The sheer scale of the project suggests one of the differences between DeFeo and the other artists considered in this chapter. Where their careers are measured by many paintings ranging across a series of different styles, DeFoe's 'evolving vision', as Michael Kimmelman has written, is manifested in the constant re-design of the piece in a multitude of superimposed reconsiderations. The final version of *The Rose* is suggestive of a combination of New York-inspired Abstract Expressionism and West Coast mysticism, and is indubitably one of the most significant works to stem from the Bay Area Beat scene. Nevertheless, although it assumed a near-legendary status in San Francisco during its prolonged creation, the painting's low profile elsewhere is indicative of what Kimmelman calls the 'prideful myopia' of a canon-creating New York art world reluctant to embrace other American art.[43] *The Rose* was finally exhibited in New York's Whitney Museum in 2003 though, in an ironic twist to the Beat notion of communal art, the disintegrating painting had to be substantially rebuilt by the museum before it could be displayed alongside a selection of her other works.

The degree to which West Coast artists of the 1940s and '50s were written out of the history of post-war American art (both institutional and countercultural) is indicative of the power wielded by New York Abstract Expressionism and theorists like Clement Greenberg and Harold Rosenberg. While fellow Beats working in other disciplines, such as poets Allen Ginsberg, Michael McClure and Lawrence Ferlinghetti, established national and international reputations and the San Francisco Poetry Renaissance heralded a new type of American verse, artists rarely accrued any more than local celebrity. It is probable that even Bruce Connor's seven-minute 1965 art film, *The White Rose*, setting the removal of *The Rose* from DeFeo's Fillmore Street studio to a Gil Evans soundtrack, was better known in New York than the painting itself, an indication of the respective attention paid to independent movies and underground West Coast art. In the 1960s, this was to change dramatically, as the countercultural 'centre' shifted from Greenwich Village to the University of California's Berkeley campus and to a San Francisco scene whose happenings now elicited international attention. For Jay DeFeo's *The Rose*, however, the shift appeared to have come too late: when the work was exhibited in Pasadena and San Francisco at the height of psychedelia in 1969, a reviewer summed it up as a 'glorious anachronism'.[44]

Notes

1. Quoted in David Anfam, *Abstract Expressionism* (London: Thames and Hudson, 1990), p. 22.
2. Referring to the work of Jackson Pollock. Quoted in Jeffrey Potter, *To a Violent Grave: An Oral Biography of Jackson Pollock* (Wainscott, NY: Pushcart, 1987), p. 221.
3. Anfam, *Abstract Expressionism* p. 192, p. 127.
4. See Lewis MacAdams, *Birth of the Cool: Beat, Bebop and the American*

Avant-Garde (London: Scribner, 2002), p. 79. Anfam also notes similar overlaps with the dancing of Martha Graham.

5. MacAdams, *Birth of the Cool* p. 82.
6. See Ann Eden Gibson, 'Abstract Expressionism: Other Politics', in Francis Frascina (ed.), *Pollock and After: The Critical Debate*, 2nd edn (London and New York: Routledge, 2000), p. 308. *Pollock and After* is an invaluable collection for anyone interested in the relationship between Abstract Expressionism and Cold War America. It contains reprints of many of the key essays that have shaped the debate since the publication of Clement Greenberg's 'Avant-Garde and Kitsch' in 1939, and illustrates the ways in which understanding of this relationship has undergone constant revision in the past half-century. I refer to several of the essays contained in *Pollock and After* in this chapter.
7. Max Kozloff, 'American Painting During the Cold War,' in *Artforum* 11.9 (May 1973). Reprinted in Frascina, *Pollock and After*, p. 131.
8. See Anfam, *Abstract Expressionism* p. 78.
9. Frascina, *Pollock and After*, p. 118.
10. Quoted in Leonhard Emmerling, *Jackson Pollock* (London: Taschen, 2003), pp. 18–19. I am drawing on Emmerling's account of the role of Native American art throughout this paragraph.
11. Frascina, *Pollock and After*, p. 116.
12. Jane de Hart Mathews, 'Art and Politics in Cold War America', first published in *The American Historical Review*, 81 (1976). Reprinted in Frascina, *Pollock and After*, pp. 155–6.
13. Ibid., p. 162.
14. See ibid., p. 171.
15. Quoted in ibid., p. 163.
16. Emmerling, *Jackson Pollock*, p. 46.
17. Clement Greenberg, 'Avant-Garde and Kitsch', in *Partisan Review*, 6.5 (Fall 1939), pp. 34–49. Reprinted in Frascina, *Pollock and After*, pp. 48–59, p. 50.
18. David and Cecile Shapiro, 'Abstract Expressionism: The Politics of Apolitical Painting', in *Prospects*, 3 (1977). Reprinted in Frascina, *Pollock and After*, pp. 181–96. See pp. 183–5.
19. Greenberg, in Frascina, *Pollock and After*, p. 52.
20. In this respect, post-war small-group jazz was probably better represented than Beat literature. In the United States, Ralph Ellison, James Baldwin and LeRoi Jones all produced significant work arguing for the sophistication of the music; a few historians and musicologists, such as Marshall Stearns and Henry Cowell, also argued that jazz had a significant place in American culture. Overseas, the identification with Existentialism contributed to the establishment of a large African-American musical community in Paris, and to strong ties between jazz and the intelligentsia. There is no doubt that white audiences and critics in France (and in

Europe more generally) took bebop and other styles of 'modern' jazz more seriously than those – the Beats aside – in the United States. Nevertheless, jazz was also exported as a weapon in the Cold War in a manner similar to Abstract Expressionist art, with an apparent blindness to the ironies inherent in the equating of an African-American art form with an ideology of 'freedom'.

21. Greenberg, in Frascina, *Pollock and After*, p. 51.
22. See David and Cecile Shapiro, in Frascina, *Pollock and After*, p. 187.
23. Ibid., p. 189. See this essay for an account of covert CIA involvement in MoMA's deployment of Abstract Expressionist art overseas.
24. See MacAdams, *Birth of the Cool*, p. 104.
25. Quoted in David Craven, 'Abstract Expressionism, Automatism and the Age of Automation', in *Art History*, 13.1 (March 1990). Reprinted in Frascina, *Pollock and After*, pp. 234–60, p. 243. I am indebted to Craven's detailed analysis of the pro- and anti-capitalist components of Abstract Expressionism.
26. Mathews, in Frascina, *Pollock and After*, p. 168.
27. Serge Guilbaut, 'The New Adventures of the Avant-Garde in America: Greenberg, Pollock, or from Trotskyism to the New Liberalism of the "Vital Center"', *October*, 15 (Winter 1980), pp. 61–78. Reprinted in Frascina, *Pollock and After*, pp. 197–210, p. 207.
28. Guilbaut in Frascina, *Pollock and After*, p. 203.
29. Harold Rosenberg, 'The American Action Painters', *Art News*, 51.8 (December 1952). Reprinted in Rosenburg, *The Tradition of the New* (London: Thames and Hudson, 1962), p. 25.
30. Anfam, *Abstract Expressionism*, p. 127.
31. See Anfam, *Abstract Expressionism*, pp. 112–13.
32. It is possible to read these works in a very different manner. Clyfford Still, for example, praised Newman's paintings because the 'intensity' of their colour symbolised an absolute rejection of the greyness of contemporary American life. See Anfam, *Abstract Expressionism*, p. 144.
33. Gibson, in Frascina, *Pollock and After*, p. 307.
34. See especially Jon Panish, *The Color of Jazz: Race and Representation in Postwar American Culture* (Jackson: University Press of Mississippi, 1997) and Peter Townsend, *Jazz in American Culture* (Edinburgh: Edinburgh University Press, 2000). I discuss my reservations about these approaches in Chapter 1.
35. Quoted in Lowery Stokes Sims, 'The African-American Artist and Abstraction', in *Norman Lewis: Black Paintings, 1946–1977* (New York: The Studio Museum in Harlem, 1998), p. 46.
36. Quoted in Sims, 'The African-American Artist and Abstraction', p. 42.
37. Interview with Norman Lewis by Vivian Browne, 1974. Quoted in Sara Wood, ' "Pure Eye Music": Norman Lewis, Abstract Expressionism and Bebop', unpublished paper, University of Birmingham. I am indebted to

Wood for alerting me to the complexities of Lewis's position as African-American Abstract Expressionist, and for conversations about the relationship between painting and jazz in the 1940s and '50s.

38. See Gibson, in Frascina, *Pollock and After*, pp. 309–10.

39. Ibid., p. 310.

40. Michael Kimmelman, 'Revisiting the Revisionists: The Modern, its Critics and the Cold War' (1994), in Frascina, *Pollock and After*, p. 298.

41. Quoted in Anfam, *Abstract Expressionism*, p. 15.

42. See www.wallyhedrick.com, www.sonoma.edu/pubs/release/2003/ 325.html, and Gretchen Giles, 'Word Play: Artist Wally Hedrick Stretches his Canvases', at www.metroactive.com/papers/sonoma/07.25.96/art-9630.html

43. Michael Kimmelman, 'An Obsession, Now Excavated', in *The New York Times*, 10 October 2003. www.jaydefeo.org/reviews1.html

44. Quoted in Kimmelman, 'An Obsession, Now Excavated', n.p.

CHAPTER FOUR

Film

> Of all the films in the fifties, it was perhaps the delinquency films that were most thoroughly shot through with omens of things to come: the generation gap and the children's crusade of the sixties.
>
> Peter Biskind, *Seeing is Believing*[1]

> Patriarchal culture relies upon the maintenance of a gender-structured disequilibrium. This involves not merely a power-based, and power-serving, cultural hierarchy of male and female, but also the establishment of normative 'gender' values which are internalised by both sexes.
>
> Frank Krutnik, *In a Lonely Street*[2]

There are, of course, differences in the respective relationships between novelists, painters, musicians and film-makers and their audiences. It was possible for Jack Kerouac to write the majority of his oeuvre in the long gap between the publication of his first book, *The Town and the City* (1950), and his second, *On the Road* (1957). He could do so because the production costs inherent in fiction-writing are insignificant and he was able to support himself via the periods of unskilled labour that counterbalanced his travels in and beyond America. Although the search for publishers was a constant source of frustration for Kerouac until *On the Road* was accepted, he managed to complete and store a sizeable literary output in anticipation of eventual acceptance. Book publishing expenses are also relatively low – particularly when texts do not include high-quality illustrations – so it was possible

97

for an independent company like San Francisco's City Lights to produce and market texts that could be distributed nationally and internationally by mail, as well as through book shops.

Painters and musicians face slightly different situations: the former require space to work and store their art – especially when, like many of the Abstract Expressionists, their paintings are large – and are unlikely to transport it across the country in a rucksack, as Kerouac did with his manuscripts; the latter, at least those involved in bebop, urban blues and rock and roll, usually perform in groups (demanding a collective commitment unnecessary to the novelist) and must have access to expensive studio equipment if they are to 'store' their work in Kerouac's manner.[3] In addition, the relationship between novels, collections of poems or records and their readers or listeners is very different to that between a painting and its viewers. Books and records are usually mass-produced and designed to withstand regular physical contact and movement: City Lights' 'Pocket Poet' series – which included Allen Ginsberg's *Howl and Other Poems* – was designed to capitalise on the sense of poetry reading being a popular activity for the disaffected young. The books were cheap, small and instantly recognisable, an ideal combination for a Beat audience with low income, commitment to travel, and a strong sense of community. Although vinyl is considerably more fragile than paper, the ubiquitous presence of jukeboxes in cafés and bars provided a similar opportunity for mass access to popular records. In contrast, a painting is a unique work that must be visited in a museum or gallery, or which provides the backdrop in a café or restaurant. In general, a distance is maintained between the work and its viewers, who – even if they are allowed to touch it, are expected to appreciate the direct bond that exists between art and artist, and to respect the qualities contained within its distinct identity.

Film-making involves even more interdependencies and, as a result, the relationship between film and the counterculture of the 1950s is probably less straightforward than those involving fiction, music and painting. The principal obstacle facing a would-be film-maker is cost: even a low-budget, non-Hollywood film in the '50s required access to expensive cameras and lighting, and corporate movies required large bankrolls to pay for the experts – camerapersons, make-up artists, set constructors, and so on – necessary to the production of commercial film, as well as money for promotion and distribution. Almost all the non-studio movies of the time are notable (often in exaggerated attempts to differ from Hollywood conventions) for their 'amateur'

– or low-budget – feel, even where the subject matter and experimental style demand attention. As a result, it tended to be extremely difficult to distribute independent films and arrange for their screening.[4]

The combination of these factors has significant consequences for the films of the time. On the one hand, Hollywood's attempts to represent youth culture depend upon the need to operate effectively within the corporate structures of a generally conservative studio system that encouraged newness only within the parameters of well-tried generic norms; on the other, the films that were produced outside Hollywood reached small audiences and – even in the case of relatively well known movies like John Cassavetes' *Shadows* or Robert Frank's *Pull My Daisy* (both 1959) – were substantially less influential on nascent youth movements than, for example, *Rebel Without a Cause* or than texts by countercultural artists working in other genres. This imbalance has determined the structure of this chapter, in which I commence with a detailed examination of three Hollywood studio films – *The Wild One*, *Rebel Without a Cause* and *The Blackboard Jungle* – that represent the juvenile delinquency which, alongside the very different Beat scene, would help to shape the counterculture of the 1960s. In the concluding section of the chapter, I offer a brief look at Hollywood's attempt to adapt Kerouac's *The Subterraneans* before turning to a summary of some of the independent films of the time in order further to assess why their profile is low in comparison to avant-garde production in other artistic genres.

Hollywood at Mid-century

At a time when McCarthyist 'witch hunts' coerced many of Hollywood's writers, actors and directors into testifying about their own and their colleagues' 'Communist' activities, scripts proffering direct criticism of dominant American ideology were virtually non-existent. Most films – whether science fiction B–movies about the invasion of small-town America by aliens, or Westerns chronicling the settling of the frontier in the face of hostile Indians and black-hatted villains – offer unproblematic endorsement of cherished 'national' values in narratives that celebrate triumph over a simplistically binary evil other. The dominant stars of the time generally reinforce aspects of this message: in many of her roles, Marilyn Monroe epitomises the fun-loving blonde who only finds true happiness by meeting the ideal mate, whereas the femme fatale epitomised by Mary Astor as Brigid O'Shaunnessy in *The Maltese Falcon* (1941) or Barbara Stanwyck as Phyllis Dietrichson in *Double Indemnity* (1944) is invariably punished for transgressing prescribed gender identities; John Wayne is the archetypal defender of national security; even the more sinister and unstable Humphrey Bogart repeatedly represents a straight-talking vernacular counter to effete or corrupt outsiders, his hard-drinking, coarse exterior concealing but not overwhelming his underlying moral decency and strength.

Of course, there were also films that challenged or subverted hegemonic faith in institutions such as the State, the individual or the family. Whereas the majority of '50s movies imagine the family as a site of strength – albeit one that must confront crisis and that requires work and, perhaps, the advice of experts in order to remain united – a director such as Alfred Hitchcock offers Freudian explorations of dysfunctional relationships. In *Psycho* (1960), for example, the encounter between an urban, modern, corrupt young woman and a man who exists in a realm buried deep in the gothic American unconscious (and away from the new freeways joining American cities) is the setting for a critique of both the contemporary United States and the disturbing legacy of Victorian values. Interest in the gothic and in the dysfunctional family were also mainstays of the counterculture-related movies of the 1950s and '60s, from *Rebel Without a Cause* to Roman Polanski's *Rosemary's Baby* (1968), but, unlike the conservatism of Hitchcock's film – in which the rather heavy-handed meting out of moral justice to the sexually and financially corrupt Marion Crane (Janet Leigh) is suggestive of deep unease with modern amorality – the movies and music of the 1960s increasing came to celebrate sexual freedom and the chance to escape from the monotony of daily life.

The few films that could be seen to offer allegorical critiques of the Cold War do so in such a way as to make their ideological stance unclear: do they attack or defend America's position? Perhaps the best example is Fred Zinnemann's *High Noon* (1952), a 'classic' Western whose ultimate ideological message remains enigmatic. In many ways, *High Noon* draws upon the generic staples of earlier popular culture, from the dime novel and other Westerns to the hard-boiled detective novel, adopting, at the most elementary level, the mythemes summed up by John Carlos Rowe as 'self-reliant individualism, masculine potency, technical ingenuity, and perseverance'[5] to construct in Will Kane (Gary Cooper) a *near*-archetypal American hero distracted by a wife who counsels against intervention and desires that he retire into the secure comfort of the domestic space. Significantly, Kane is alienated from the community by the very qualities that make him appear 'heroic' to the viewer and he does not discover the extent of his isolation until moments of crisis, when he is unable to rely upon social solidarity to support his actions. The plot stages a series of meetings in which a range of potential allies refuse to assist in confronting the enemy. Kane has to go it alone because he is stripped of his official position and serves, effectively, as a vigilante, acting on the principle that in moments of crisis, as Richard Slotkin puts it in his detailed reading of the film, 'the defence of "civilization" is more important than the procedures of "democracy"'.[6] Finally, there is a sense that Kane overcomes his nemesis, Frank Miller (Ian MacDonald) – who has returned to Hadleyville to kill those who overthrew him and put him in jail – because he embodies a particular brand of 'masculine' virtue – a combination of 'knowledge, skill, and power' coupled with a conscience that, to quote Slotkin once more, holds that (in cases like this) 'possession of the power to act entails an absolute responsibility to act, whether or not the action is legal or acceptable to the public'.[7] Kane's triumph is represented through a form of doubling between 'hero' and 'villain' – there are many clues that suggest Kane has his own dark side – but he is redeemed by his '"essential" goodness and manliness' of character, which provide an authority to which he 'can appeal in justification of his actions'.[8]

Although *High Noon* is hardly a 'countercultural' movie – even if it can be read as a damning critique of Cold War America – I mention it here because many of the values that it cherishes are also endorsed by the youth movies of the early to mid-1950s that established Marlon Brando and James Dean as iconic screen rebels. Although both *The Wild One* (1953) and *Rebel Without a Cause* (1955) construct heroes who are perceived as threats by respectable members of the communities they inhabit, Brando and Dean play characters whose beliefs and actions are closer to those of Will Kane than Frank Miller. Likewise, in *The Blackboard Jungle* (1955), the English teacher Rick Dadier (Glenn Ford) learns that he cannot depend upon other teachers representing a spectrum of ideological positions to assist him in his own battle with a gang of – in his case – delinquent teens, and there is no doubt that his triumph depends upon the 'self-reliant individualism, masculine potency . . . and perseverance' identified in Kane by John Carlos Rowe.

There are various reasons for the similarities across genres, all of which are useful when we consider how (and why) the film industry responded to the hysteria over juvenile delinquency in the 1950s. It is important to remember that Hollywood was then largely governed by an oligarchy of major companies, such as Warner Brothers, Paramount Pictures, Metro-Goldwyn-Mayer, RKO and Twentieth-Century Fox, and that this cartel was able to control both production and distribution. Leonard Quart and Albert Auster note that, at this time,

> Eight major studios [were] producing 99 percent of all films screened in North America and almost 60 percent of films shown in Europe. In addition, there were almost 90 million tickets sold each week in the US. Indeed the film industry was the sixth most important industry in the United States in 1945.[9]

As a result of the HUAC hearings of the late 1940s, which had increased institutional and public suspicion about Hollywood, there was a general nervousness in the studios about what could be produced, reinforced by a sense that the majority of cinema-goers endorsed the repressive policies of the Cold War. In addition, these companies had been established for several decades and were more responsive to scripts that operated within the parameters of successful, low-budget formulae than to those that appeared more radical.

Oddly, this combination made films about juvenile delinquency attractive to the big studios, especially since plots could easily be constructed around variations not only on the Western, but also on the standard heterosexual love story and an updated version of the public enemy gangster narratives of the '30s and '40s, now transposed to represent out of control youths terrorising urban communities. Moreover, juvenile delinquency was highly topical. The early '50s saw near-hysteria about the 'problem' of unruly teenagers: in 1954, there was a Senate Subcommittee on Juvenile Delinquency, and the educationalist and journalist Benjamin Fine published his far-reaching study, *1,000,000 Delinquents*. For some critics, this is not enough to explain the turn to teen films: Peter Biskind has suggested that, 'considering that 1954 was the year that Dulles announced the policy of massive retaliation, the year that three Puerto Rican nationalists shot up the House of Representatives, wounding five Congressmen, the year that Ike considered (and decided against) nuking Ho Chi Minh to bail the French out of Dien Bien Phu, and the year the Supreme Court decided that segregated schools were separate but unequal', studio obsession with juvenile delinquency is 'peculiar, to say the least'. For Biskind, the interest reflected 'the first wave of conservative backlash against what William Whyte called the "filiarchy" . . . an autonomous youth culture, not delinquency per se'.[10]

There is some truth in this assertion and there is no doubt that the youth culture soon to discover its own language in rock and roll appeared to represent a challenge to hegemonic American self-satisfaction that – in its alienation amidst abundance – could prove highly disturbing. And yet, the very factors that made juvenile delinquency seem threatening could also make it appealing for the Hollywood studios. In an essay about the Hollywood Ten – the writers and directors who had testified as 'unfriendly' witnesses during the 1947 HUAC investigation of Hollywood – Stephen Vaughn has noted the 'virtual impossibility of bringing an openly anticapitalist picture to the screen'.[11] Vaughn's argument is that the studio system precluded writers offering well-disposed representations of radical causes, such as the labour movement, and that even when such a movie was made, its distribution would be stymied. Thus, for example, Herbert Biberman's *Salt of the Earth* (1954), a sympathetic and accurate portrayal of working-class life in the United States, was delayed while he was imprisoned (following the HUAC investigation) and, despite winning numerous awards in Europe, was discredited by the Motion Picture Industry Council, while Roy Brewer's International Alliance of Theatrical and Stage Employees projectionists would not show it. The movie only received proper national distribution in 1965.[12]

In contrast, even movies that appeared to side with youth against institutional or familial oppression, such as *The Wild One* and *Rebel Without a Cause*, seemed safe, since, as the latter's title implies, their protagonists' alienation lacked any kind of leftist dimension. In addition, the studios were quick to recognise a burgeoning market for such films: a youth culture with disposable income unthinkable during their parents' Depression-era childhood offered an untapped market for films about teenagers. Although Hollywood studios were driven by the conservative desire not to offend long-term loyal patrons, they also recognised the need to develop this potential new audience. This conundrum contributed to what Biskind accurately calls the 'bewildering array of contradictory attitudes'[13] in films about juvenile delinquency, including – in addition to those mentioned above – *Crime in the Streets* (1956), *Jailhouse Rock* (1957) and *High School Confidential* (1958). Given the scope of this book, I will focus on the three movies that appealed most to the new youth audience, rather than those that adopted overly hostile or simplistic positions. These examples are also particularly useful in establishing connections with films of the 1960s, produced at a time when the counterculture wielded more power through cinema than through any other medium.

Hollywood's Wild Rebel Jungle

During the mid-twentieth century, Hollywood displays a near-obsessive concern with a perceived crisis of masculine identity. I have already cited two films – *High Noon* and *Psycho* – in which this crisis surfaces, first, in Will Kane's need to 'prove' himself against the wishes of his (soon-to-be) wife and, second, in Norman Bates's (Anthony Perkins) transgressive identification with his dead mother, but the 'problem' is also enacted elsewhere, as in the hard-boiled detective's attempts to resist the temptations of the femme fatale in pictures like *The Maltese Falcon* and *The Big Sleep* (1946). It would be possible to argue that such a crisis is also pervasive in the countercultural arts of the time in areas including Charlie Parker's anxiety of influence over the legacy of Lester Young, in the Abstract Expressionist persona of the 'manly' artist, or even – more mundanely – in Kerouac's early battles with his father and in his unusually close relationship with his mother. Here, however, I focus on movies in which the tension between attempts to socialise young men and these men's efforts to articulate their alienation and discontent are explored. The films adopt differing approaches to the topic. *The Wild One* is, in many ways, close to the Western in its representation of a small town terrorised by a gang of outlaws, although its efforts to understand why Johnny (Marlon Brando) cannot assimilate to a dominant culture tainted by its intolerance of difference are closer to late-'60s countercultural movies such as *Easy Rider* and *Alice's Restaurant* (both 1969) than to narratives in which order is restored with the eradication of an external threat. *Rebel Without a Cause* also revolves around an alienated outsider – in this case, Jim Stark (James Dean) – but is propelled by interest in the effects of dysfunctional middle-class parents on their offspring. In some ways, *The Blackboard Jungle* is the most ambitious of the movies: it offers a more systematic attempt to explain the phenomenon of juvenile delinquency in socio-historical terms, assesses the limitations of a range of ideological approaches to the problem and, rather than being focalised around a figure of alienated youth, confronts the topic through the experiences of a teacher in an inner-city high school that is as wild as Will Kane's West.

Of the three films, Laslo Benedek's *The Wild One* now looks the most dated. In part, this is because of its setting in Wrightsville, a small-town American community that – apart from the jukebox in the bar where Kathie Bleeker (Mary Murphy) works – appears to be fixed in time in the early years of the twentieth century in both attitudes and appearance. Indeed, this sense of a community doing its best to cling to its faith in traditional ideals in the face of threatening modernity is confirmed when the old-timer bar tender, Jimmy (William Yedder), replies to the question 'Do ya like TV?' with the answer 'Oh, pictures! No, no pictures. Everything these days is pictures. Pictures and a lot of noise. Nobody even knows how to talk. Just grunt at each other.' In a further instance of the movie's datedness, the plot is too straight-forward to be particularly gripping: the attraction between Johnny and Kathie (who, formulaically, is the sheriff's daughter) and the involve-ment of the hyperbolically implausible Chino (Lee Marvin as the leader of another motorcycle gang) offer little of interest when juxtaposed with later biker movies.

The film is as significant for the reactions that it generated at the time as for what we can see in it now: remarkably, the British Board of Film Censors only allowed its general release in 1968 and American critics feared that it would incite copycat riots in impressionable viewers. It is true that *The Wild One* has assumed a cult status with biker gangs, and that Brando's pouting 'What've you got?' response to the question 'What are you rebelling against?' is probably the most famous and succinct expression of youthful alienation from core 'American' values of the time, but the reasons for institutional hostility towards the film also have much to do with its systematic deconstruction of the mythology of Main Street. At the heart of *The Wild One* is a 'typical' American community that is as hypocritical and intolerant of outsiders as the Hadleyville of *High Noon* (or, much later, as the reactionary citizens represented in *Pleasantville*), but Wrightsville lacks a Will Kane to save it. Instead, its own sheriff is weak and unable to outflank the town bullies, and it is Johnny who – despite flaws that stem from his own apparent insecurity – has the authority and 'masculinity' to control his gang, attract Kathie and stand up both to the rival bikers and to the town's vigilante element. The script that accompanies the film's opening shots of an empty road, just before the arrival of the Black Rebels Motorcycle Club (Johnny's gang), reads,

> This is a shocking story. It could never take place in most American towns, but it did in this one. It is a public challenge not to let it happen again.

Although the message initially appears to be offering a warning about the terrors brought to the community by a band of nomadic outsiders, it becomes increasingly clear that the real threat implied here is of self-destruction caused by bigotry and suspicion – a genuinely subversive assessment of national life at a time when people were told to look out for any kind of un-American activities in their midst.

The other reason for the movie's ongoing relevance is the casting of Marlon Brando as Johnny. As a Midwesterner who drifted around the West Coast before arriving in Greenwich Village in the 1940s, Brando resembles other iconic figures from the counterculture, such as Jackson Pollock and Neal Cassady. His 'Method' acting also bears similarities with the other art forms of the immediate post-war arts discussed in this book, especially in its focus on conveying emotional intensity rather than developing sophisticated intellectual perspectives. At the time of *The Wild One*'s release, Brando was already known for performances as an outsider or misfit in movies including, *A Streetcar Named Desire* (1951), creating an image that was further cemented with his characterisation of Terry Malloy in *On the Waterfront* (1954), and was becoming identified with a persona that transcended individual screen roles. Like Dean Moriarty in *On the Road*, the men played by Brando in the early 1950s were characterised by an untameable, 'natural' opposition to an overcivilised hegemonic culture, and were particularly threatening to that culture because of their ability to attract sexually repressed women – like Kathie Bleeker – starved of any kind of passion in their own communities. Peter Biskind has pointed out that Brando's characters are 'punished for [their] raw power and masculinity in almost every film he ever made, being badly beaten in films as different as *The Wild One, On the Waterfront* . . . and *The Appaloosa*',[14] suggesting an ambivalence to his type even on the part of directors sympathetic to the concept of the alienated outsider, but it is also clear that Johnny – like Stanley Kowalski in *A Streetcar Named Desire* or Terry Malloy in *On the Waterfront* – is more tormented by inner demons than by the threat of physical attack.

Ultimately, Brando himself was dissatisfied with *The Wild One* for reasons that indicate the flaws inherent in most studio productions of the immediate post-war period. Describing the film's conception and development, he said, 'We started out to do something worthwhile, to explain the psychology of the hipster. But somewhere along the way we went off the track. The result was that instead of finding why young people tend to bunch into groups that seek expression, all that we did was show the violence.'[15] The pre-history to the film – in which the 'invasion' of Hollister, California, by biker gangs over the Fourth of July weekend in 1947 was adopted for a short story called 'The

Cyclists' Raid' (1951) by Frank Rooney, before being turned into a movie script – helps to explain why it failed to meet Brando's expectations. The historical incident was newsworthy but relatively uneventful, and did not involve direct confrontations between the bikers and townspeople; the short story added melodramatic twists to the original narrative; and the movie opted to focus on the dramatic spectacle inherent in biker gangs riding in formation or becoming engaged in physical battles with locals rather than providing many insights into the source of their alienation or into their own ideology. In contrast, two films released in 1955 both sought to provide a fuller understanding of the psychological profile overlooked – according to Brando – in *The Wild One*.

It would be easy to assert that *Rebel Without a Cause* has endured as much because of the death of James Dean in the year of its release – and, to a lesser extent, the early demises of its other stars, Natalie Wood and Sal Mineo – as because of anything exceptional about the movie. Dean's early death, like those of Charlie Parker, Jimi Hendrix and others, has ensured that he will remain, to follow Bob Dylan, 'forever young', and will not have his reputation as symbol of counter-cultural youth undermined by the problems that confronted contemporaries who survived, like, for example, Brando or Eric Clapton (Hendrix's greatest rival as 'king' of the guitar heroes of the 1960s).

In some ways, this would be a valid argument: Dean's leather-jacked persona, frozen in black and white posters on bedroom walls around the world, is an iconic image even for many people who have never seen his films. Indeed, many first-time viewers of *Rebel Without a Cause* express surprise at some of its features, most notably the fact that it is in colour and that it lacks a rock and roll soundtrack. And yet, such a reading would do a disservice to one of the most influential – and interesting – films about juvenile alienation. Although *Rebel* sometimes offers a rather confused attitude to the reasons – and possible remedies – for teenage discontent, and although its 'delinquents' seem rather less menacing than those witnessed in *The Wild One* or *The Blackboard Jungle*, its focus on the children of the affluent, suburban middle class introduces a challenge to the culture of consumption that is closer to the Beat sensibility than to the other films discussed here.

All three of *Rebel*'s central teenage characters are from 'respectable' families, and all experience forms of alienation from their parents: Jim (Dean) is drunk in the opening scene and it is soon suggested that his troubles stem from living with a domineering mother and a 'feminised' father who is torn between his own mother and his wife. According to her father, Judy (Natalie Wood) is a 'problem' and a 'dirty tramp', although it seems that his hostility stems from anxieties about his own (repressed) attraction to a newly sexualised daughter rather than from her activities, and it is striking that the relationships between the teenagers are devoid of overt sexual activity. Plato (Sal Mineo) lives in a large house, but is looked after by a maid and is seen as a nameless financial burden by his absent father. He is driven by the search for alternative father figures, such as the imagined identities he attaches to his biological father, the picture of Alan Ladd he has pinned in his locker and, finally, Jim himself.

The source of Jim's construction of masculinity is never made clear, although it seems close to the model idealised in Westerns. Not only does he cherish physical courage – and is only roused by accusations that he is 'chicken' – Jim is also attracted to a code of strong moral rectitude and action from principle. Thus, he is drawn into the 'chicken run' that will result in Judy's boyfriend Buzz's (Corey Allen) death because he must prove his 'manhood', but is also eager to go to the police and admit to his role in the incident, a stance that his parents label 'idealistic'. This combination of physical and moral strength marks him as the opposite of his father, a classic representation of the overcivilised man in a grey flannel suit that many in the '50s feared had lost touch with the conception of 'true' American manhood. Mr Stark's emasculated persona is marked from the first scene of the film (in which Jim, Judy and Plato are all detained at the local police station), when his efforts at male bonding with Ray (Edward Platt) – a sympathetically portrayed cop who tries to act like a surrogate father to the teens – remain unrequited when Ray refuses the offer of a cigar.[16] The sense that Mr Stark is over-feminised is confirmed repeatedly throughout the film: he is indecisive, appears comically dressed in an apron as he cleans the house, and at one point exclaims 'Hello, Jimmy, you thought I was mum?'

When the film is summarised this way, it appears that *Rebel* recognises youth as embodying core 'American' values that have been forgotten by a post-war generation obsessed with material gain. Mr Stark even asks Jim, 'Don't I buy you everything you want?', as if the commodified relationship between parent and child makes Jim's behaviour inexplicable. The sterile, standardised interiors of Jim and Judy's homes, which resemble pictures from good housekeeping magazines, are contrasted not only with Buzz's response to Jim's question, 'Why do we do this?' / 'You gotta do something', but also with a sense that an earlier generation also cherished an individualism that has now been lost. Jim's grandmother, for example, compares her own home-made (and therefore, personal) contribution to his school lunch with the staple peanut butter sandwiches provided by his mother. Later, the idiosyncratic deserted house to where Jim, Judy and Plato retreat to enact their fantasies of familyhood provides a sharp contrast with their real homes.

And yet, this identification is problematised in a number of ways. First, the school outing to the Griffith Park Observatory introduces a form of cultural and existential relativism that undermines the ideological strength of Jim's opposition to his parents' values. The focus on the vastness of space and the insignificance and meaningless of individual existence is reiterated by the guide's assertion that, in contrast, Man's problems are 'trivial and naïve'. Even if the Big Bang that terrorises Plato at the end of the show is a reminder of the constant threat of nuclear annihilation during the Cold War – and thus an endorsement of the need to experience life for the moment, rather than slip into the hypocritical complacency adopted by the parental figures in a society that encourages passivity – this is not the same as attesting that the 'something' undertaken by Jim and Buzz is a genuine alternative. In this context, there is pertinence in the manner of Buzz's death: he is unable to jump from his car before it goes over the cliff because his leather jacket – the symbol of his rebellion – catches on the door handle. If an automobile plunging into the Pacific serves as a metaphor for the destruction at the end of the American Dream (an image returned to by Kerouac in *Big Sur* (1962)), there is no sense that the car-loving counterculture we witness in *Rebel*, as much as with Kerouac's Dean Moriarty, will provide a remedy.

More importantly, the film suggests that rebellion is unsustainable and that the more extreme the symptoms of alienation are, the more quickly they will be exterminated. Thus, it is unsurprising that Plato is killed near the end of the movie: it seems that his 'problems' are incurable and – with repeated hints that his attachment to Jim is driven as much by homosexual desire as by the search for a father – that the position he represents is too far from society's norms to be redeemed. In addition, the film makes clear that the yearning for an undefined 'something' is insufficient protection against the flawed alternative seen in middle-class American suburbia: when Jim secretly removes the bullets from Plato's gun, he compromises the integrity of his earlier stance. With Plato's death, following on from that of Buzz, Jim appears to be dragged back towards the norms of that society because he cannot imagine any other alternative, and it is significant that even in the deserted house, Jim, Judy and Plato are conditioned to act out conventional familial roles. It comes as little surprise, therefore, when Jim is reunited with his parents (and they with one another) in the closing scene. Despite the implication that Mr Stark has been restored to 'true' manhood by the night's events, such closure implies that Jim's reinvention in a grey flannel suit is not far away.

As such, critics have tended to read the conclusion to *Rebel Without a Cause* as a conservative retreat into the values of the traditional family. Jim and Judy's relationship is seen as an accommodation with heterosexual 'normality' that is made possible by the necessary death of the queer-coded Plato. Although Peter Biskind overlooks the gay subtext, he is representative in suggesting that Plato is 'too rebellious, too disaffected' and has to die, and in arguing that it is the 'parents who have the last laugh, who define the values of the film, not the rebellious children'.[17] Nevertheless, this kind of reading is misleading and depends upon unproblematic assumptions linking narrative point-of-view and what happens to Jim. Thus, while there is no doubt that Jim *does* renounce his ideals – as we have seen – by removing the bullets from Plato's gun without telling him and in his reconciliation with his parents, the resolution is more complex and ironic than such a summary would suggest. First, it is perverse to accept the premise that Jim and Judy's relationship encourages the belief that they will experience long-term happiness: even by Hollywood's standards, Judy's ability to overcome any grief felt at Buzz's death and announce that she loves Jim (all in the space of a few hours) seems indecently hasty. Although, given the standards upheld by Hollywood at the time, the pairing lacks the sexual activity that we witness with Dean Moriarty's serial marriages in *On the Road*, the suspicion lingers that this liaison will be equally impermanent, or will be as unhappy as that of Jim and Judy's parents. Likewise, the removal of Jim's red jacket – now worn by the dead Plato – is hardly indicative of a 'happy' ending: beyond a more general identification with passion, red has played a particularly significant role in American culture from *The Scarlet Letter* (1850) through *The Red Badge of Courage* (1895) to *The Wizard of Oz* (1939), and its removal suggests a return to an America as grey as Dorothy's Kansas but lacking the sentimental attachment to locale for which she longs. The cop who encourages Plato to come out of the Griffith Park Observatory with the words 'Come here, son' thus summarises a deception that goes beyond the death of Plato to serve as a damning assessment of the damage done to children by their parents in the 1950s.

In contrast to *Rebel Without a Cause*'s fascination with families, *The Blackboard Jungle* presents a world in which parents are almost entirely absent. The opening script announces that the film is 'concerned with juvenile delinquency – its causes – and its effects,' and it is plain that many of the teenagers in Rick Dadier's class have grown up with the gang rather than the family providing the closest social ties. Whereas *Rebel Without a Cause* represented a world of weak fathers, *The Blackboard Jungle* has no fathers at all (bar Dadier himself at the movie's end), as if they had gone to war a decade before and never returned. Like Will Kane in *High Noon*, Dadier has to make this environment safe by removing the most violent, threatening elements; and, like Kane, he must do so while choosing between two women, a dark 'temptress' (here a fellow teacher) and a blonde wife who, while initially opposed to his actions, is ultimately 'converted' to the cause. Like Kane, Dadier has the chance to abandon the (often ungrateful) community to its fate: he is offered the chance to work in a suburban high school where children conjugate Latin verbs and sing the national anthem but chooses to stay and complete his mission. Of course, there has never been any real doubt about what he would do. Dadier is given the job after reciting lines from Shakespeare's *Henry V* and is contrasted throughout with a bespectacled, swing-loving idealist who is clearly not man enough for the job and who quits after his record collection has been destroyed by the teens.

Beyond the famous, pioneering use of Bill Haley and the Comets' 'Rock Around the Clock' over the credits, it is hard to see why *The Blackboard Jungle* appealed so strongly to rebellious elements of the youth market. Although the most actively anti-Establishment youth, Artie West (Vic Morrow), articulates the draft-dodging benefits of a criminal record in a manner that would be adopted by the counter-culture of the late 1960s (as, for example, in Arthur Penn's *Alice's Restaurant*), he is shown to have no redeeming qualities. As Ronald Reagan, then head of the Screen Actors Guild, succinctly summarised, 'Any juvenile . . . would have to have a feeling of disgust for the bad boy.'[18] Whereas both *Rebel Without a Cause* and *The Wild One* offered fairly broad critiques of mainstream American values and provided ambiguously framed endings, it is hard to identify any irony in the way the Star Spangled Banner is used as a weapon to restrain West's co-agitator and enforce a form of social control.

The Blackboard Jungle can best be considered as a liberal intervention within the then evolving civil rights debate. At the start of the movie, it appears that the principal troublemaker in Dadier's class will be the African-American Gregory Miller (Sidney Poitier). Several scenes enact moments of racial tension and suggest ways to overcome divisions in a multi-ethnic community, and it is noteworthy that Dadier's own low-point comes as he approximates the racism that he has condemned in others, shouting, 'Why, you black . . .' at Miller. Ultimately, however, this narrative is also predictable, with Miller switching from T-shirt to collar and tie, offering his musical talents for Dadier's school Christmas show and, finally, agreeing to stay on at school rather than becoming a mechanic. The film's heavy-handed (and improbable) message is that race does not matter in an America of equal opportunities and – while it is an overstatement to follow Biskind's lead and claim that Miller is simply an Uncle Tom[19] – there seems little doubt that it endorses melting-pot ideologies of assimilation rather than imagining forms of dissent, or even the 'lateral synthesis' advocated by LeRoi Jones in *Blues People*,[20] that could re-shape hegemonic norms. As the similarities to *High Noon* suggest, *The Blackboard Jungle* does little more than transplant pre-existing Hollywood plots into a new environment, whilst failing to deliver the veiled critique of 'American' values evident in the former's complexly ambiguous narrative.

Beat Film

My focus on movies about juvenile delinquency should not be taken to imply that there were no films about – or by – the Beats. Within Hollywood, Roger Corman's *Bucket of Blood*, E. T. Greville's *Beat Girl* and Charles Haas's *The Beat Generation* (all 1959) are examples of movies that sought to cash in on the 'beatnik' phenomenon at the end of the 1950s. More interesting is Ranald MacDougall's adaptation of *The Subterraneans* (1960), the only one of Jack Kerouac's novels to be turned into a movie. Although the film abandons the mixed-race relationship that is at the core of the book, it is not entirely without merit. In particular, as Preston Whaley has pointed out, *The Subterraneans* is unique (for Hollywood of the time) in the manner in which it depicts jazz and jazz musicians. All of the film's musicians are identified prominently in the opening credits and, unusually, the jazz performances are carefully dubbed to ensure that the music and visual image are in synch. From the opening scene, in which the major characters listen to a jazz combo uninterrupted by dialogue, it is clear, as Whaley continues, that 'the film values musical authenticity'. Although the musicians are all white, the fear that racial questions will be entirely erased from a Hollywood adaptation of a book *about* race is removed when the African-American singer, Carmen McRae, takes the stage to perform 'Coffee Time'.[21] While Whaley is right to qualify the film's 'equality of representation', noting that the African-American musicians are generally at the edge of the screen, his observation that Art Farmer's trumpet solo at a key moment in the movie is at least as important as the dialogue in conveying the 'loneliness, regret, unrequited love, and the perplexed difficulty of communication between the sexes'[22] emphasises the degree to which *The Subterraneans* moves beyond other Hollywood depictions of the Beat world.

There are also numerous examples of work by Beat film-makers. As with literature, even a brief listing of a few examples illustrates the fact that individual members of the Beat Generation pursued a wide range of interests. In San Francisco, the poet ruth weiss produced the experimental film *The Brink* (1961), a movie that echoes the free jazz of the time in its focus on sounds above 'meaning' or 'structure' in a process whereby, as Whaley suggests, 'the priority of the aesthetics of tone color subordinates the mechanics of signifying chains'.[23] Similarly, Ron Rice's *The Flower Thief* (1960) anticipates the combination of innocence and knowingness about the world that would characterise the city's hippie community a few years later. In New York, Jack Smith and Ken Jacobs produced films such as *Blonde Cobra* (1959) and *Flaming Creatures* (1962) that questioned distinctions between art and life, and served as models for the pop art of the 1960s.

The two best-known Beat films – Robert Frank's *Pull My Daisy* and John Cassavetes' *Shadows* – were also made in New York. The former, an adaptation of Jack Kerouac's play, *The Beat Generation*, narrated by Kerouac and featuring Beats Ginsberg, Peter Orlovsky and Gregory Corso, as well as the artist Larry Rivers, offers a fine visual representation of Beat lifestyle, as well as witty juxtapositions of the counterculture with a bishop, his sister and his mother who visit the East Side loft where the Beats have assembled. While *Pull My Daisy* remains closely based on Kerouac's script and conveys the illusion of improvisation, the original version of *Shadows* was almost entirely improvised. Part-funded by public donations sent after Cassavetes made a request for funds during a radio interview, and scored by jazz bassist Charles Mingus, *Shadows* is an example of the ways in which the Beats attempted (and, to a degree, failed) to transcend hegemonic attitudes to race. Although the film was a success with the New York avant-garde, its low-budget production and lack of plot also created problems that led to Cassavetes shooting a revised – and better funded – version (released in 1961) that included an hour's new material (and only thirty minutes of the original), in which the director believed that a clearer narrative emerges.[24]

Even more adventurous is Jonas Mekas's *Lost, Lost, Lost* (1949–63), a decade-and-a-half-long diary of the film-maker's experiences from his arrival in New York from Lithuania to his encounters with Beats including Allen Ginsberg and LeRoi Jones, and featuring – in another demonstration of the inter-disciplinarity of Beat artistic production – a series of filmic haikus. Mekas is perhaps the most significant figure in East Coast independent cinema throughout the 1950s and '60s: in addition to his own films, he also served as cameraman on Andy Warhol's eight-hour study of the Empire State Building, *Empire* (1964), founded the influential independent cinema quarterly, *Film Culture*, and was the first film critic for *Village Voice*. As such, he was largely responsible not only for championing independent American movies such as the original version of *Shadows*, but also for disseminating information and opinion about French *Nouvelle Vague* films such as Fraņois Truffaut's *Les Quatres Cents Coups* (*The 400 Blows*, 1959), Jean-Luc Godard's *A Bout de Souffle* (*Breathless*, 1960) and Alain Resnais's *Hiroshima, Mon Amour* (1959), all of which were cult hits in the United States and major influences on American underground cinema.[25]

If anything can be said to unite these films, it is the sense that to be an artist in the 1950s was necessarily to be an outsider in a nation deeply suspicious of challenges to hegemonic norms. All of the movies imagine worlds that bear little or no relation to the suburban 'ideal' ceaselessly promoted in television shows and commercials, and all chronicle examples of defiant otherness. Given this level of marginalisation, it is unsurprising that many avant-garde artists elected to live outside the United States: some of the most notable Beat films were produced by the expatriate community in Europe, where the collaborative team of William Burroughs, Brion Gysin, Antony Balch and Ian Sommerville worked on *Towers Open Fire* (1963; a loose adaptation of Burroughs's novels *The Soft Machine* and *Nova Express*) and on Balch and Burroughs's *Cut-Ups* (1967), a film that, as the title suggests, applies Burroughs's technique of slicing and reassembling materials to disturb or destroy familiar links between images and reality.[26] Burroughs would return to America and apply his revolutionary techniques not only to his fiction but also to playfully subversive gestures such as the splicing and reconstruction of speeches made at the Democratic Convention in Chicago in 1968,[27] but the fact that, like so many other American artists, he chose to spend so much of his professional career away from the United States is further proof of the alienation experienced by the cultural avant-garde in the mid-twentieth century.[28]

Notes

1. Peter Biskind, *Seeing is Believing: Or How Hollywood Taught Us to Stop Worrying and Love the 50s* (London: Bloomsbury, 2001), p. 197.
2. Frank Krutnik, *In a Lonely Street: Film Noir, Genre, Masculinity* (London and New York: Routledge, 1991), p. 75.
3. Of course, this is less true of solo performers such as the Southern bluesmen and the folksingers who could travel more freely (and cheaply) than ensemble performers.
4. This is still true of most independent films from the 1950s today. Most are hard to obtain and hardly ever screened, and some, like the original version of John Cassavetes' *Shadows* (1959), no longer survive. The best collection of Beat films, transferred to video, is probably that held in the Moffitt Library at the University of California, Berkeley.
5. John Carlos Rowe, *Literary Culture and U.S. Imperialism From the Revolution to World War II* (Oxford: Oxford University Press, 2002), p. xi.
6. Richard Slotkin, *Gunfighter Nation: The Myth of the Frontier in Twentieth-Century America* (Norman: University of Oklahoma Press, 1992), p. 393. I am indebted here and below to Slotkin's reading of *High Noon*, pp. 391–6.
7. Ibid., p. 393.
8. Ibid., p. 394.
9. Leonard Quart and Albert Auster, 'Hollywood Dreaming: Postwar American Film', in Josephine G. Hendin (ed.), *A Concise Companion to Postwar American Literature and Culture* (Oxford: Blackwell, 2004), p. 151.
10. Biskind, *Seeing is Believing*, p. 197.
11. Stephen Vaughn, 'Political Censorship During the Cold War: The Hollywood Ten', in Francis G. Couvares (ed.), *Movie Censorship and American Culture* (Washington, DC and London: Smithsonian Institution Press, 1996), p. 246.
12. See Vaughn, 'Political Censorship During the Cold War' p. 246.
13. Biskind, *Seeing is Believing*, p. 198.
14. Ibid., pp. 260–1.

15. Quoted in Jeff Stafford's review of *The Wild One* at http://turnerclassic-movies.com/ThisMonth/Article/
16. In a mark of the extent to which he differs from his father in his ability to establish homosocial ties, Jim shares a cigarette with Buzz immediately before the contest that results in the latter's death.
17. Biskind, *Seeing is Believing*, p. 210, p. 211.
18. Quoted in Biskind, *Seeing is Believing*, p. 216.
19. Biskind, *Seeing is Believing*, p. 215.
20. LeRoi Jones, *Blues People: The Negro Experience in White America and the Music That Developed From It* (New York: William Morrow, 1963), p. 191. See Chapter 1 for a more detailed examination of Jones's point.
21. Preston Whaley, Jr., *Blows Like a Horn: Beat Writing, Jazz, Style, and Markets in the Transformation of U.S. Culture* (Cambridge, MA and London: Harvard University Press, 2004), p. 103.
22. Ibid., p. 106.
23. Ibid., p. 71.
24. See Ray Carney, *American Dreaming: The Films of John Cassavetes and the American Experience* (Berkeley: University of California Press, 1984), passim, for the definitive account of the history of the film's production.
25. See Lewis MacAdams, *Birth of the Cool: Beat, Bebop and the American Avant-Garde* (London: Scribner, 2002), pp. 227–8.
26. See Jack Sergeant's discussion of *Cut-Ups* in 'A Brief Introduction to the Beat (in) Film', at www.sensesofcinema.com/contents/00/9/beat.html
27. See Terry Southern, *Now Dig This: The Unspeakable Writings of Terry Southern, 1950–1995* (London: Methuen, 2002), p. 123. According to Southern – covering the convention with Burroughs and Jean Genet for *Esquire* magazine – it was 'Burroughs's belief that if these [cut-up and reassembled] tapes were played constantly in the Convention Hall, the subliminal effect – of the repetitions, the non sequiturs, and the general idiocies – would so confound any chance listener as to possibly snap his mind, and thus become a profoundly disruptive factor in the overall "Convention profile"'.
28. This phenomenon was not, of course, limited to a single period. From writers such as Washington Irving and Nathaniel Hawthorne, through Henry James and Edith Wharton, to the 'Lost Generation' of F. Scott Fitzgerald and Ernest Hemingway's Paris in the 1920s, innumerable artists had relocated to Europe in efforts to find an alternative to a national culture that they perceived as wilfully hostile to their craft. In the early Cold War years, Paris again became a refuge, not only for Beats but also for jazz musicians appreciating the chance to perform away from the racial discrimination they experienced at home.

Part Two
1961–1972

Introduction

We see the hope of tomorrow in the youth of today. I know America's youth. I believe in them. We can be proud that they are better educated, more committed, more passionately driven by conscience than any generation in our history.

Richard Nixon, 20 January 1969[1]

You see these bums, you know, blowing up the campuses. Listen, the boys that are on the college campuses today are the luckiest people in the world, going to the greatest universities, and here they are burning up the books, storming around.

Richard Nixon, 1 May 1970[2]

Tin soldiers and Nixon's comin'
We're finally on our own
This summer I hear the drummin'
Four dead in Ohio

Crosby, Stills, Nash & Young, 'Ohio' (1970)[3]

Following the death of the Grateful Dead guitarist Jerry Garcia on 9 August 1995, a tie-dye flag was flown at half-mast over San Francisco's City Hall. Tributes were paid by legions of Dead Heads, including then President Bill Clinton, and a few days after the funeral fans gathered in Golden Gate Park to listen to the group's music and share personal and collective reminiscences.[4] In keeping with the ideology of (many of) his generation, some of Garcia's ashes were scattered in the Ganges, the rest in the sea by the Golden Gate. The '60s had been over for a quarter of a century, but the death of the best-known member of the quintessential countercultural band of the era made the national news and seemed – especially with the subsequent painful yet very public dissolution of The Grateful Dead – ironically to show that nostalgia for the spirit of the decade lived on. The point was reinforced soon after by the launch of 'Cherry Garcia' ice cream by Ben and Jerry's, a company whose environmental and social policies have placed it at the meeting-post of countercultural and corporate America.

The attention paid to Garcia's death would appear to suggest that the cultural and political upheavals of the '60s had changed America for good, and there is much to support that assertion. The popular culture of the United States and beyond is still marked by allusions to the decade's music, film, art and literature; iconic groups of the time, including Crosby, Stills, Nash & Young and The Velvet Underground re-form from time to time – more often than not with disappointing or disastrous artistic results – largely because of the enormous financial incentives to do so. Andy Warhol's work is as popular as ever, and continues to be exhibited around the world, and many of the novelists that were required reading for the counterculture, such as Kurt Vonnegut, Ken Kesey and Thomas Pynchon, were quickly placed – and have remained – at the core of undergraduate reading lists by academics who themselves came of age in the Baby Boomer generation. Post 9/11, and with the wars in Iraq and Afghanistan, prominent anti-Vietnam War protestors such as Joan Baez have spoken out strongly against renewed American aggression around the world. At another extreme of the cultural spectrum, it is rare to view an episode of *The Simpsons* without spotting playful references to '60s culture. Nor is it only ageing Baby Boomers who attend the gigs and the galleries: Bob Dylan's US tour in late 2001 drew large numbers of teenagers and early-twentysomethings – young enough to be the grandchildren of his first fans – and many of the top bands of the new millennium are openly indebted to the sounds of forty years ago.

When the political climate of the nation is scrutinised, however, a different pattern emerges. While the countercultural art of the 1960s has become virtually a new orthodoxy in the academy and the market-place, many of the political advances that accompanied it have been reversed or halted. Recent elections at national, state and local levels have largely resulted in shifts to the right, and there is little sign of a strong New Left inheritance in current mainstream debates. Although the feminist and gay rights activism of the 1960s and '70s did result in greater freedoms and legal protection for women and for homosexuals, growing public opposition to abortion and same-sex marriage (and even to heterosexual sex outside marriage), alongside a heightened profile for conservative Christianity – with concomitant political power – indicates a fading of the counterculture's ideological message as revisionist historians seek to discredit its memory. After Hurricane Katrina had destroyed much of New Orleans in 2005, television news around the world transmitted images of impoverished African-Americans apparently left to fend for themselves by state and federal governments still imbued with institutional racism half a century or more after civil rights became the focus of national and international attention. When musicians, actors or novelists speak out against the nation's foreign policy, they can face coordinated assaults on their work – as has been the case with, for example, The Dixie Chicks, Sean Penn and Steve Earle – and are told to steer clear of issues they 'don't understand'. While the latter point provokes the obvious question, what is the purpose of art if it doesn't ask awkward or challenging questions about the culture within which it is produced?, it also goes some way to explaining the apparent anomaly I describe above, in which the cultural artefacts of the '60s are canonised but the political agenda that accompanied them is discredited or overlooked.

In some ways, this indicates an effort on the part of many Americans to erase awkward memories of a decade that saw the United States confront issues that had been repressed throughout much of its history. In my Introduction to the period 1945–60, I argued that the movie *Pleasantville* pretends that the '60s never (or *should* never have) happened and this attitude is also frequently found in the conservative political agenda put forward under the presidency of George W. Bush. The difference is that recent Republican moral campaigns on sexuality, for example, eulogise the very same mythical '1950s' America that *Pleasantville* deconstructs, but are blind to the movie's playful exposé of the era's problems. The art of the '60s survives in a manner that is often stripped of its historical context, or – as with Dylan's civil-rights-era anthems such as 'Blowin' in the Wind' – placed within such narrow confines that it is seen to have done its work and becomes a kind of museum piece with no relevance to the present (implicitly 'equal opportunity') nation.

In what follows I attempt to provide an overview (albeit selective) of the place of the counterculture in the 'long '60s' – the period from the Woolworth's lunch-counter sit-in in Greensboro, North Carolina, in

February 1960 and Kennedy's election later that year, to the Nixon presidency and the end of the Vietnam War – that explains why protest was so pervasive and (increasingly) so violent. Given the extraordinarily rapid changes that took place during this time, and the sheer quantity of dramatically newsworthy stories – civil rights and Black Power, the assassinations of John and Bobby Kennedy, Martin Luther King and Malcolm X, the introduction of the (contraceptive) pill and the 'sexual revolution', the first moon-landing, the Cuban Missile Crisis, the construction of the Berlin Wall, the escalation of the war in Vietnam, San Francisco's 'Summer of Love', campus protests, the Charles Manson murders, Woodstock, Altamont and 1968's Chicago Democratic Convention (as well as events in Europe and Mexico that year), to name but some of the best-known reference points – my narrative will focus on those moments most pertinent to the emergence of the counterculture and New Left as significant social forces, and especially on those occasions when the two were most closely linked.

From JFK to Kent State: Protest and the Counterculture

The turbulence of the late 1960s would have been inconceivable when John F. Kennedy was elected President in 1960. In his inaugural address, Kennedy urged Americans to 'ask not what America will do for you – ask what you can do for your country',[5] appealing to the idealism of many young people at a moment when the election of a youthful President seemed to symbolise the transfer of power to a new generation. Kennedy himself – and, more importantly, his image alongside the glamorous and 'sophisticated' Jackie in 'Camelot' – made a major contribution to the feeling that, as Fredric Jameson sums up, 'in the 60s, for a time, everything was possible; that this period . . . was a moment of universal liberation, a global unbinding of energies'.[6] Thus, although the reality of Kennedy's short presidency included bearing much of the responsibility for subsequent US involvement in Vietnam as well as the failed 1961 Bay of Pigs invasion and the brinkmanship of the Missile Crisis, his legacy, as Jameson reminds us, includes the 'rhetoric of youth and of the "generation gap" . . . which outlived him and dialectically offered itself as an expressive form through which the political discontent of American students and young people could articulate itself'. Kennedy's assassination further contributed to this division, seeming for many young Americans to 'mark the decisive end of the well-known passing of the torch to a younger generation of leadership, as well as the dramatic defeat of some new spirit of public or civic idealism',[7] and contributing to the historical conditions within which the radicalised counterculture of the 1960s developed.

As the summary above suggests, Kennedy's 'New Frontier' was more often located in foreign than in domestic policy and, unlike his successor Lyndon Johnson's 'Great Society', was not characterised by any great enthusiasm for pushing through civil rights legislation. In one way, this is unsurprising: global events such as the move towards independence for many nations in Africa and the Caribbean were enacted within an ongoing Cold War environment where Kennedy initiatives such as the Peace Corps offered the opportunity to demonstrate the 'benevolence' of the United States and strengthen its position vis-à-vis the Soviet Union. The Peace Corps (if not his decisions involving Cuba and Vietnam) can be seen as a shrewd effort to strengthen the nation's standing with potential allies. Nevertheless, the lack of attention to domestic issues meant that, even during his short presidency, opposition was mobilising – and forming alliances – that would become the mainstays of anti-Establishment protest throughout the decade. Ironically – in the light of Kennedy's ambitions – throughout the 1960s, events in the Third World (for example, in Cuba, Vietnam and China) would also come to play an unprecedented part in influencing activism within the US, from civil rights to Black Power and the anti-war movement.

Although Kennedy's role in deepening American involvement in Vietnam was a significant factor in the escalation of the conflict, the war barely registered as the target for protest before his assassination. Likewise, despite the fact that the Missile Crisis did help to mobilise the anti-nuclear lobby, protest was relatively minor compared to that of, for example, the Campaign for Nuclear Disarmament in the United Kingdom, and most people participated in air-raid drills without complaint. The Missile Crisis did, however, instil a sense of a generation gap: remembering the events of 1962, Charles Kaiser (who was then a schoolboy) suggests that the incident 'eliminated our confidence in our parents' ability to control the world or protect us from its wickedness. It's the kind of experience that works subliminal wonders for one's willingness to question the wisdom of one's elders.'[8] Likewise, the fear of irresponsible political and military leaders destroying the world in a nuclear holocaust contributed to the rise of satirical critiques such as Stanley Kubrick's *Dr. Strangelove* (1964), a movie disowned by

Columbia Pictures for many years following its release, but which was eventually selected by the Smithsonian Institution as one of the fifty greatest American films of all time.[9] This kind of satire became an essential component of countercultural commentaries on the Establishment in the 1960s, being a key element of the New Journalism developed by Terry Southern, Tom Wolfe and Hunter S. Thompson, as well-being deployed repeatedly by musicians such as Bob Dylan, The Beatles, Arlo Guthrie and Country Joe and the Fish, and in movies like *Easy Rider* and *Alice's Restaurant*.

Overwhelmingly, however, it was civil rights that provided the focus – and, subsequently, the model – for the waves of protest that would beat incessantly against the Government for the remainder of the decade. Although the sit-in at Woolworth's whites-only lunch-counter in Greensboro was by no means the first of its kind, and the National Association for the Advancement of Colored People (NAACP) and the Congress of Racial Equality (CORE) had offered support for many other similar actions since the mid-1950s, the rapid spread and mass publicity accorded to the Woolworth's campaign led both to the creation of the Student Nonviolent Coordinating Committee (SNCC) and to increasingly widespread use of the sit-in as a form of protest. It is probably not a coincidence, for example, that anti-HUAC demonstrators adopted the same tactic in San Francisco in May 1960, and Todd Gitlin illustrates the extent to which the sit-in became 'the main dynamo that powered the white movement', pointing out that 'without the civil rights movement, the beat and Old Left and bohemian enclaves would not have opened into a revived politics'.[10] Subsequent acts such as James Meredith's arrival at the all-white University of Mississippi in 1962, Mohammed Ali's refusal to fight in Vietnam in 1967 and the Black Power salutes given by athletes Tommie Smith and John Carlos on the medal podium at the Mexico Olympics in 1968 all acted as inspiration and motivation to elements of the white anti-war movement throughout the '60s.

Equally, the civil rights movement reactivated the coupling of the arts and political protest, a practice common before HUAC turned its focus on Hollywood in the late 1940s, but – with the exception of a few activists such as Paul Robeson and Pete Seeger, who suffered enormous hardship for their efforts – largely dormant since. The folk music boom of the late 1950s and early '60s provides perhaps the strongest link between Old and New Left, but its more overtly political dynamics only resurfaced nationally with its affiliation to civil rights, the first of a series of single-issue struggles that would characterise New Left identity. Although the 28 April 1963 gathering at the Lincoln Memorial is, of course, best remembered for Martin Luther King's 'I have a dream' speech, it also featured an appearance by Bob Dylan, by then unchallenged as the new poet of the countercultural left. Dylan's combination of a white folk tradition epitomised by Woody Guthrie and the African-American rural blues of the Deep South matched the multi-racial mix of an audience that had gathered from across the nation.

Dylan is a pivotal figure in the transformation of the counterculture from groups like the Beats – who constituted a small minority of the population, largely limited to enclaves in New York, San Francisco and a few other large cities – into a collection of larger overlapping movements with shared agendas. These groups, though still a minority, had a significant public profile that was often at the centre of national attention. Gitlin summarises Dylan's early significance in a way that is worth quoting at length:

> The Zimmerman boy from up-country Minnesota had adopted a name that was both literary (the besotted and lyrical Dylan Thomas) and true-gritty American (*Gunsmoke*'s Marshall Matt Dillon), had gone to Greenwich Village and picked up a following with his folk anthems and antiestablishment gags. The tiny New Left delighted in one of our own generation and mind singing earnest ballads about racist murderers ('The Lonesome Death of Hattie Carroll'), the compensatory racism of poor whites ('Only a Pawn in Their Game'), Cold War ideology ('Masters of War' and 'With God on Our Side'). Insiders knew Dylan had written the chilling 'A Hard Rain's Gonna Fall' during the Cuban Missile Crisis, evoking the end of the world . . . To make it all more marvellous, Dylan did all this not on the marginal, faintly do-it-yourself Vanguard or Folkways label, redolent of Pete Seeger and the fight against the blacklist, but on big-league commercial Columbia Records. Teased by the idea of a popular movement, we admired Dylan's ability to smuggle the subversive into mass-circulated trappings.[11]

I cite Gitlin not only because of the concise manner in which he links Dylan's early songs to particular aspects of American culture, but also because of his ability to recollect what the artist meant to the then tiny New Left and, in particular, to the Students for a Democratic Society (SDS), at that time in its infancy, but subsequently to become the centre of student protest throughout the decade. Although Dylan himself would rapidly disown association with the movement, 'go electric' and engage in a series of reinventions that has continued throughout his career, Gitlin's summary demonstrates his unparalleled significance to the fusion of art and politics in the 1960s. Although other musicians – most notably The Beatles and The Rolling Stones – would also provide a soundtrack to encounters between protestors and the Establishment, Dylan's role as not just a chronicler but also a shaper of youth culture in the '60s is indubitably unique.

If the Lincoln Memorial gathering demonstrated the possibilities for peaceful racial integration, however, much of the remainder of the decade was marked by an escalation of violence both against – and later by – elements of both black and New Left communities. In addition, as the decade progressed, it became increasingly clear that political affiliations that crossed race and class lines were hard to sustain. The ghetto race riots that erupted in the summers of 1964–8 – including, most famously, that in Watts in August 1965 – suggested that the civil rights legislation introduced by Lyndon Johnson did not go far enough to satisfy many African-Americans. Although New Left activists such as Tom Hayden continued to advise black communities in Newark and elsewhere, their presence eventually caused conflict with separatist Black Power groups. In 1966, SNCC activist Stokely Carmichael told a rally in Greenwood, Mississippi, 'We need Black Power', and stated that he distrusted all white organisations and that African-Americans should stay at home and fight rather than going to Vietnam; for Carmichael, integration was a 'subterfuge for the main-tenance of white supremacy'.[12]

The shift from civil rights to Black Power and anti-war protests that marked the Johnson presidency was also distinguished by ruptures: there is no doubt that the anti-war *movement* of the late 1960s – as characterised by an uneasy alliance of the increasingly fragmented SDS and groups like Abbie Hoffman and Jerry Rubin's Yippies – was highly unpopular with the majority of Americans who were opposed to the war, as well as with those who supported it. In addition to the fragmentation along racial lines, it was evident that the movement would not be able to establish the kinds of lasting, significant alliances across class barriers for which it had hoped. Hunter S. Thompson identifies one instance of these tensions when he highlights the break-down of relations between the SDS and the Hell's Angels in California:

> The Angels blew it in 1965, at the Oakland–Berkeley line, when they . . . attacked the front ranks of an anti-war march. This

proved to be an historic schism in the then Rising Tide of the Youth Movement of the Sixties. It was the first open break between the Greasers and the Longhairs, and the importance of that break can be read in the history of the SDS, which eventually destroyed itself in the doomed effort to reconcile the interests of the lower/working class biker/dropout types and the upper/middle, Berkeley/student activists.[13]

Thompson's point is significant and illustrates the volatile relationship between the counterculture and the Angels (especially in the Bay area) throughout the 1960s. Although bands like The Grateful Dead and later The Rolling Stones employed the Angels as security for many of their gigs, there were many accounts of overly physical crowd control, culminating, of course, in events at the Stones' gig at Altamont in December 1969. The Angels also acquired control of much of the drugs market in the area in the late '60s and were significant players in the increasing trade in cocaine and heroin that contributed to the decline of Haight-Ashbury around the end of the decade.

More widely, it was clear that popular constructions of counter-culture lifestyle depicted patterns at odds with working-class American ideals based on patriotism and self-improvement. In a recent study of the Chicago police and the 1968 Democratic Convention, Frank Kusch suggests that the police – like others in their urban working-class communities – saw the 'hippie movement . . . [as] the antithesis of [Chicago's] creed of hard work and loyalty to tradition; hippies and antiwar activists were likened to godless transients without respect for traditional values'.[14] Within the popular stereotype, almost any male with long hair was a drug-taking 'commie' subversive, whose anti-war stance manifested un-American attitudes, and whose idleness – and even disrespect for money – indicated an incompatibility with the core values of 'real Americans' who (as summed up by police officer Eddie Kelso) 'worked hard every day to build this country, who paid their taxes, kept their neighbourhoods clean, and wanted a better life for their children than they had themselves'.[15] Although Kusch's study does not exonerate the police for their violent actions at the convention, it does go some way towards explaining them: there is no doubt that, like many members of working-class communities, the police resented what they saw as an abuse of privilege by white college students, who came from (or were perceived to come from) affluent families, but who seemed to reject the society that had provided them with a comfortable lifestyle. Although, in part, the conflict was generational, with those who had grown up during the Depression in the 1930s enraged by young Americans unwilling to appreciate how lucky they were, traditional cross-generational ties remained strong in most ethnic urban working-class communities, and the majority of younger people were also hostile to protesters.

The civil rights movement was clearly marked by the presence of artists as well as activists, and the presence of figures like Bob Dylan was a significant force in creating mass protests. The same is true of the anti-war movement, but the relationship functioned in a rather different manner, with the Yippies, for example, incorporating self-consciously theatrical performance – learned from countercultural groups like the anarchist collective, the Diggers – into their strategies for disrupting events like the Democratic Convention. The Diggers themselves emerged out of the San Francisco Mime Troupe in 1966 and gave away food to those who wanted it every afternoon at the Fell Street Panhandle of Golden Gate Park. This concept soon developed into a wider 'free' project, in which people would be transported, without charge, around the city in buses and trucks, and which included the 'Free Frame of Reference', a store providing free clothing and other items in a gesture that, as Michael William Doyle sums up, 'parodies capitalism even while redistributing the cornucopian bounty of that system's surplus'.[16] The Diggers also offered a free medical centre and distributed free acid, free housing and free legal services.

As Doyle points out, the Diggers would be 'unimaginable without their having been able to draw upon the vaunted affluence of a postscarcity society. Surplus goods were more easily available during the economic boom of the mid-1960s, which followed a long period of postwar prosperity.'[17] This does not mean, however, that their actions were without a significance that extended well beyond the Bay region. Although the 'Free Network' was clearly an important local service and did much to facilitate San Francisco's 'Summer of Love', their street theatre provided a wider and more lasting legacy for the counterculture. Again, Doyle provides an astute and concise summary of Digger performance:

> The Diggers took theatre into the streets. In the process they attempted to remove all boundaries between art and life, between spectator and performer, and between public and private. The resulting technique, which they referred to as 'life-acting,' punned on the dual meaning of the verb 'to act,' combining the direct action of anarchism with theatrical role playing.[18]

For my present purposes, I am less concerned with developing a detailed history of the Diggers than with stressing their import to the establishment of inseparable ties between the artistic and political wings of the counterculture, especially through their influence on the Yippies. The latter were created as an East Coast equivalent to the San Francisco group, and – even before adopting the 'Yippies' moniker – appropriated its strategies in efforts to expose the greed inherent in free-market capitalism, most notably when they threw money from a balcony onto the floor of the New York Stock Exchange and then burnt dollar bills in front of the press in what Todd Gitlin astutely sums up as a 'politics of display'.[19] Such actions, however, both signified a crucial difference between Yippie and Digger ideology and led the West Coast group to disown their New York would-be counterparts. Whereas the Diggers functioned within and sought to extend the countercultural community, the Yippies were equally concerned with taking their 'guerrilla theater' into the heart of American capitalism, usually alerting the press in advance and seeking as much publicity as possible. For the Diggers, such behaviour was little more than self-promotion, and marked an irreconcilable rupture.

There is much truth in the accusation of publicity-seeking: among the Yippies' best-remembered stunts were the attempt to levitate the Pentagon and the planned nomination of a pig (Pigasus) as Democratic presidential candidate in Chicago. Nevertheless, their antics were underpinned by an incisive understanding of the power of the media and the ease with which the authorities could be panicked into responses that made them appear brutal, stupid, or both. As Gitlin points out, 'since revolutionaries couldn't count enough real allies for a revolution, they conjured images . . . that permitted them to elude, for a while, the difficulties of practical politics'.[20] Such activities reached their climax with the Chicago convention, with highly publicised promises to spike the city's water supply with LSD and to plant disguised Yippie women in hotels and at the convention centre to seduce delegates.[21] Although there was never any chance – or even intention – of realising these actions, the threat was enough in itself to raise the sense of the event as spectacle and to ensure that 'the whole world [was] watching' as police (perhaps deliberately provoked by the Yippies) clubbed demonstrators in the city's streets.

Although the Yippies were perceived as posing a revolutionary threat to hegemonic American values – and Rubin and Hoffman were two of the 'Chicago Eight' tried on conspiracy charges as a result of events at the convention – their stance was, in many ways, characteristically 'American'. Rubin's doctrine was 'Act first. Analyze later. Impulse – not theory – makes the great leaps forward',[22] a philosophy that not only transplants the Beat mantra, 'First thought, best thought', into a more directly political arena, but also resurrects that Transcendentalist ideology of Emerson and Whitman. Like the Transcendentalists, the Yippies made little or no distinction between theory and practice, and both groups sought to shake 'ordinary' Americans out of their overcivilised existences and effect individual and social transformation. Further, their belief in self-reliant non-conformity as an antidote to what they perceived as the stultifying norms of middle-class America, and their opposition to the domestic and imperialistic injustices of racism and the Vietnam War, matched Transcendentalism's own doctrine of non-conformity and many of its advocates' opposition to slavery and the war with Mexico. Unsurprisingly, and unfortunately for the Yippies, their actions failed to win over the support of a conservative America for the most part outraged by satirical deconstructions of national symbols (especially the flag) and by radicals who were perceived to support the North Vietnamese in their struggle with the United States, rather than demonstrating the kind of patriotic zeal expected in times of war.

Ironically, the actions of the Yippies and other groups in Chicago – and subsequently during Democratic presidential candidate Hubert Humphrey's election campaign – contributed to Richard Nixon's election victory and to the escalating force used against protestors. Chicago was a Democrat city and its mayor, Richard J. Daley, was an old-school party boss determined to protect delegates from what took place outside the convention, but the actions of his police force shocked many of the people who witnessed events on television. Even if the majority of those polled supported the police's action,[23] it is likely that significant numbers of potential left-leaning Democrat voters were put off by what they had witnessed, by the convention's rubber-stamping of Humphrey as candidate and by the heavy-handed treatment of supporters of the movement's preferred candidate, Eugene McCarthy. At the other extreme of the party, it is also probable that wavering voters were disturbed by what they perceived as the party's inability to control its more unruly members, and voted for Nixon. Either way, the fact that the protestors had converged on Chicago and continued to trail Humphrey enabled Nixon to conduct a campaign that was largely free of major incidents. In what proved to be a close election, the actions of the Yippies and other factions emerging from a dissolving New Left were possibly decisive factors in sealing Nixon's triumph.

In the light of events that followed, Yippie plans for Chicago and the police response seem relatively tame. The People's Park confrontation in Berkeley, the most radical campus environment in the United States, developed after the local community's attempt to transform university waste ground into a space to be enjoyed by the people was met by California Governor Ronald Reagan's dispatch of several thousand armed National Guardsmen into Berkeley and the death of one man from police buckshot wounds. Following Nixon's announcement of American movement into Cambodia on 30 April 1970, there were mass student protests at campuses across America. Three days after Nixon attacked 'these bums ... blowing up the campuses', four students were shot dead by National Guardsmen at Ohio's Kent State University, precipitating a nationwide student strike supported by unprecedented numbers that led to further violent clashes and to the deaths of two black female students at Jackson State College, Mississippi. Although protests on this scale were not repeated, they did have an effect, with Henry Kissinger believing that Nixon had succumbed to the pressure when he announced the withdrawal of US forces in Cambodia that summer.[24] By this time, however, the political organisations that had emerged from the fragmentation of the SDS were also increasingly violent, bombing and burning university and other buildings with connections to the war. Although the playful manipulation of the media deployed by the Yippies did not disappear immediately, the artistic countercultural strategies that had been in the foreground as late as People's Park had little connection with these attempts to meet violence with violence.

Beyond Protest: San Francisco, the 'Summer of Love' and the Counterculture in the '60s

The rapid transformation of the counterculture's engagement with national and international political campaigns was matched by equally swift changes at local levels, as well as in terms of public recognition for its musicians and other artists. For example, by the mid-1960s the hub of the San Francisco counterculture was shifting from the North Beach (the epicentre of the Beat community) to Haight-Ashbury. North Beach was increasingly overrun with tourists and was also regularly subjected to police intimidation and maltreatment, whereas Haight was (around 1965–6) what Dennis McNally calls a 'charming neighborhood', made up of a mixture of African-Americans, Russian immigrants, San Francisco State students and bohemian refugees from the North Beach. As McNally continues, in his biography of The Grateful Dead,

> Early in 1966 the city's voters rejected a freeway that would have destroyed the Haight, and it stayed popular. Something special grew there, a new attitude. There was 'a fantastic universal sense that whatever we were doing was *right*,' wrote the journalist Hunter Thompson, 'that . . . our energy would simply *prevail*.' America had once been about freedom and possibility, and now it was choked in bureaucracy. Dropping out had become a most reasonable social statement.[25]

The Dead themselves established a commune at 710 Ashbury Street in September 1966, and became integral to the new San Francisco sound. But they also reflected the attitude that dominated the city's counterculture at the time, sharing as much because it was all they could afford as because of any particular ideology, and immersing themselves in the area's LSD culture to the extent that they were supported financially by Owsley 'Bear' Stanley, whose mass production of extremely pure LSD was the catalyst for the area's psychedelic scene. For the Dead, the efforts of the Yippies and other protest groups were both misguided and largely irrelevant, suggesting that broad swathes of countercultural San Francisco were not interested in alliances with the politics of protest. At the Human Be-In held in Golden Gate Park on Saturday 14 January 1967, for example, the crowd were largely indifferent to what Jerry Rubin had to say and preferred to drop acid and listen to San Francisco bands including Quicksilver Messenger Service and The Grateful Dead, and to poets such as Allen Ginsberg, Gary Snyder and Michael McClure. Jerry Garcia felt that, when Rubin spoke, 'the words didn't matter. It was that angry tone. It scared me, it made me sick to my stomach', and – probably summing up the thoughts of most of the audience – asked 'Why enter this closed society and make an effort to liberalize it . . .? Why not just leave it and go somewhere else?'[26]

The fact that, at the time of the Be-In, The Grateful Dead lived in a commune in the heart of the bohemian Haight-Ashbury district illustrates the local nature of the San Francisco scene as late as early 1967. At Ken Kesey's Acid Tests, the band provided the music but tended not to draw attention to themselves with stage lights or a show, since there were many other visual attractions for the crowd, and they were not regarded as celebrities. Instead, in an association that would form the basis for the band's subsequent career, the relationship would be what McNally calls a 'partnership of equals, of companions in an odyssey'.[27] Nevertheless, this kind of cohabitation was remarkably short-lived, and the explosion of interest in the 'hippie' scene in 1967's Summer of Love led to the rapid destabilisation and disintegration of the Haight-Ashbury community, with most of the leading musicians, including The Grateful Dead, relocating to Marin County by 1968.

Ironically, the principal cause of this transformation was the raised national profile of the bands themselves, especially after the Monterey International Pop Festival held in June 1967. Monterey made national stars of artists such as Jimi Hendrix and Big Brother and the Holding Company (featuring Janis Joplin), and brought Otis Redding (one of the few black artists to perform there) to the attention of a large white audience, but its particular focus on San Francisco bands and sounds drew overwhelming media attention to the city. This, alongside the arrival of so many young people, placed intolerable pressures on Haight-Ashbury, which was also subject to greatly increased police presence, often concentrated around 710 Ashbury Street. The mass influx of young white Americans also created tensions between the counterculture – accurately described by Greil Marcus as a 'very white scene'[28] – and the neighbourhood's African-American residents. As Alice Echols has pointed out, 'There was virtually no connection between San Francisco's black community and white countercul-ture',[29] and it is noteworthy that the few leading non-white musicians in the counterculture – such as Jimi Hendrix, Arthur Lee of Love and even the long-time Bay area resident Sly Stone – chose to base themselves in Los Angeles or New York. In any case, the place of rock music in American culture was changing rapidly: *Rolling Stone* was launched that November and its founder, UC Berkeley student Jann Wenner, seeking to distance the magazine from the by then thriving underground press, announced, 'This is not a counterculture paper, this is an industry paper.'[30]

In a further twist, the Dead themselves also abetted the changing relationship between San Francisco's musical counterculture and cor-porate America. Although their management included communal discussion and could be chaotic, the band's dealings with Warner Bros. provide a significant index of how big business and the under-ground could accommodate one another's best interests. By this, I do not simply mean that the Dead 'sold out', although they were quick to rename a double live album when Warner/Reprise pointed out that a product titled *Skull Fuck* would not be stocked by most retailers and that the band would suffer financially. Instead, their presence in the Warner stable gave enormous countercultural kudos – and, despite the poor sales of the group's own early records, financial profit – to the label. As Fred Goodman has pointed out, The Grateful Dead were 'authentic American bohemians, the acid-munching standard bearers of the underground. The Dead challenged convention – and now, by inference, Warner Bros. did as well.'[31]

Although drug use had been widespread among Beats and jazz musicians in the 1940s and '50s, and heroin addiction was common in their acquaintances around Times Square, more general consumption of non-prescription substances was relatively limited and tended (for obvious reasons) to be carried out discreetly. In contrast, the major countercultural festivals of the '60s, such as Monterey and Woodstock, were marked by open use of marijuana and LSD, and by the organisers' presumption that many of the audience would take drugs and that help should be available for those experiencing bad trips or other negative effects. LSD had been publicised by Dr Timothy Leary and his colleagues in the Harvard Psychedelic Research Project in the early '60s (and Leary coined the famous slogan, 'Tune in, turn on, drop out'), but its significance to the counterculture was at least as pronounced in San Francisco, where Ken Kesey and his Merry Pranksters set out to explore what the world was like when experienced on acid. The Pranksters had travelled in a repainted school bus driven by Neal Cassady (the model for Dean Moriarty in *On the Road*) from San Francisco to New York in 1964, in the process – foreshadowing the Yippies later in the decade – confusing and enraging many citizens with their take on the presidential election and the norms of American culture. When they returned to San Francisco, Kesey and the Pranksters offered to 'turn on' anyone who cared to join them in their 'Acid Tests', where people were encouraged to 'freak freely' to the multi-media backdrop of poetry, light shows, film loops and the music of the house band, the Warlocks – soon renamed The Grateful Dead.[32]

It should be clear just how far the counterculture had moved from the anti-modern ideology espoused by many Beats: as Todd Gitlin notes, the Acid Tests were an attempt to 'electrify [the world] courtesy of the advanced products of American technology', whether these were the purest LSD available or state-of-the-art sound and vision systems.[33] For Alice Echols, LSD was the final component in establishing the historical conditions for the 'hippie revolution', linking with the nation's unprecedented prosperity, the British invasion led by The Beatles and The Rolling Stones, and by Bob Dylan going electric.[34]

Likewise – if more sceptically – for 'gonzo' journalist Hunter S. Thompson, LSD was a symbol of the inability of the counterculture to escape the norms of consumer capitalism; its users were 'pathetically eager acid freaks who thought they could buy peace and understanding for three bucks a hit'.[35] In any case, at the Acid Tests, LSD – still legal in California at the time – was distributed freely and everything was done to encourage a collective spirit that contrasted with dominant society's emphasis on private familial consumption. As David Farber sums up, in an important essay on drugs in the 1960s counterculture, the Pranksters 'took their acid visions as a sign of the immensely entertaining, challenging, and occasionally enlightening free spaces people could create if they cared to'.[36]

Although the mass use of hallucinogenic drugs like LSD was contemporaneous with the anti-war movement, and – even allowing for the reservations of Jerry Garcia – many individuals bridged the line between political protest and the search for personal enlightenment, there are clear differences between the two experiences. While Kesey and others believed that if politicians took acid their world-view would change and wars would end, the possibility of this happening was obviously remote. Trips were either an individual experience or part of a shared happening involving the like-minded. While civil rights or anti-war protest sought to change the world for all, LSD offered the promise of transcendence of that world. In some ways, the difference marks differing responses to an issue raised by Herbert Marcuse in *One-Dimensional Man* (1964), a text that became a key shaper of countercultural ideology. For Marcuse,

> It seems that the persistence of these untranslatable universals [Beauty, Justice, Happiness] as nodal points of thought reflects the unhappy consciousness of a divided world in which 'that which is' falls short of, and even denies, 'that which can be.' The irreducible difference between the universal and its particulars seems to be rooted in the inconquerable difference between potentiality and actuality – between two dimensions of the one experienced world. The universal comprehends in one idea the possibilities which are realized, and at the same time arrested, in reality.[37]

Marcuse himself was dubious about the efficacy of 'bohemian' alternatives to the norms of daily life, regarding them as being 'quickly digested by the status quo',[38] and was also pessimistic about possibilities of overturning the dominant social order. Thus, for young radicals, *One-Dimensional Man* became more of a summary of what was wrong with American society than a guide to how to change it. As my discussion of civil rights and anti-war activism has indicated, there were large numbers of Americans who, while accepting Marcuse's analysis of how late capitalism functioned, would not accept his totalising model. If such a model truly existed, then where did Marcuse himself find the space to critique it? In a different way, his scepticism about the 'irreducible difference' between potential and actuality was no obstacle to the large numbers of young people willing to seek Truth through drugs, even if they – unlike those in the movement – did not expect to overthrow the prevailing social order. Despite these differences, however, both the movement's campaigns against the State and the counterculture's searches for transcendental escapes from it – each of which was much more widely practised than the models assessed by Marcuse in what is essentially a study of the 1950s in America – implied a rejection of the notion that capitalism's control of the individual and the collective was all-embracing.

In the chapters that follow, I will develop this point, looking at the counterculture's accommodations with, rejections of and attempts to chronicle and transform American society. My discussion of fiction assesses the ways in which authors such as Diane di Prima, Richard Brautigan and Ken Kesey bridged the gap between Beat and hippie, extending the former's critique of American society and imagining ways to effect widespread social change. The chapters on music and art focus on the rapid pace of change in countercultural practice in the 1960s, and on how (and how far) artistic experimentation could be coupled with a discourse of protest. Finally, I offer readings of films that suggest the partial empowerment of the counterculture within Hollywood, with directors such as Arthur Penn and Dennis Hopper making films that took it seriously, even if they did not always represent it in a favourable light. Movies like *Easy Rider* (1969), *Alice's Restaurant* (1969), *Woodstock* (1970) and *Deliverance* (1972) are significant both as examples of texts that attracted large youth (and, in most instances, more general) audiences, and as documents that are sensitive to the reasons for the counterculture's fragmentation around the end of the 1960s.

Notes

1. Richard Nixon, 'Inaugural Address,' 20 January 1969, at www.yale.edu/lawweb/avalon/presiden/inaug/nixon1.htm
2. Quoted in Mark Feeney, *Nixon at the Movies: A Book About Belief* (Chicago: University of Chicago Press, 2004), p. 185.
3. Neil Young, 'Ohio', released by Crosby, Stills, Nash & Young as a single in 1970 and on the album *Four Way Street* (Atlantic, 1971). Copyright © 1970, 1993 Cotillion Music, Inc. and Broken Fiddle.
4. See Dennis McNally, *A Long Strange Trip: The Inside History of the Grateful Dead and the Making of Modern America* (London: Corgi, 2003), pp. 817–18.
5. Quoted in M. J. Heale, *The Sixties in America: History, Politics and Protest* (Edinburgh: Edinburgh University Press, 2001), p. 19.
6. Fredric Jameson, 'Periodizing the 60s', in Jameson, *The Ideologies of Theory: Essays 1971–1986, Volume 2: The Syntax of History* (Routledge: London: 1988), p. 207.
7. Ibid., p. 183.
8. Charles Kaiser, *1968 in America: Music, Politics, Chaos, Counterculture, and the Shaping of a Generation* (New York: Grove Press, 1988), p. xvii.
9. See Terry Southern, *Now Dig This: The Unspeakable Writings of Terry Southern, 1950–1995* (London: Methuen, 2002), pp. 72–85.
10. Todd Gitlin, *The Sixties: Years of Hope, Days of Rage* (New York: Bantam, 1987), p. 83.
11. Gitlin, *The Sixties*, p. 197.
12. See Kaiser, *1968 in America*, p. 136; Heale, *The Sixties in America*, p. 122.
13. Hunter S. Thompson, *Fear and Loathing in Las Vegas* (London: Flamingo, 1993), p. 179. Several members of the West Coast counterculture, including Jerry Garcia and Michael McClure, distinguish between the Angels' San Francisco chapter, who were close to The Grateful Dead, and what they see as the less disciplined Oakland chapter, whose behaviour at Altamont brought widespread condemnation.
14. Frank Kusch, *Battleground Chicago: The Police and the 1968 Democratic National Convention* (Westport, CT: Praeger, 2004), p. 15.
15. Ibid., p. 152.
16. Michael William Doyle, 'Staging the Revolution: Guerrilla Theater as a Countercultural Practice, 1965–68', in Peter Braunstein and Michael William Doyle (eds), *Imagine Nation: The American Counterculture of the 1960s and '70s* (London: Routledge, 2002), p. 80.
17. Ibid., p. 81.
18. Ibid., p. 80.
19. Gitlin, *The Sixties*, p. 233.

20. Ibid., p. 235. Gitlin is highly critical of the Yippies, arguing that they were 'trapped in a media loop, dependent on media standards, media sufferance, and goodwill. These apostles of freedom couldn't grasp that they were destined to become clichés' (p. 237).

21. See Kaiser, *1968 in America*, pp. 232–3.

22. Quoted in Gitlin, *The Sixties*, p. 237.

23. See Kusch, *Battleground Chicago*, p. 155. According to Kusch, 'the *New York Times* reported that a nationwide poll conducted with 1,000 people overwhelmingly supported the police. Television networks were also inundated with mail condemning the media's coverage and interpretation of the convention. Letters to CBS were eleven-to-one in favour of police action. A Gallup poll two weeks after the convention suggested that Americans supported police fifty-six percent to thirty-one percent.'

24. See Gitlin, *The Sixties*, pp. 409–11.

25. McNally, *A Long Strange Trip*, p. 227.

26. Quoted in McNally, *A Long Strange Trip*, p. 254.

27. Ibid., p. 175.

28. Greil Marcus, *Mystery Train* (London: Faber, 2000), p. 75.

29. See Alice Echols, *Shaky Ground: The Sixties and Its Aftershocks* (New York: Columbia University Press, 2002), p. 33.

30. Quoted in McNally, *A Long Strange Trip*, p. 316.

31. Fred Goodman, *The Mansion on the Hill: Dylan, Young, Geffen, Springsteen and the Head-On Collision of Rock and Commerce* (London: Pimlico, 2003), p. 75.

32. See Tom Wolfe, *The Electric Kool Aid Acid Test* (New York: Bantam, 1969) for the best account of Kesey's Acid Tests.

33. Gitlin, *The Sixties*, p. 207.

34. See Echols, *Shaky Ground*, p. 27.

35. Thompson, *Fear and Loathing in Las Vegas*, p. 178.

36. David Farber, 'The Intoxicated State/Illegal Nation: Drugs in the Sixties Counterculture', in Braunstein and Doyle, *Imagine Nation*, p. 26.

37. Herbert Marcuse, *One-Dimensional Man* (London: Ark paperbacks, 1986), pp. 209–10.

38. Ibid., p. 14.

CHAPTER FIVE

Fiction

> Maybe the target nowadays is not to discover what we are, but to refuse what we are.
> > Michel Foucault, 'The Subject and Power' (1982)[1]

> 'Close the book, man, what's the matter with you, don't you know you're liberated?'
> > Unnamed student protestor in E. L. Doctorow, *The Book of Daniel* (1971)[2]

There are both ruptures and continuities between the Beat Generation and the countercultural fiction of the 1960s. Jack Kerouac – whose *On the Road* is unquestionably the iconic Beat novel – seemed both to him and to many others to belong in another America. On the one hand, *On the Road* celebrates the kind of individualism increasingly challenged by the more collective ideals of the '60s; on the other, the explosion of anti-Establishment movements that rejected his largely conservative views about the United States appalled Kerouac. At heart, he remained the small-town Catholic child of French Canadian joual-speaking parents, eulogising such staples of national life as baseball and apple pie and ice cream, and becoming ever more angry at what he saw as the hippies' crass betrayal of the Beat ideals of 'conviction' and 'spirituality'.[3] In any case, he was a reluctant prophet, withdrawing into alcoholism and life with his mother and his third wife, Stella, the sister of a childhood friend.

Kerouac's reactionary anger notwithstanding, however, '60s counterculture should not be seen as a 'progressive' advance on all Beat attitudes and, in some ways, it was closer to hegemonic white America than had been the case in the previous decade. The Beats embraced (albeit problematically) forms of African-American culture such as jazz and were broadly conducive to the concept of mixed-race relationships, even if these couplings tended to be short-term. In addition, as I make clear in Part One of this book, many Beat writers envisaged artistic creativity occurring as a consequence of strong homosocial and homo-sexual ties between men. In contrast, while some women did achieve – or were believed to have achieved – greater freedoms with the sexual revolution of the 1960s, the 'hippie generation' was overwhelmingly white and was often demonstrably hostile to homosexuality. Black Power, the women's movement and gay rights were all shaped in part by fractured relationships with political and artistic elements of this counterculture.

Emerging tensions about race are apparent in the bohemian New York scene of the early mid-'60s. Although Kerouac's fellow Beat LeRoi Jones, for example, continued (later as Amiri Baraka) to be a major poet, playwright and critic throughout the decade and beyond, his turn to separatist Black Nationalism led to rifts with acquaintances in the white counterculture (including his divorce from the Jewish Beat poet, Hettie Cohen), and, after the assassination of Malcolm X, to his relocation from Greenwich Village to Harlem and then to Newark. Baraka's reinvention is more 'personal' than most, but his poem 'Black Dada Nihilismus' (1964) provides a good example of the extent to which, even before abandoning the Village, he was questioning the worth of the multi-racial Beat sensibility that is still evident in *Blues People*, published the previous year. In the poem, Baraka seems to imagine a complete and disturbing split from white America, including the racially mixed world of bohemian lower Manhattan, calling,

Come up, black dada

nihilismus. Rape the white girls. Rape
their fathers. Cut the mothers' throats.

Black dada nihilismus, choke my friends

in their bedrooms with their drinks spilling
and restless for tilting hips or dark liver
lips sucking splinters from the master's thigh.[4]

In a detailed and nuanced reading, Daniel Wong-gu Kim has recently highlighted the extent to which Baraka's apparently direct call to violent Black Nationalism is qualified by the poem's structure, pointing out that

> the invocation of black Dada nihilismus to murder begins haltingly, marked off from the stanzaic body of the incitement contained within the prior stanza. Furthermore, that stanza break coincides with a disjunctive enjambment that disrupts the unity of the phrase 'black Dada nihilismus.' This phrase is enjambed only here – at the apparent apex of violence – and not in its other three appearances. 'Come up, black Dada' would have been syntactically sufficient, yet the invocation stutters across the stanza gap to add 'nihilismus.' The gap here only readmits the ironizing connotations of -ismus, undermining the murderous impulse from the outset.[5]

I think that Wong-gu Kim is right to develop a close reading that pays as much attention to form as to content in a manner that emphasises the stuttering irony of the poem and to challenge critics who have seen only its violence. Nevertheless, when 'Black Dada Nihilismus' is considered in the context of Jones's work in the late 1950s and early 1960s, not only as a writer, but also as editor of *Yugen* magazine, of the literary newsletter, *The Floating Bear* (co-edited by Diane di Prima) and of a series of books for Totem Corinth that contained work by (among others) Kerouac, Gary Snyder, Allen Ginsberg and Philip Whalen, it is unsurprising that these ironies risked being overlooked. The bohemian arts community of the time was still small and Jones was an integral member of what Ginsberg called the 'black white hip'[6] Greenwich Village art crowd, making his calculated rejection of familial and professional ties – emphasised here in the line, 'choke my friends' – particularly traumatic for erstwhile lovers and colleagues.[7] Clearly, Baraka takes James Baldwin's concerns about the multiracial Village community (as represented in *Another Country*) on a path that is considerably more militant. As such, it is striking that Jones's new radicalism coincided (somewhat ironically) with the critical and commercial success of his play, *Dutchman* (1964), in which a naïve black college student is tormented and finally murdered by an abusive white woman in a subway car symbolic of a deeply disturbed national racial unconscious.

While Kerouac and Baraka distanced themselves from the '60s

counterculture, many of the other members of the early New York and West Coast Beat scene became pivotal to the next generation's artistic community: Ginsberg served not only as sometime mentor to Bob Dylan, but also as a leading figure in areas such as green and anti-nuclear movements, gay rights and anti-war campaigns, in addition to continuing to produce important and widely read poetry. Likewise, fellow readers at the Six Gallery on the night in October 1955 when Ginsberg first performed 'Howl' were at least as prominent in the '60s countercultural scene as they had been in the previous decade: Gary Snyder and Michael McClure, in particular – both of whom featured at San Francisco's 1967 Human Be-In – brought interests in Eastern philosophy and in environmentalism to a much larger hippie community. McClure was also one of several countercultural figures to become friends with the Hell's Angels, working with 'Freewheelin Frank' (Reynolds), the secretary of the San Francisco chapter, on the latter's autobiography (1967) and on efforts to set McClure's poetry to music in the mid-'60s, as well as establishing close links with a new generation of artists such as Jim Morrison and Ray Manzarek of The Doors. Diane di Prima, too, bridges the gap between Beat and hippie, and William Burroughs – though his unique brand of subversive dissidence hardly fits the archetype of the '60s countercultural rebel – became not only one of the most popular novelists among young activists but also an idiosyncratic figure present at several key moments in the decade's turbulent history.[8] Writers like Terry Southern and Kurt Vonnegut, who had begun their careers in the 1940s, were more famous in the '60s than ever before, and even Norman Mailer – perceived as too 'square' by many of the Beats – was a significant actor-reporter at events such as the 1967 anti-Vietnam War demonstration in Washington (chronicled from this perspective in *Armies of the Night: History as a Novel, the Novel as History*, 1968) and the 1968 Chicago Democratic Convention, and published *Why are we in Vietnam?* (1967), a novel that explores the pathological violence Mailer identifies at the heart of American masculinity.

Oddly, however, recent studies of 1960s counterculture have largely erased literature from its history. The otherwise comprehensive collection, *Imagine Nation* (2002), contains essays on music, film, the New Left and many other dimensions of alternative lifestyle in the decade, but makes no mention of Thomas Pynchon, Diane di Prima or Vonnegut and only refers to Mailer, Burroughs and Richard Brautigan in passing (and without allusion to their fiction). The same is true of Alice Echols' otherwise excellent *Shaky Ground* (2002), which covers areas similar to *Imagine Nation* and is marked by similar omissions. Where the fiction and poetry of the Beat Generation remain central to critical reconsiderations of '50s counterculture, it is as if the hippie generation had no interest in books.

This is, of course, a major misrepresentation of the decade: while it is certainly true that visual and aural performance were integral to '60s counterculture, literature by no means disappeared, and many of the elements of what subsequently became known as 'postmodernist' fiction stemmed from the experimentalism inherent in the movement's primary authors. Thematically, Pynchon's novels, *V.* (1963) and, even more so, *The Crying of Lot 49* (1966), articulate a sense – shared by large numbers of young people – of alienation amidst abundance in a world where it is ever harder to locate the centres of oppressive control. In a nation that increasingly appeared to be becoming overrun by the 'unwarranted influence' of the 'military-industrial complex'[9] warned of by President Eisenhower in his 1961 Farewell Address, Oedipa Maas's (the protagonist of *Lot 49*) scrutiny of each piece of evidence that she uncovers in her quest to understand the 'reality' of America offered a model that would be echoed – paranoia, conspiracy theories and all – by many of those who dropped out of mainstream society. Near the novel's end, musing on whether or not an underground postal system named the Tristero exists and offers an alternative to the banality of California life, Oedipa speculates:

> Either you have stumbled indeed, without the aid of LSD or other indole alkaloids, on to a secret richness and concealed density of dream; on to a network by which X number of Americans are truly communicating whilst reserving their lies, recitations of routine, arid betrayals of spiritual poverty, for the official government delivery system; maybe even on to a real alternative to the exitlessness, to the absence of surprise to life, that harrows the head of everybody American you know, and you too, sweetie. Or you are hallucinating it.[10]

Oedipa never discovers whether the Tristero is real, but her desire to imagine other worlds is a dream shared – and practised – by the counterculture of the time, especially in West Coast communities like the San Francisco of the Diggers and The Grateful Dead, who were keen to develop networks as independent of hegemonic institutions as possible. In a different way, Vonnegut's *Slaughterhouse-5* (1969), with its invocation of science fiction and other popular genres, makes what has come to be seen as the quintessentially postmodernist gesture by destabilising traditional distinctions between 'high' and 'popular' culture. For Vonnegut, the popular and the fantastic serve as the best weapons in an effort to represent alternatives to the master narrative of American scientific, military and economic triumphalism that, for him and many others in the anti-war movement of the late 1960s, had become depressingly self-perpetuating.

Linda Hutcheon has observed that *The Crying of Lot 49* provides a 'social commentary about the loss of relevance of traditional values in contemporary life',[11] and the point could also be applied to *Slaughter-house-5*, as well as to many other writings of the time. For Diane di Prima, Ken Kesey and Richard Brautigan, these values are not only irrelevant, but are also obstacles blocking out the possibility of realising full human potential. Di Prima's investigation of her Italian-American heritage, Kesey's representation of the nation as asylum (as well as his subsequent trip across the country with his Merry Pranksters) and Brautigan's literary assaults on the oppressive behemoths he encounters (and runs from) whenever he comes up against hegemonic America all suggest the need to escape tradition if meaningful selfhood is to be achieved. Importantly, each offers not just a transcript of the efforts to invent 'free' space in a landscape deeply marked with official accounts of national history – statues and monuments, but also master narratives of assimilation and, more darkly, of social control – but also proposes forms of representational practice that are posited as *examples* (rather than the more prescriptive *models*) of how to construct other worlds.

In what follows, I provide a detailed reading of di Prima's *Memoirs of a Beatnik*, before moving to briefer discussions of Kesey's *One Flew Over the Cuckoo's Nest* and, more generally, of Brautigan's fiction from the 1960s. I focus primarily on di Prima both because she provides an exemplary instance of the transition from Beat to hippie and because, as one of the (very) few female artists to have a high profile in both movements, she is ideally placed to commentate on the sexual dynamics of the counterculture. I turn to Kesey both to illustrate a different vision of how to change America and because of the extent to which his vision of freedom is engrained with the sexism that di Prima had to overcome. Finally, my reading of Brautigan illustrates how an author largely ignored by literary critics served not just as a chronicler of '60s counterculture, but also as one of its most significant experimental artists.

'Last-of-the-Beats/First-of-the-Hippies':[12] di Prima, Kesey and Brautigan

Although Diane di Prima's hybrid novel-autobiography, *Memoirs of a Beatnik*, was not written until the late 1960s and was first published in 1969, it can usefully be compared with *On the Road* in its representations of the gender politics of Beat culture at mid-century. Whereas Kerouac's women tend to be subordinate to the desires of the male characters and are labelled as 'whores' when they reject the values imposed upon them by Sal and Dean, di Prima is eager to celebrate female sexuality. It is also plain that, unlike the women in *On the Road*, who spend much of their time looking after the male Beats, di Prima's younger self is a serious artist working towards the publication of her first collection of poems. In *Memoirs*, di Prima is dedicated to her craft and willing to make emotional and economic sacrifices in order to develop it. Unlike Sal Paradise, she is independent of her family through a combination of her choice and their ethnic Italian-American rejection of her lifestyle. On the other hand, her freedom has gender-determined limits: she lacks the kind of geographical mobility that is available to Paradise – almost the entire book takes place in New York – and di Prima can only escape the city in the company of friendly males. It would be virtually inconceivable for a woman to be able to travel alone 'on the road' in the manner available to Sal.

Memoirs of a Beatnik is a curious book in that its tone shifts as the narrative progresses. In an Afterword written in 1987, di Prima recalls that in 1968 she was the sole breadwinner in a nightmarish California commune, and that she started to write *Memoirs* in response to Olympia Press publisher Maurice Girodias's request for a pornographic 'potboiler', as the best way to make quick money to provide 'seaweed and brown rice and miso soup' for all.[13] Most of the first half of *Memoirs* fits the requested pornographic pattern, with highly clichéd representations of the 1950s Village scene interspersed with lengthy descriptions of many different kinds of sexual encounter. As the book progresses, however, the tone starts to shift: at one point near the end of the narrative, di Prima revisits the pornography of the opening chapters, but introduces an element of postmodern playfulness to tease the reader, contrasting 'what you would like to hear' (more sex) with 'what actually happened' (reading in a cold room).[14] The second half of *Memoirs* is a detailed résumé of Beat life in New York in the 1950s, dominated by a somewhat idiosyncratic feminist analysis of what it meant to be a woman at the time, and by assessments of the relation-ship between the Beats and the Italian-American community that was battling with the new artistic counterculture for control of Village space. These narratives are supplemented by accounts of the then subversive potential of homosexuality (contrasted to what di Prima calls the 'gay liberation' of the late 1960s, with which – for di Prima, living and writing in San Francisco – 'the social stigma has gone out of homosexuality') and of the 'neo-fascist city planning'[15] that trans-formed an area of lower Manhattan from home to ethnic Americans and Beats into the Lincoln Center, both of which illustrate the pace of change during the decade between the mid-1950s and mid-'60s.

As I suggested above, however, the most noteworthy element of *Memoirs* is the degree to which it offers a contrast to the narratives written by male Beats. Di Prima's argument that 'The real horror, the nightmare in which most of us are spending our adult lives, is the deep-rooted insidious belief in the one-to-one world'[16] may initially seem like little more than a version of Ginsberg's attitude to sex extended to liberate women from the shackles of male-dominated marriage. Her account of the various forms of contraception available at the time, however, provides a detailed examination of the obstacles placed in the way of women's sexual pleasure, as well as hinting that the 'sexual liberation' of the 1960s has been a mixed blessing for women.[17] *Memoirs of a Beatnik* shares elements of Kerouac's view of society, and the more general Beat desire to escape (or, in Kerouac's case, sustain) the dysfunctional family, but her narrative, like her autobio-graphy, *Recollections of My Life as a Woman* (2001), also illustrates the complicity of many male Beats in patriarchal attitudes to women, and makes clear that it was not easy for female writers to be accepted as artists within this community.

Memoirs of a Beatnik uses the hippie sensibilities of the 1960s to reconsider the significance of Beat. In her celebration of 'being a chick to three men, and each of them on his own trip', di Prima not only adopts the language of a later counterculture to describe her experiences, but also launches an attack on the 'one-to-one world' that was, for Kerouac, and even for his serial relationship-seeker Dean Moriarty, as much part of Beat as mainstream American life.[18] This section of the book, in which she cherishes the domestic rituals of catering for 'her' men while they go out to work, risks replicating elements of more conventional housewifery, but it is important to remember that di Prima always envisages her participation as a temporary arrangement. While the community of Italian-American women within which she was raised considered it to be an 'inconceivable breach of etiquette' ever to 'complain of their sex life or marriage', which are lifelong commitments, di Prima is unashamed to answer the 'restlessness' that calls her away from the men and back to New York.[19] Even if such attitudes were – just about – permissible for a woman in the San Francisco counterculture of the late 1960s, when they are contrasted with male Beat thoughts about their female companions in the 1950s, they illustrate once again the radical nature of di Prima's lifestyle.

By dropping out of college, di Prima breaks the contract whereby many first- and second-generation ethnic Americans worked hard on the assumption that their children would be both better educated and wealthier than themselves. Post-Second World War Italian-American fiction was dominated by novels such as Michael DeCapite's *The Bennett Place* (1948) and his brother Raymond's *The Coming of Fabrizze* (1960), in which 'Americanisation' is charted through social and economic advance.[20] In contrast, di Prima's rejection of the usual route to success is – like that of the male Italian-American Beat, Gregory Corso – marked by the adoption of a different American ideology, preached most famously by Henry David Thoreau in *Walden* (1854). Like Thoreau, di Prima inverts Benjamin Franklin's blueprint for the American Dream of wealth through hard work, seeking the minimum employment necessary to support herself in her writing. Di Prima, however, reformulates the Transcendentalist use of nature – as what Richard King has called the 'vehicle, the mediating term, for the moral and the spiritual' – adding a countercultural revision in which, as King continues, 'Nature, as the sexual and the erotic, becomes the touchstone of individual and collective virtue and health.'[21] Instead of upward mobility from a childhood in a 'block that just avoided being a slum',[22] *Memoirs* charts a plot of economic and social decline into a freezing, rat-infested East Side tenement, alongside spiritual *and* sexual enlightenment uniting nineteenth-century Transcendentalism and 1960s counterculture.

The freedom inherent in di Prima's persona provides a significant contrast to the oppression of women she sees within outwardly more conventional families. Although the decision to abandon an identity based on tradition appears to come easily to her, and she offers little detailed information about her own parents, di Prima does make clear the problems that such a rupture can entail for women, even where their families are severely dysfunctional. One friend, Lee, is unable fully to use the close friendships that, for di Prima at college, 'kept one from stepping off the edge into the abyss of boredom and despair', and (unsurprisingly) remains so traumatised by memories of being raped by one of her father's employees and 'frequently bullwhipped' by her father that she 'could not bear to be touched at all'.[23] Another, Tomi, is represented as facing an almost intolerable dilemma in choosing whether to join di Prima in the move to bohemian Greenwich Village. Tomi's family serve as representatives of everything that the counter-culture of the 1950s and '60s despised in the United States: superficially enacting the nation's obsession with consumerism – living 'beyond their means in expensive Darien', and shopping in 'Gristede's where everything cost three times as much as it did in the local supermarket' – the family's private life reads like a catalogue of American gothic. Tomi's father is a drunk who rapes di Prima; her aunt is 'some kind of a witch',[24] and her brother, 'Sweet William', has been abused by their uncle and is now involved in an incestuous relationship with Tomi. Ultimately, however, Tomi feels forced to abandon the plan to move to the Village because she cannot leave her mother to face these traumas alone. Once more, di Prima reiterates the differences inherent in men and women's ability to 'drop out': the former are generally spared the psychological manipulation that left many young women with a deep commitment to familial responsibilities incompatible with the freedom promised by the counterculture.

Towards the end of *Memoirs of a Beatnik*, di Prima recollects an orgy involving Allen Ginsberg and Jack Kerouac.[25] Alongside her rape by Tomi's father, this is one of the most troubling representations of sexual politics in the book since, in the former, di Prima suggests that she feels 'pleasure', 'in spite of myself',[26] and in the latter is goaded into action by a circle of chanting males. Experiencing her period, di Prima plans to go to sleep and leave the men to themselves but, after Ginsberg delivers a 'long speech on the joys of making it while menstruating', she provokes the 'cheer of the whole gang' by 'pull[ing] out the bloody talisman [her Tampax] and [flinging] it across the room'.[27] The episode is of note for several interconnected reasons. First, its representation of sex is very different from that found elsewhere in the novel. Here, pornographic clichés are largely replaced by a more naturalistic lan-guage that – rather than heightening the significance of this coupling with the 'King of the Beats' – suggests that Kerouac is not much of a lover. Significantly, the encounter takes place a few pages after di Prima decides that she 'wanted to have a baby' and just before the discovery (in the book's final paragraph) that she is pregnant.[28] While the resolution to become a single parent is clearly a radical gesture within the climate of 1950s America, di Prima's emphasis on her menstrual blood here suggests anger at *not* being pregnant – and a blaming of this upon her community of male Beat lovers – that could explain the odd nature of this sex scene.

At the end of *Memoirs*, di Prima's wish is fulfilled and she relates how,

> when the full moon shone on the fire-escape again, I didn't get my period as I should have. And as the moon waned, my breasts grew and became sore, and I knew I was pregnant. And I began to put my books in boxes, and pack up the odds and ends of my life, for a whole new adventure was starting, and I had no idea where it would land me.[29]

Although it is unclear where di Prima will head, it is evident that the process of reinvention that has defined her (constantly fluid) sense of self is leading her away from the 'cool' persona required within the Beat scene and towards something approximating the 'Earth Mother' of the 1960s counterculture.[30] Remembering Ginsberg's representation in 'Howl' of women as the oppressive force stifling the male homosocial and homosexual bonding that is at the root of male creativity, and bearing in mind Kerouac's refusal to acknowledge that he was the father of Joan Haverty's daughter, Jan (born in 1952), there is a sense that a single motherhood arrived at by choice offers an escape from a patriarchal Beat community resistant to women's ambitions. While the new life hinted at in the conclusion to *Memoirs* insists on ongoing non-conformity (in the guise of a poet who elects to be a single mother), it also imagines a new and different space for di Prima within a counterculture moving beyond Beat ideology.

As the foregoing discussion suggests, if di Prima's ability successfully to transcend the generation gap between Beat and hippie writer is unusual, the fact that she is a woman makes this doubly so. Written in the year that *Memoirs* was published, the 'Redstocking Manifesto' argued that women are 'considered inferior beings, whose only purpose is to enhance men's lives', making no distinction between culture and counterculture in the assertion that '*All men* have oppressed women' (emphasis in original),[31] and thus reinforcing the sense that women's groups did not feel that New Left and 'alternative' communities were doing enough to further women's rights. The emergence of Redstockings and other radical feminist organisations in the late 1960s is indicative both of the manner in which strategies for protest that had been developed in the civil rights and anti-war movements were being adopted by other causes and of a growing feeling that women were systematically marginalised within political and artistic communities. In the counterculture of the late '60s, this is indubitably true of a writing and publishing fraternity that was still dominated by a sexist culture evident, for example, in Terry Southern's repeated eulogies to Hugh Hefner and *Playboy*. For San Francisco poet ruth weiss, the small independent publishers such as City Lights and Auerhahn Press that released many of the most famous countercultural texts of the Beat and hippie eras 'were not interested in women poets'.[32] While musicians and actors such as Grace Slick, Janis Joplin, Jane Fonda and Julie Christie maintained high profiles, few female authors achieved success or profile to match di Prima's.

This does not mean, of course, that there were no other female writers working within the counterculture of the time. Of those reaching adulthood in the early years of the decade, both Janine Pommy Vega and Anne Waldman shared di Prima's confidence in their status as women *and* artists, while work by older women such as Jane Bowles, Adrienne Rich and Denise Levertov remained influential. Likewise, Ann Bannon's series of Beebo Brinker novels (1957–62) provides a rare lesbian counterpart to the more familiar Beat narrative of the hetero- or homosexual male leaving small-town America to experience a process of self-discovery in Greenwich Village.

Re-readings like those recently offered by the contributors to Roanna C. Johnson and Nancy M. Grace's edited collection, *Girls Who Wore Black: Women Writing the Beat Generation* (2002), clearly contribute significantly to the challenges to male-dominated literary canons that have been undertaken since the 1970s, when scholars growing up within or alongside a counterculture questioning most forms of institutional authority started to assume influential academic positions.[33] They do not, however, fully explain how the literary gender politics of the counterculture were perceived at the time. Thus, while Betty Friedan's *The Feminine Mystique* (1963) articulates middle-class women's alienation in a manner that is strikingly close to a Beat sensibility (whilst also making clear why women like di Prima's friend, Tomi, find it so hard to escape the source of their despair), Kate Millett's pioneering and influential approach to feminist literary theory in *Sexual Politics* (1969) hints at women's discontent with countercultural, as well as hegemonic, norms.

The key tenets of Millett's argument – and of the numerous criticisms that have been levelled at it – are well known and do not require detailed re-telling here. Broadly, Millett identifies 'patriarchy' as a pervasive 'political institution' whereby 'one group of persons [women] is controlled by another [men]'.[34] In a wide-ranging literary historical analysis, Millett illustrates the degree to which patriarchy has become so pervasive that it tends to be regarded as part of a natural order, rather than a historical manifestation of particular cultures. One consequence of this misapprehension is, for Millett, the extent to which women have internalised an ideology that defines them as passive and willing to be controlled by men. For her critics, Millett's argument is naïve – depending upon simplistic identification of authors and their protagonists – and overly dismissive of writing by women, which is almost entirely ignored.[35]

What has been overlooked in readings of *Sexual Politics* is that two of the three authors Millett uses to explicate her argument most fully – Henry Miller and Norman Mailer – are closely aligned to the counter-culture and articulate an extreme form of sexually explicit discourse championed as part of the movement's expression of free speech but patently offensive to most Americans at the time. Miller, in particular, can be seen as a forerunner of the sexual revolution of the 1960s (and a hero to many Beats and hippies), whose 1930s novels such as *Tropic of Cancer* and *Tropic of Capricorn* were banned in the United States for several decades. While Millett's aim in selecting these writers is clear – their graphic descriptions of male sexual prowess and female submission are represented as demonstrations of what is generally concealed by polite discourse – the fact that she looks to the countercultural canon is indicative of the degree to which she (and many other women affiliated to the emergent radical feminism of the late 1960s) believed that the counterculture's advocacy of resistance to hegemonic norms did not preclude its complicity with mainstream imposition of patriarchal authority.

Some of the reasons for the marginalisation experienced by women writers are apparent in Ken Kesey's *One Flew Over the Cuckoo's Nest* (1962), a novel in which opposition to panoptic surveillance and control is deeply rooted in the kinds of masculine literary nationalism advocated by the Transcendentalists. While the book was written several years before Kesey's acid trips and jaunts with the Merry Pranksters established him as a central figure of the '60s counter-culture, it is an anticipatory statement of much of the movement's sexual politics. For Chief Bromden – a Native American narrator whose paranoiac introductory warning, 'They're out there', fore-shadows Oedipa Maas's slightly later conspiracy-theory narrative –

freedom and enlightenment come from men. *Cuckoo's Nest* imagines only two types of women: those like Nurse Ratched, the matriarchal overseer of the asylum ward where Bromden is detained, whose role is to keep men in a perpetual state of infantile submission to seemingly senseless rules; and the hookers who provide the therapeutic sexual healing that is deemed to make '*men*' (italics in original) out of the inmates.[36]

This negative introductory summary should not be taken, however, to indicate that the novel is without value as an example of the counterculture's changing strategies for resisting social control. Conceived while Kesey was a graduate student in creative writing, *Cuckoo's Nest* deploys many of the mainstays of 1950s myth/symbol American Studies in its representation of the nation. Thus, it characteristically juxtaposes the liberation found in nature (in particular, through a fishing trip organised by the book's central character, Randle P. McMurphy) with the alienating effects of a mechanical modern world, here allegorised by the institution. Key tropes of national identity are enacted through McMurphy, a cross between the archetypal cowboy and Marlon Brando's Johnny from *The Wild One*; through Bromden, who needs to grow back into his massive frame in order to rediscover his heritage; and through the highly problematic stereotyping of African-Americans as either Uncle Toms or threateningly sexual operatives of State control. In allowing Bromden to narrate the story, Kesey advocates a re-voicing of the Indian that ultimately offers what is portrayed as an attractive alternative to the overcivilised world of white America.

Although Kesey adopts the discourse of myth/symbol American Studies, he puts it to unconventional use. Instead of constructing a national narrative along the lines of those proposed by scholars such as Richard Chase and R. W. B. Lewis,[37] in which archetypes are deployed to demonstrate the superiority of the nation in the context of Cold War polarities, Kesey's position is more akin to that of contemporary social theorists such as Paul Goodman in his critique of the damage done to individuals by a State that in *some* ways resembles the totalitarian Soviet Union posited by myth/symbol Americanism. The big difference – as with *The Crying of Lot 49* – is that the American version of the totalitarian state is driven, ironically, by the plethora of post-scarcity brand names ('Tupperware' for Oedipa, the reified screen presence of Marilyn Monroe and the 'Walt Disney World'[38] for Kesey's inmates), that promise 'freedom' yet seem to preclude the possibility of genuine human relations.[39]

But where *Lot 49* concludes indeterminately, with no verdict on whether or not an alternative America exists, Kesey deploys a clearly marked Christian allegory to suggest – perhaps in anticipation of the Pranksters' mission to 'convert' ordinary Americans – that national rejuvenation is not beyond the realms of possibility. McMurphy himself functions as a Christ-like figure: he takes his twelve 'disciples' on the fishing trip, is betrayed by the Judas-like Billy Bibbit, who commits suicide after stuttering 'They m-m-made me!' in defence of his sexual awakening, is wearied by his efforts to help others and is symbolically 'crucified', asking 'Do I get a crown of thorns?' as he 'spreads his arms out' to receive electric shock therapy.[40] McMurphy even experiences a kind of ghostly resurrection when he is returned to the ward after his lobotomy and before being smothered by the Chief. At the end of the novel, Bromden uses the strength he has acquired from McMurphy's teachings to escape, while most of the other surviving 'disciples' return to the outside world to convert the masses to his gospel of manly solidarity in what functions as a reminder of the revolutionary nature of an original Christianity contrasted with its ersatz American alternative.

Cuckoo's Nest's narrative of redemptive empowerment assumes particular significance when read within the context of shifting countercultural ideologies. When he arrives on the ward, McMurphy closely resembles Dean Moriarty in his con-man individualism. Unbothered by the welfare of others, his sole concerns are with discovering a more comfortable alternative to jail and sharking the other inmates out of their valuables with a pornographic deck of cards identical to Dean's. As we have seen, however, McMurphy acquires a sense of responsibility to the community, in which he is willing to sacrifice himself for the greater good. That is, Kesey proposes a model that anticipates the communal ideals of '60s alternative culture to replace the individualism of Kerouac's Beat protagonist.

While it could be argued that the group ethos is present in other Beat texts, such as 'Howl', there are also key differences. First, although *Cuckoo's Nest* stresses the importance of strong homosocial ties, it rejects the validity of homosexual ones. One inmate's confession that he 'indulged in certain practices that our society regards as shameful' receives only 'half hearted' recognition from McMurphy,[41] and he only discharges himself once he has learned how to behave like a 'man' and exert authority over Nurse Ratched. His departure with his wife signifies control over women rather than the Beat desire to escape female entrapment.

Cuckoo's Nest is also useful in articulating a later split in counter-cultural approaches to the mainstream. Where the Beats conducted themselves discreetly in their travels across the continent and generally expressed both their kicks and their alienation in the company of the like-minded, Kesey's conclusion imagines McMurphy's legacy as the start of what will ultimately be a large-scale, national conversion. While there is no sense that McMurphy's disciples will indulge in the kinds of outlandish behaviour adopted by the Merry Pranksters or the Yippies to shock Americans out of their complacency, their departure is underpinned by a proselytising principle absent from the Beat Generation. Where some '60s countercultural groups – most notably, San Francisco's Diggers – continued to advocate as full a removal as possible from engagement with hegemonic America, Kesey outlines the prototype of an interactive, transformative agenda. At the end of the novel, Bromden escapes by throwing a control panel though a window, 'baptizing the sleeping earth' with the broken glass in a gesture that turns the tools of institutional control against his oppressors and reconfirms his spiritual bond to the landscape. Once more revisiting the central tenets of Transcendentalism in a celebration of nature as therapeutic alternative to a sterile culture, Kesey imagines Bromden returning to his Indian friends, who have resisted the Government's efforts to 'buy their right to be Indians' by appropriating the 'big million-dollar hydroelectric dam' responsible for the flooding of their land and 'spearing salmon in the spillway'.[42] A small moment of resistance in itself, the act serves as a symbolic start to the recovery of meaningful engagement with the land that Kesey suggests is possible if people can be persuaded to see beyond the limits of acquiescence to consumer capitalism. Appealing to the mythic possibility of America and to the 'authentic' culture of the indigenous population in a manner that would be imitated by numerous communes throughout the decade, Kesey concludes *Cuckoo's Nest* with possibly the most opti-mistically utopian vision of the nation's future to emanate from the counterculture.[43]

While Kesey resurrects Christian mythology to escape the confines of military-industrial America, Richard Brautigan goes even further in launching what Marc Chénetier describes as 'an assault on all fixed representational forms, from myths and codes to moral messages and ideological assertions'. For Chénetier, one of very few critics to engage seriously with Brautigan's fiction, novels such as *Trout Fishing in America* (1967) echo Kesey in contrasting 'longing for an authentic (if problematic) pastoral vision with the multiple expressions of a corrupted, modern pseudo-tradition, thus denouncing the destruction of the country's soul and its recuperation by the hypocritical messages of a commercialised, falsified present'.[44]

The point can be illustrated by a brief look at one of the stories collected in *Revenge of the Lawn* (1972) and at episodes from *Trout Fishing in America*, although the themes that I discuss emerge in Brautigan's first novel, *A Confederate General From Big Sur* (1964) and are at the heart of most of his fiction written in the 1960s. In 'The Wild Birds of Heaven', Mr Henly's children coerce Henly, a 'simple American man', into purchasing a new television by warning him that if he refuses they will 'become juvenile delinquents'. Having been shown a picture of 'five juvenile delinquents raping an old woman', Henly agrees and – in a moment characteristic of Brautigan's surrealist ability to combine objects with their social purposes – finds a 'video pacifier that had a 42-inch screen with built-in umbilical ducts'.[45] In a world where having a large debt is an index of being a good creditor, and where a 'beautiful girl' is measured by the fact that 'she looked like a composite of all the beautiful girls you see in all the cigarette advertisements and on television', it comes as only a minor surprise when a blacksmith removes Henly's shadow and replaces it with the shadow of a bird that will remain until he has paid for the television. When, as he leaves, the 'beautiful girl' speaks to him, Henly thinks of sex, reaches for his cigarettes and, to his embarrassment, finds that he has 'smoked them all up'. The story concludes with her staring 'at him as if he were a small child that had done something wrong'.[46]

To summarise 'The Wild Birds of Heaven' in this way illustrates both Brautigan's view of an America distorted by consumer capitalism and the linguistic strategies he deploys in order to reveal the hidden mechanisms of control. For Brautigan, relationships with things have replaced those with other people, so that children will become juvenile delinquents not because of absent parents but because of a broken television. Purchasing a new set that is more maternal than a biological mother can (at least for the 'simple American man') avert crisis. Beauty is no longer one of what Herbert Marcuse calls the 'untranslatable universals': instead, it is stripped to its commodity form, what Marcuse calls 'the music of salesmanship'.[47] Sex is no longer a pleasure to be enjoyed in itself or a means of reproduction; rather, it is a tool of the corporation, its meaning reduced to standardised images prompted by internalised associations with advertisements and movies. When the blacksmith nails the bird's shadow to Henly's feet, the process suggests a two-dimensional crucifixion, in which the body and colour of the natural world have been entirely removed without Henly even realising what he has lost.[48] It is only when he cannot perform the function of the 'simple American man' – because he is out of cigarettes – that Henly is embarrassed into feeling like a child. Until that point, he is convinced of his own power and freedom.

Brautigan's use of the surreal echoes William Burroughs's novelistic cut-ups or Bob Dylan's mid-1960s lyrics in its ability to highlight the absurdities of 'everyday' American life. By describing a familiar object in an unusual way – a 'video pacifier that had a 42-inch screen with built-in umbilical ducts' – or, as with the bird's shadow, representing the common (and seemingly even desirable) condition of good credit rating and large debt with singular symbolism, Brautigan exposes the ideological patterns that dictate individual and collective behaviour. Reading his fiction, it is apparent that Brautigan detects narratives and monuments that limit human freedom everywhere he looks, and that he believes escaping the control they wield requires constant vigilance and imagination.

The point is made most directly in *Trout Fishing in America*. The novel's cover depicts Brautigan and a woman in front of a statue of Benjamin Franklin in San Francisco's Washington Square. Franklin, of course, serves as the epitome of the disciplined American subject, rising from obscurity to wealth and power through strictly managed ambitions and efforts. His articulation of the American Dream has been used as the model for the success myth at the core of national identity. For Brautigan, such control represents nothing but danger. As a recollection near the start of the book makes clear, he understands that the displacement of the natural by the cultural begins in early childhood:

> One spring afternoon as a child in the strange town of Portland, I . . . saw a row of old houses, huddled together like seals on a rock . . . At a distance I saw a waterfall come pouring down off the hill. It was long and white and I could almost feel its cold spray.
>
> There must be a creek there, I thought, and it probably has trout in it.
>
> Trout.
>
> . . . But as I got closer to the creek I could see that something was wrong. The creek did not act right. There was a strangeness to it. There was a thing about its motion that was wrong. Finally I got close enough to see what the trouble was.
>
> The waterfall was just a flight of white wooden stairs leading up to a house in the trees.[49]

In order to discover the 'real' America of the boy's imagination – achieved through rare, cherished moments of union with nature – Brautigan recognises the need to dismantle the scaffolding that supports national mythologies. In *Trout Fishing*, the process involves an (deliberately) unsystematic deconstruction of Franklin's *Autobiography* (1793), probably the most famous representation of hegemonic Americanism. Instead of a chronological account of an individual's gradual development, tracing a path from obscurity to success, Brautigan's protagonist, 'Trout Fishing in America', is a fragmented assemblage of many 'characters' whose story illustrates an inversion of the usual markers of progression and results in a withdrawal from conventional American life. Where Franklin constructs charts and lists to discipline himself into a particular shape, Brautigan leaps from one anecdote to another, often seemingly at random, celebrating particular moments for themselves rather than seeing them as points on a path that will only reach its deferred fulfilment at the end of the book. The closing word of *Trout Fishing in America* offers an ironic and witty undermining of such narratives: instead of a grand statement of social success, the novel ends with the understated 'mayonaise', a misspelled gratification of the 'human need . . . to write a book that ended with the word Mayonnaise'.[50] Where Franklin, the trained typesetter, uses his trade as a metaphor for the need to correct the 'errata' in his life, Brautigan finishes with a typographical error that symbolises a freedom from American discipline that embodies the countercultural ideal.

Brautigan is probably the most 'writerly' of the novelists I have discussed in this chapter. His defamiliarising language and constant signposting of inter-textual allusions to other writers provide a self-consciously systematic literary investigation of the textual strategies that underpin forms of social control. Such inter-texts are also apparent, however, in di Prima's own rejection of the Franklinian model and in the realignment of pornography that aids in her empowerment in the second half of *Memoirs of a Beatnik*, as well as in Kesey's turn to the revolutionary potential of original Christianity. While each writer encounters resistance not only in the shape of external figures of authority, but also from internalised patterns of thought and behaviour that must be unlearned if an approximation of freedom is to be realised, all finally suggest an optimism that is absent from totalising political models such as Marcuse's *One-Dimensional Man* and, as the following chapters will illustrate, from many of the countercultural texts that engaged more directly with the dominant political issues of the 1960s.

Notes

1. Michel Foucault, Afterword, 'The Subject and Power', in Hubert L. Dreyfus and Paul Rabinow, *Michel Foucault: Beyond Structuralism and Hermeneutics* (London: Harvester, 1982), p. 216.
2. E. L. Doctorow, *The Book of Daniel* (London: Picador, 1982), p. 309.
3. Jack Kerouac, 'About the Beat Generation', in *The Portable Jack Kerouac*, ed. Ann Charters (New York: Penguin, 1996), p. 559.
4. Amiri Baraka, 'Black Dada Nihilismus', in *The Selected Poetry of Amiri Baraka/LeRoi Jones* (New York: William Morrow, 1979), p. 41.
5. Daniel Wong-gu Kim, 'In the tradition: Amiri Baraka, black liberation, and avant-garde praxis in the U.S.', in *African American Review*, Summer–Fall 2003, at www.findarticles.com/p/articles/mi_m2838/is_2-3_37/ai_110531676
6. Quoted in Barry Miles, *Allen Ginsberg: A Biography* (London: Virgin, 2002), p. 249.
7. See, for example, Hettie Jones (Hettie Cohen), *How I Became Hettie Jones* (New York: Dutton, 1990) for a highly personal account of the effect that Baraka's retreat from the mixed-race Greenwich Village community had on his (then) wife.
8. Oliver Harris has pointed out that, 'Of course, Burroughs has always been tangential to the movement . . . He was never completely there or quite belonged but always marked a limit, a point of excess, a kind of strange inner extremity.' Harris is describing critical constructions of Burroughs's role in the Beat Generation of the 1950s, but the observation is equally relevant to his indeterminate relationship to the counterculture of the 1960s. Oliver Harris, *William Burroughs and the Secret of Fascination* (Carbondale: Southern Illinois University Press, 2003), p. 3.
9. Dwight D. Eisenhower, 'Farewell Address'. 17 January 1961. At www.mindfully.org/Reform/Eisenhower-Farewell-Address-17jan61.htm
10. Thomas Pynchon, *The Crying of Lot 49* (London: Picador, 1979), pp. 117–18.
11. Linda Hutcheon, *A Poetics of Postmodernism: History, Theory, Fiction* (London: Routledge, 1988), p. 130.
12. I am taking the phrase from Duncan McLean's Introduction to Richard Brautigan, *A Confederate General From Big Sur* (Edinburgh: Rebel Inc, 1999), p. xvii.
13. Diane di Prima, *Memoirs of a Beatnik* (London: Marion Boyars, 2002), p. 191. This narrative is further complicated by the addition of footnotes to the 1988 edition updating hippie attitudes to sexual freedom to take account of AIDS.
14. Ibid., p. 148, p. 150.
15. Ibid., p. 14, p. 174.

16. Ibid., p. 109.
17. Ibid., pp. 104–6.
18. Ibid., p. 108, p. 109.
19. Ibid., p. 48, p. 110.
20. For an overview of these narratives, see Fred L. Gardaphé, 'Italian American Literature and Culture', in Josephine G. Hendin (ed.), *A Concise Companion to Postwar American Literature and Culture* (Oxford: Blackwell, 2004), pp. 299–322. In a mark of the continuing centrality of the American Dream narrative to ethnic Italian fiction, di Prima only receives passing mention in Gardaphé's essay.
21. Richard King, *The Party of Eros: Radical Social Thought and the Realm of Freedom* (Chapel Hill: University of North Carolina Press, 1972), p. 174.
22. Di Prima, *Memoirs*, p. 48.
23. Ibid., p. 45, p. 46.
24. Ibid., p. 51.
25. Ginsberg also recollects this incident, although, unlike di Prima, he includes Kerouac in its homosexual elements. See Miles, *Allen Ginsberg*, p. 215.
26. Di Prima, *Memoirs*, p. 68.
27. Ibid., p. 182.
28. Ibid., p. 180.
29. Ibid., p. 187.
30. Anthony Libby provides a provocative reading of di Prima's poetry, noting the significance of motherhood and the 'degree of evil' that di Prima suggests is involved in abortion. See 'Diane di Prima: "Nothing Is Lost; It Shines In Our Eyes" ', in Roanna C. Johnson and Nancy M. Grace (eds), *Girls Who Wore Black: Women Writing the Beat Generation* (New Brunswick, NJ and London: Rutgers University Press, 2002), pp. 45–68.
31. The 'Redstocking Manifesto' (1969) is freely available at numerous web sites, for instance, http://fsweb.berry.edu/academic/hass/csnider/berry/hum200/redstockings.htm) and in Miriam Schneir (ed.), *Feminism In Our Time: The Essential Writings, World War II to the Present* (New York: Vintage Books, 1994), pp. 125–9.
32. Quoted in Preston Whaley, Jr., *Blows Like a Horn: Beat Writing, Jazz, Style, and Markets in the Transformation of U.S. Culture* (Cambridge, MA and London: Harvard University Press, 2004), p. 68.
33. Johnson and Grace have highlighted the significance of women in the Beat and post-Beat counterculture. Although there are dangers in their approach – most notably in the manner that they offer reductive definitions of male writers so that, for example, the gay Jewish Allen Ginsberg becomes part of a 'white male hegemonic norm' – Johnson and Grace's work does illustrate the range of writing by women that has been subsumed beneath the Kerouac, Ginsberg, Burroughs canon. Roanna

C. Johnson and Nancy M. Grace, 'Visions and Revisions of the Beat Generation', in Johnson and Grace (eds), *Girls Who Wore Black*, pp. 1–24, p. 4.

34. Kate Millett, *Sexual Politics* (London: Virago, 1977), p. xi, p. 23.
35. A good, concise summary of the pros and cons of Millett's argument is provided by Douglas Tallack in *Twentieth-Century America: The Intellectual and Cultural Context* (London and New York: Longman, 1991), pp. 294–7.
36. Ken Kesey, *One Flew Over the Cuckoo's Nest* (London: Picador, 1973), p. 9, p. 241.
37. See Richard Chase, *The American Novel and Its Tradition* (New York: Doubleday, 1957) and R. W. B. Lewis, *The American Adam: Innocence, Tragedy and Tradition in the Nineteenth Century* (Chicago: University of Chicago Press, 1955).
38. Kesey, *Cuckoo's Nest*, p. 55.
39. For a discussion of Pynchon in these terms, see Peter Currie, 'The Eccentric Self: Anti-Characterization and the Problem of the Subject in American Postmodernist Fiction', in Malcolm Bradbury and Sigmund Ro (eds), *Contemporary American Fiction* (London: Edward Arnold, 1987), p. 65.
40. Kesey, *Cuckoo's Nest*, p. 222.
41. Ibid., p. 241, p. 242.
42. Ibid., pp. 254–5.
43. See Philip Deloria, 'Counterculture Indians and the New Age,' in Peter Braunstein and Michael William Doyle (eds), *Imagine Nation: The American Counterculture of the 1960s and '70s* (London: Routledge, 2002), pp. 159–88, for an account the versions of Indian–white ethnic succession imagined by communalists in the 1960s.
44. Marc Chénetier, *Richard Brautigan* (London: Methuen, 1983), p. 32.
45. Richard Brautigan, *Revenge of the Lawn: Stories 1962–1970* (Edinburgh: Rebel Inc., 1997), p. 38, p. 39.
46. Ibid., p. 39, p. 41.
47. Herbert Marcuse, *One-Dimensional Man* (London: Ark paperbacks, 1986), p. 209, p. 57.
48. The removal of the man's own shadow assumes even greater significance when it is remembered that Brautigan links the person's shadow to her or his 'personality'. *Trout Fishing in America* (London: Vintage, 1997), p. 148.
49. Brautigan, *Trout Fishing in America*, pp. 4–5.
50. Ibid., p. 151, p. 150.

CHAPTER SIX

Music

One generation got old
One generation got soul
This generation got no destination to hold
Pick up the cry
Hey now it's time for you and me
Got a revolution
Jefferson Airplane, 'Volunteers' (1969)[1]

During the 1960s the music of the counterculture was transformed rapidly and repeatedly. At the start of the decade, the revival of interest in traditional American songs led to a folk boom coupling political protest with a near-obsessive insistence on the use of acoustic instruments in a quest for 'authenticity'. By 1969, the year of Woodstock, a much larger countercultural community would think nothing of a festival combining Joan Baez with Jimi Hendrix, Richie Havens with The Who. Although such transformations involved a large element of accommodation to the American corporate economy, they also signalled a more overtly political slant to 'youth' music than had been the case in the 1940s and '50s. Bebop had been 'alternative' primarily in its experiments with musical orthodoxies and in the lifestyles of many of its performers – a combination that was, of course, political in the manner that it helped to redefine the African-American as musician rather than entertainer – and in its appeal to a relatively small number of listeners. Rock and roll had troubled the adult white hegemony because of its overt sexuality, perceived identification with juvenile delinquency and reliance on African-American art forms – as well as the racial integration of its audience – rather than for any demands for major political change in its lyrics. Although few rock artists had the musical training and dexterity of the leading jazz players, the music of the '60s would also be revolutionary, but in the double sense that it would combine formal experimentation with overt calls for major ideological transformation that had been largely absent from instrumental '50s jazz and most rock and roll songs. Artists such as Bob Dylan, Jimi Hendrix, Jefferson Airplane, Sly Stone, Neil Young and The Grateful Dead performed in ways that mounted direct challenges to an older conservative generation, although, ironically, these challenges were accompanied by the incorporation of rock music and uneasy relationships between artists, managers and record companies.

At the start of the decade, however, the situation was very different and it was the folk revival associated with Greenwich Village and other urban artistic communities that provided the major forum for political protest. In one way, this was the result of directions taken by the dominant genres of the 1950s: although Miles Davis was gaining 'crossover' success with albums such as *Porgy and Bess* (1958), *Kind of Blue* (1959) and *Sketches of Spain* (1960), the turn to free jazz by John Coltrane, Archie Shepp, Cecil Taylor and others led to a loss of commercial interest. Davis himself attributed this to the role of white critics who, he claimed, encouraged free jazz because they resented the popularity of black musicians, knowing that its complexity and lack of identifiable melodies would alienate audiences. For Davis, 'all of a sudden jazz became passé, something dead that you put under a glass in the museum and study'.[2] There is possibly some truth in this assertion, but it is more likely that in 1964 (the year that Davis is writing about) the 'British Invasion' led by The Beatles was a greater factor in taking musical audiences in new directions. In any case, Coltrane, in particular, served as a major musical and spiritual influence on bands such as The Byrds, and Davis became increasingly rock-orientated in both his music and his audience, performing at such major late-'60s festivals as the Isle of Wight and making unrealised plans to record with Jimi Hendrix.

As for the other musical forms from the 1950s that would be significant precursors of '60s rock, urban blues had a tiny white following in the United States until British bands like The Rolling Stones and The Animals arrived talking about Muddy Waters, and rock and roll was becoming safe and institutionalised. Buddy Holly and Eddie Cochran had died in plane and car crashes, Chuck Berry was jailed in 1961 under the Mann Act for transporting a minor across state lines (in a case possibly motivated by resentment at the success of his racially integrated nightclub in St Louis), and the post-army Elvis, under the direction of his manager 'Colonel' Tom Parker, was heading for Hollywood and Las Vegas.

From Folk to the 'Fab Four'

In some ways, the folk boom of the early '60s seems anomalous: the election of John F. Kennedy as President suggested a nation wanting to cast off the conservatism of the Eisenhower years, and Kennedy's call for a New Frontier and a man on the moon by the end of the decade indicated the acceleration of the technocratic society. The growth of the university system provided opportunities for young people to explore new ideas, and the widespread television coverage of the violent responses to civil rights protests in the South alerted many Northern white Americans to the ongoing need to modernise the nation. Blues, jazz and, more widely, rock and roll had demonstrated the possibilities opened up by electronic instruments (especially, of course, the guitar), and even artists subsequently identified with the folk boom, such as Bob Dylan, drew much of their initial musical inspiration from figures like Chuck Berry and Elvis.

For many people associated with folk music in the early 1960s, however, identification with such progress was equivocal: although Kennedy was popular with the young and the call for civil rights (addressed more enthusiastically by Lyndon Johnson than by Kennedy) was vociferously championed in folk circles, interest in new musical technology was deemed to be almost treasonable. Instead, the movement looked to the acoustic songs of the South (both black and white) as antidotes to the modernity that surrounded them, and which was resisted in actions such as the successful campaign by Greenwich Village residents to save Washington Square from development and in opposition to the proliferation of nuclear weapons. Thus, the folk movement was in the vanguard of calls for progressive social change but was suspicious of technological revolution and centrally planned urban regeneration. Long-forgotten blues artists such as Mississippi John Hurt, Son House and Skip James were 'rediscovered' and celebrated for their 'authenticity' often decades after they had recorded the tracks that now attracted the attention of a young white audience, but musical innovation tended to be discouraged. Although the folk elders accepted electric music played by African-American artists such as Muddy Waters, Lightnin' Hopkins and John Lee Hooker, attempts to go electric by white artists were strongly resisted, and the most popular recordings by younger artists were acoustic songs like 'Where Have All the Flowers Gone' by The Kingston Trio and covers of Bob Dylan songs by Joan Baez and Peter, Paul and Mary.

The hostility to the excesses of the modern world clearly had some benefits: in terms of social history, it is likely that the acoustic music of the rural American South would have been forgotten without the energies of cultural anthropologists including John Hammond, Alan and John Lomax, Mack McCormick and Sam Charters, and compilation recordings such as Harry Smith's *Anthology of American Folk Music* (1952). Apart from such historical value, the music also suggested an alternative vision of what America could be. The *Anthology* became a kind of bible to what Jon Pankake calls 'the questing youth of the 1950s and 1960s, those post-Eisenhower seekers after an America somehow more authentic than the plastic version they saw being offered to them in the mass media.'[3] Greil Marcus goes even further, describing Smith's collection as a 'seductive detour' away from what was known in the 1950s

> not as America but as Americanism. This meant the consumer society, as advertised on TV; it meant vigilance against all enemies of such a society and a determination never to appear as one; it meant what Norman Mailer . . . described as the state of mind of the republic: the coexistence of the fear of 'instant death by atomic war' and the fear of 'a slow death by conformity with every creative instinct stifled' . . . The *Anthology* was a mystery – an insistence against every assurance to the contrary, America itself was a mystery.[4]

Marcus's description sounds overly romantic but, for Baby Boom artists like Bob Dylan, who were teenagers in the 1950s and reached adulthood around 1960, this rediscovery came in the nick of time: for Dylan, watching elderly folk and blues performers such as Dock Boggs, Skip James, Mississippi John Hurt and Maybelle Carter at the 1963 Newport Folk Festival was like witnessing 'the end of the traditional people',[5] as modern America became standardised and monochrome. For many in the folk community, Dylan appeared to be the best hope of keeping the memory alive.

The folk boom's legacy also contributed in other ways, such as with the emergence of environmentalism as a key tenet of countercultural ideology in the 1960s and '70s. Environmentalism became a topic adopted by musicians as diverse as Neil Young on the title track of his *After the Gold Rush* (1970) and Marvin Gaye on 'Mercy Mercy Me (The Ecology)' from *What's Going On* (1971), and writers like James Dickey, whose novel, *Deliverance* (1970) – a text combining environmentalist themes with Vietnam War allegory and with a less-than-favourable view of Dylan's 'traditional people' – was later made into a movie by the British director John Boorman (1972). Although the ideals of environmental responsibility were not always upheld in practice – as the litter-strewn fields displayed at the end of the *Woodstock* movie (1970) make clear – the basis for much green politics did stem from the folk movement's search for meaningful alternatives to a modern lifestyle that threatened the individual, the nation and the planet.

Nevertheless, this kind of anti-modernism also had faults that ultimately led to the end of the folk boom and contributed to the fragmentation of 1960s counterculture. In particular, the desire for the 'purity' of acoustic instruments and hostility to electric guitars resulted in one of the most notorious bust-ups in countercultural history when Bob Dylan took the stage at Newport with a band in July 1965. Although Muddy Waters had performed at the previous year's festival with an electric band without significant opposition (and The Paul Butterfield Blues Band and The Chamber Brothers did likewise at the 1965 festival before Dylan), the reaction to Dylan's short set was hostile. As Robert Shelton sums up in *No Direction Home* (1986),

> As Dylan led his band into '[Like a] Rolling Stone,' the audience grew shriller: 'Play folk music! . . . Sell out! . . . This is a folk festival! . . . Get rid of that band!' Dylan began 'It Takes a Train to Cry,' and the applause diminished as the heckling increased. Dylan and the group disappeared offstage, and there was a long, clumsy silence. Peter Yarrow [a member of top folk act, Peter, Paul & Mary] urged Bob to return and gave him his acoustic guitar. As Bob returned on the stage alone, he discovered he didn't have the right harmonica. 'What are you doing to me?' Dylan demanded of Yarrow. To shouts for 'Tambourine Man,' Dylan said: 'OK, I'll do that one for you.' The older song had a palliative effect and won strong applause. Then Dylan did 'It's All Over Now, Baby Blue,' singing adieu to Newport, good-bye to the folk-purist audience.[6]

There are conflicting reports about the intensity of the animosity directed at Dylan, and some members of the audience did applaud his performance, but there is no doubt that this incident – and many more like it as Dylan toured the United States and Europe in 1965 and '66 – marked the end of folk's hegemony and the turn to rock as the music of the counterculture.[7] Although leading folk artists such as Joan Baez and Pete Seeger continued to perform and protest, their influence waned as acid and blues rock bands dominated festivals such as Woodstock.

In a way, the ideology of the folk boom contained the seeds of its own destruction, since it encouraged young people to challenge authority and think for themselves. By the time that Dylan led his band onstage at Newport, such challenges could be turned against the rigid codes implicit in the preservation of folk's purity, as well as in the challenges to the Government over civil rights, nuclear weapons and the already escalating conflict in Vietnam. Moreover, external factors were conspiring against those who sought to keep folk at a distance from popular culture. The arrival of The Beatles had made an impression on many of the younger members of the folk community, and encouraged them to experiment with electric instruments and drums. In his autobiography, *Long Time Gone* (1988), for example, David Crosby recounts how hearing early Beatles records on the jukebox suggested new directions for folk musicians and led him to form The Byrds with other early converts Jim (later Roger) McGuinn and Gene Clark.

The Beatles, at least in their early guise, were heavily influenced by American artists such as Buddy Holly and The Everly Brothers (and also had several years' experience playing covers of US rhythm and blues and rock and roll standards), and, as Crosby points out, did little to challenge the clichéd lyrics of other pop songs in their early releases. Nevertheless, several aspects of their music and image would have a profound impact on the music that became the soundtrack to '60s counterculture. For Crosby, the 'Fab Four . . . took rock 'n' roll beats and instead of having the usual three chord change . . . they had put folk music changes in them. They had relative minors and real music . . . In the songs they wrote there were infinitely better chord changes and melodic content.'[8] At a time when it was still unusual for bands to write their own material, the compositional abilities of John Lennon and Paul McCartney would encourage many American artists to perform and record their own songs. George Harrison's use of an electric twelve-string Rickenbacker guitar would also be copied by

The Byrds (and many other American bands of the time), leading to the distinctive sound of their version of Dylan's 'Mr. Tambourine Man' and also assisting in the highly innovative integration of the music of John Coltrane and Ravi Shankar (played on the twelve-string), and to reciprocal influencing of later Beatles work. The arrival of The Beatles in the US on 7 February 1964 – and their debut on *The Ed Sullivan Show* two days later, watched by an estimated 73 million people[9] – confirmed their new status not only as the most important band of the twentieth century, but also as the prime shapers of American music for the remainder of the decade.

The legacy of The Beatles to the American counterculture is too great to explore in full here. At one extreme, the release of *Sgt. Pepper's Lonely Hearts Club Band* (1967) steered Brian Wilson in new musical directions that transformed (at least temporarily) The Beach Boys from surf pop teen idols into psychedelic experimentalists; at the other, the lyrics to songs such as 'Piggies', 'Revolution', 'Blackbird' and 'Helter Skelter' from the 'White Album' (*The Beatles*, 1968) were interpreted by Charles Manson as direct messages that helped to formulate an ideology that seemed to mark the implosion of the counterculture. Somewhere in between, Crosby, Stills, Nash & Young would become the most successful supergroup of the late 1960s, covering 'Blackbird' at Woodstock and attempting to position themselves as America's answer to the Fab Four. In addition, The Monkees' television series, inspired by the success of the Beatles' movie *A Hard Day's Night* (1964), launched by NBC in 1966, demonstrated the extent to which major broadcasting corporations sought to appropriate youth culture, and even Frank Sinatra (who remained resolutely hostile to almost all aspects of the counterculture) featured George Harrison's 'Something' as a staple of his live act.

Bob Dylan

Bob Dylan is probably the only major countercultural artist whose profile and standing in the mid-1970s was as high as it had been in the early 1960s. He is also the American musician who comes closest to matching The Beatles as composer of songs covered in significant ways by other artists in the past forty years. Dylan tracks from 'Blowin' in the Wind' on would be sung at seminal events such as the 1963 March on Washington; the Byrds' version of 'Mr. Tambourine Man' effectively marks the beginning of a new form of countercultural West Coast pop; Hendrix's 'All Along the Watchtower' has now become a clichéd soundtrack to myriad documentaries about urban unrest and anti-war protest in the late 1960s. Like The Beatles, Dylan could appeal to a wide spectrum of American culture, with even a single song such as 'Subterranean Homesick Blues' providing both the name for the Weathermen – the post-Students for a Democratic Society terror group responsible for the 'Days of Rage' in Chicago in November 1969 and for a subsequent bombing campaign in support of causes including the Black Panthers and the antiwar movement – and serving as inspiration for a string of television commercials in the 1980s and '90s.

Dylan's electric performance at Newport had met with such opprobrium because of his iconic status within the folk movement. 'Blowin' in the Wind' had become virtually a civil rights anthem, recorded by African-American artists including Sam Cooke and inspiring Cooke to write his own civil rights masterpiece, 'A Change is Gonna Come'. In addition, other early songs such as 'Don't Think Twice, It's Alright' had become staples of the folk repertoire. It is unsurprising, however, that Dylan should reject the role of 'leader' of a movement: in his autobiography, he claims that he felt 'ominous forebodings' when he was introduced as such at an earlier Newport festival. Dylan's Transcendentalist inheritance was always of the Emersonian kind, based upon being 'true to yourself' and unafraid to change direction and antagonise others.[10] In addition, even before he became nationally famous, he was immersing himself in a host of cultural experiences, including off-Broadway theatre, Impressionist art and modern architecture, as well as maintaining his teenage enthusiasm for rock and roll, all of which would encourage him to look beyond the simple structures of most folk music.

There is no doubt that Dylan was ambitious for greater fame and financial rewards than could be provided by the relatively small folk community, but making this too self-evident would have risked harming his status as countercultural artist. As a result, his relationship with Albert Grossman, who managed him for most of the 1960s, enabled him to appear to focus solely on his art, and became the blueprint for many other countercultural artists then and since. Jazz musicians like Miles Davis had generally handled their own financial affairs, receiving money directly from club owners and paying their bands themselves. Rock and roll managers – most notably Elvis's 'Colonel' Tom Parker – had steered their clients towards mainstream show business in the belief that the pop phenomenon would be short-lived and that this was the best way to maximise earnings. Grossman's approach was entirely different and immensely appealing to someone in Dylan's position. As Fred Goodman has argued in *The Mansion on the Hill*, an important study of the relationship between rock music and big business, Grossman's 'greatest achievement . . . was creating a commercial environment in which his clients could make a lot of money but preserve their integrity'.[11] By taking care of business, Grossman could make it appear that Dylan was uninterested in such matters and was merely pursuing his muse. The approach was staggeringly effective and would be imitated by the likes of Elliot Roberts with Neil Young and John Landau with Bruce Springsteen, as well as being extended to a stable of other artists by Grossman himself.

This does not, however, undermine the extent to which Dylan's performances and songwriting both helped to shape the music of the 1960s. His switch to electric guitar – and the rawness of his live sound in his early days playing with a band – prompted many young musicians to make the same move, and his songs were as significant as those of The Beatles in channelling rock in new directions. The release of the six-minutes-long 'Like a Rolling Stone' in June 1965 shattered the notion that pop songs should last two or three minutes, and took Dylan's ability to impose sophisticated messages on simple structures to a new level. Likewise, albums such as *Highway 61 Revisited* (1965) and *Blonde on Blonde* (1966) led many critics to argue that rock music could be regarded as 'true art' and destroyed any residual notion that pop music was always ephemeral.

In addition to his other interests, Dylan was also well versed in Beat fiction and poetry, and was close to (and championed by) Allen Ginsberg, who had been in the vanguard of the Beat movement in the 1950s and was an active and respected presence at many of the countercultural happenings of the 1960s. Importantly, Ginsberg was reported as refuting the notion that Dylan had sold out by going electric, suggesting instead that he had 'sold out to God. That is to say, his command was to spread his beauty as wide as possible. It was an artistic challenge to see if great art can be done on a jukebox. And he proved that it can.'[12] Although some Beats were hostile to the new counterculture, with Kerouac attacking it repeatedly, Ginsberg's support is unsurprising: Dylan's enthusiasm for *On The Road*, 'Howl' and especially for Gregory Corso's poem 'Bomb' (1958) provided inspiration for his own lyrics and album sleeve notes and established an important link between the Beats and a '60s counterculture that differed from them in many ways. The backing of a figure like Ginsberg made Dylan's switch to rock music palatable to other young people whose ideology had been shaped by Beat literature, and added credence to the notion that pop did not have to be lightweight.

But Dylan's profile as (reluctant) prophet of the folk boom in the early '60s and high-profile campaigner against social injustice in the mid-'70s (most notably with 'Hurricane', a song protesting against the framing of the boxer Rubin Carter) masks the extent to which he virtually vanished for several years at the height of the counterculture and, even when he did re-emerge, received at best mixed reviews for his new material before the release of *Blood on the Tracks* (1975) and *Desire* (1976). The reasons for this disappearance are still shrouded in some mystery: it is known that Dylan was injured in a motorcycle crash near his Woodstock home in late July 1966, but there have been differing accounts of the severity of his injuries. Dylan himself suggests that the pressures of raising a young family, coupled with a desire to 'get out of the rat race' – itself a revealing phrase with which to describe his position – and an inability to muster 'any real interest' in events outside his immediate circle prompted the retreat.[13] Although Dylan was a prime source of inspiration for events that were starting to take place in California, he remained on the East Coast, playing songs that owed as much to the 'traditional people' as to the counterculture. Made with members of The Band in the basement of their communal house, Big Pink, the material recorded over the summer of 1967 sounds, as Greil Marcus notes in *Invisible Republic*, like 'certain bedrock strains of American cultural language' that have been 'retrieved and reinvented'.[14] A steady flow of covers and bootlegs would appear in the next few years, but the 'Basement Tapes' reveal a Dylan inhabiting a very different underground from the one emerging within the countercultural rock community in California at the time, and a selection of the songs was only officially released in 1975.

Jefferson Airplane and the San Francisco Sound[15]

The barrage of feedback that introduces 'The Ballad of You and Me and Pooneil', the opening track on Jefferson Airplane's *After Bathing at Baxter's* (1967), shows how well they had absorbed Dylan's electric message. The sound is an obvious rejection of the purity of folk music (at least, as imagined by the leading ideologues of the folk boom) and announces that, although many of the group had emerged from the folk scene, they were no longer a part of it. In contrast to the studied veneration surrounding the production and reception of acoustic, largely rural folk music, the feedback suggests something modern, urban, and slightly out of control. It also, however, serves another purpose, demonstrating that although the Airplane *are* modern and urban, they are aware of what this entails and will appropriate the products of corporate America – such as electric guitars and amplifiers – and put them to their own use. Designers of guitars and amplifiers devoted much energy to modifications that would eliminate feedback and allow for a clean sound, but guitarist Jorma Kaukonen delivers something at odds with those aims. The album's introduction thus provides a dramatic moment of self-staging, positioning the San Francisco sound at a distance from both earlier forms of the counter-culture and the America of nine-to-five jobs and disciplined, careful accumulation. Although the remainder of *After Bathing at Baxter's* moves through acoustic interludes, moments of free jazz, and loose jams more characteristic of San Francisco's psychedelic rock, the tone is set by an introduction that, recorded in May 1967 – at the start of the city's 'Summer of Love' – marks a dramatic departure from the Airplane's first two considerably more polished albums.

The feedback now seems prescient of the more disturbed environ-ment and ideology that consumed the Haight-Ashbury district later that year, as thousands of (often deeply troubled) young people descended on San Francisco in the wake of its new fame as the 'hippie capital' of America. When *After Bathing at Baxter's* was released in the autumn of 1967, it certainly did reflect the more sombre mood – even the album's cover, with its red, white and blue colours and images of the extremes of American cultures of consumption and decay, point, to the particular conditions facing San Francisco at the time, as much as to a wider national malaise. Although the Airplane's lyrics had always contained darker messages alongside trippy homilies on love and peace – 'Pooneil' was recorded around the time that 'Somebody to Love', with its famous couplet, 'When the truth is found to be lies / And all the joy within you dies'[16] was in the charts – they also probably captured the essence of a distinctively San Francisco music more than any other band, with the possible exception of The Grateful Dead.

In part this was due to the unique vocal harmonies generated by the three principal singers, founding members Marty Balin and Paul Kantner, and Grace Slick, who joined the band in September 1966 and entirely re-shaped its sound and dynamics; in part, it was the presence of several talented songwriters composing a range of material that could still be stamped with a clear group identity. For example, 'Somebody to Love' and Slick's 'White Rabbit' – a song in which, as Jeff Tamarkin summarises, 'Lewis Carol meets Ravel meets [Miles Davis's] *Sketches of Spain*', and which epitomises the 'impenetrably, exclusively coded' lyrics that Todd Gitlin identifies with that summer's youth music[17] – had both been performed by Slick in her earlier band, The Great Society, but were arranged entirely differently when Jefferson Airplane recorded them.

After Bathing at Baxter's is an album that charts the many dimensions of San Francisco's Summer of Love, from celebrations of communal spirit through the sounds of urban hustle to psychedelic weirdness and lengthy passages of instrumental jamming. Nevertheless, Jefferson Airplane were as keen as Dylan to maximise the financial rewards that stemmed from their success, producing radio advertisements for Levi's and being involved in unsavoury squabbles over money at Woodstock and other gigs. Allen Ginsberg's endorsement of Dylan's switch to electric rock (cited above) was important in ensuring that such actions did not alienate the band's core audience, even if they did sometimes cause ill feeling between the Airplane and other artists. His profile as the pre-eminent Beat poet meant that his assertion that art and commerce could be reconciled in the large San Francisco bohemian community would garner wide support. In the period around 1965–7, the idea that it was acceptable to be a countercultural musician and be very well paid for it would become a significant aspect of the city's musical culture – led by artists such as Jefferson Airplane, Quicksilver Messenger Service, The Grateful Dead, Country Joe and the Fish, and Big Brother and the Holding Company – that would draw many times more followers than the folk scene or the political New Left had ever managed.

LA

Although San Francisco and, in particular, the Haight-Ashbury district became synonymous with the Summer of Love and with the countercultural sound and lifestyle of the late 1960s, this does not mean that all the significant musicians of the time migrated there. New York remained a centre of artistic production and radical bands like The Fugs were often more directly involved in political action than their better-known West Coast counterparts. Singer-songwriters such as the

Canadian Leonard Cohen and groups like Pearls Before Swine (originally from Florida) relocated to New York (in Cohen's case, to the artistic-Beat Chelsea Hotel), rather than heading West. Jimi Hendrix, born in Seattle but living in London when he had his first hit single, also chose New York as his American base, although his ascendancy to countercultural superstardom had been precipitated by his appearance at Monterey. Other New York groups – most notably, The Velvet Underground – offered an often dark, ironic counterpoint to Flower Power, although their role in Andy Warhol's multi-media Exploding Plastic Inevitable, and later stints at famous centres of West Coast countercultural music such as LA's Whisky-a-Go-Go, illustrate the degree to which they overlapped with the artistic ambitions of the counterculture even where their image, name and songs suggested an alternative, 'underground' commentary on its values. Although Dylan did eventually move to Malibu in the 1970s, his departure from New York City – allegedly in an attempt to control his use of alcohol and amphetamines[18] – initially took him to Woodstock in upper New York State.

The Velvet Underground remained relatively unknown during the 1960s (and their records have sold many times more copies since the 1970s than they did at the time), in large part because they refused to repeat the more clichéd nuances of a countercultural sound that was becoming very big business by the time they released their first album in 1967. In contrast, many other artists not usually associated with either political protest or radical musical innovation wrote and performed songs that sought (and sometimes captured) the political zeitgeist. For example, the generally musically and politically conservative Canadian singer Gordon Lightfoot issued 'Black Day in July' as a commentary on the 1967 riots in Detroit, offering an ironic parody of Lyndon Johnson's aggressive response in the lines:

> There's really not much choice you see
> It looks to us like anarchy
> And then the tanks go rolling in
> To patch things up as best they can[19]

The Bronx-born Dion DiMucci, who had had a series of pop hits in the early '60s as frontman for Dion and the Belmonts, and as a soloist (most famously, 'Teenager in Love' and 'Runaround Sue'), also reinvented himself as a countercultural folksinger and had a major success with 'Abraham, Martin, and John', a song lamenting the souring of the American Dream and referencing the deaths of the Kennedys and Martin Luther King. Unlike Lightfoot, Dion's transformation was longer-lasting and more credible, although he was reunited with the Belmonts by the early 1970s.

But while New York remained home to a wide range of counterculture-leaning artists (and while most large North American cities had their own local scene and their own bands[20]), there is no doubt that Los Angeles emerged as the major alternative to San Francisco as home to what was fast becoming a major rock industry. In part, the reasons were economic: as the market for 'youth'-targeted music grew, it was almost inevitable that the management of the business would gravitate to a city whose movie industry was already helping to transfer much artistic capital away from New York. Even the quintessential New York duo Simon and Garfunkel spent more time in California, with Paul Simon serving on the board of directors for the Monterey Festival, Art Garfunkel devoting increasing energy to a Hollywood acting career, and with their music becoming indelibly associated with the LA-staged Mike Nichols movie, *The Graduate* (1967).

The extra resources associated with movie-making gave LA a head start over cities like San Francisco in the provision of recording studios with the most up-to-date technology – a major consideration as (in the wake of *Sgt. Pepper*) more and more artists moved from 'live' studio recording to multiple overdubs and increasingly sophisticated production values. Recording quality was becoming particularly important with the opening up of FM radio from 1964, when a law was passed banning stations from duplicating their AM shows on FM. As Jeff Tamarkin notes, the waveband offered 'clean, static-free sound, often in stereo', and quickly resulted in a new breed of DJs willing to play an eclectic mix of musical genres that roamed far from the restrictions of AM chart shows.[21] Even the major San Francisco bands like Jefferson Airplane travelled to LA to record most of their albums, and new FM stations like San Francisco's KMPX were essential to the spread of the underground music scene.

In addition, however, it must be remembered that the LA of the mid-'60s was a very different sort of urban space to that which emerged from the 'regeneration' of the 1970s and '80s. Roy Marinell, at the time a member of the folk-rock band The Gentle Soul, recalls that

> The old Ocean Park area and the old Venice Canal area were the world's chicest slums . . . There were these wonderful old homes that were built as beach houses that you could rent relatively

cheaply, right on the beach. There were a couple of coffeehouses in the area. Ocean Park wasn't developed like it is now. Main Street is now one Starbucks after another.[22]

Marinell looks back (perhaps too nostalgically) to a pre-urban-planning 'Golden Age' of communal living: by the mid-'60s, more and more young people were gathering at and around clubs such as the Whisky-a-Go-Go on Sunset Strip, and Laurel Canyon was developing a party and drug culture to rival that in San Francisco. Bands such as The Byrds and, for a shorter time, Buffalo Springfield (who featured both Stephen Stills and Neil Young) helped to attract large numbers of teenagers to the Strip. Nevertheless, the battle to determine LA's future design had already commenced, with confrontations between police and youth focusing on rival claims on public space as much as on the lifestyle choices of the young. The issue was marked by complaints about overcrowding from local businesses, and about overly aggressive policing from club-goers and musicians. A protest about the introduction of a curfew and increased police mistreatment of 'longhairs' – with Neil Yong becoming one victim of a beating – led to further conflicts and subsequently to Buffalo Springfield's first hit single, 'For What It's Worth'.[23] Although the song's subject matter may seem insignificant in comparison to the later shooting of students by National Guardsmen at Kent State University – the subject of Crosby, Stills, Nash & Young's 'Ohio' – Richie Unterberger is accurate in his claims that 'For What It's Worth' is a strong contender for 'best protest rock song of the 1960s', and that its defence of the right to self-expression (learnt to a large degree from the civil rights movement) helped to halt the more extreme attempts to harass youths on the Strip.[24]

The 'Long '60s'

By the end of the '60s – and despite the many claims to the contrary inspired by (somewhat distorted) utopian memories of Woodstock – the countercultural rock scene was in crisis. To a large degree, this was due to external factors that propelled the nation into one of its most turbulent periods in a century. The condition is captured in 'The End' by The Doors, another of the iconic LA countercultural groups, in their ironic refrain, 'The west is the best / The west is the best / Get here, and we'll do the rest.'[25] Vietnam, Black Power, urban riots, the assassinations of Robert Kennedy and Martin Luther King, the violence surrounding the Democratic Convention in Chicago and the brutal suppression of student protests at Berkeley, Kent State and elsewhere – the final two especially significant in illustrating the fact that being white and middle class no longer guaranteed immunity from institutional assault – all pointed to what Todd Gitlin has called the 'demolition of a fraudulent consensus', and the normalisation of confrontation and extremism (both cultural and countercultural) at a time when The Rolling Stones' 'Street Fighting Man' became the must-play track at dance parties.[26]

Nevertheless, tensions more specific to the music scene also contributed to the virtual destruction of the kind of community that had existed around 1966–7. One factor was the issue of class that had plagued the counterculture throughout the '60s and never been resolved. The mixed reaction to Dylan at Newport illustrated (among many other things) that other social groups who preferred rock and roll were joining the festival's stock audience of students and left-leaning artists and professionals, who tended to be traditional in their musical tastes. The counterculture's inability to connect across class barriers never really disappeared and, in some ways, would later be responsible for violent clashes such as that between the Hell's Angel 'security' and the crowd at 1969's notorious Altamont festival. During the mid- to late 1960s, the counterculture had maintained an uneasy relationship with the Hell's Angels in the San Francisco area – largely because the Angels were the major providers of drugs – but at the concert Meredith Hunter, an African-American member of the crowd watching the Stones, was stabbed to death by members of the Oakland chapter of the Angels and Marty Balin of Jefferson Airplane was beaten unconscious as he attempted to stem the violence. Altamont is often signalled as a symbolic end to the 1960s (and, rather too simplistically, as a contrast to the ideals of Woodstock[27]), and is recorded in detail in *Gimme Shelter* (1970), Albert and David Maysles's movie chronicling the Stones' 1969 US tour.

Further factors were precipitated by the downside of drug use: while social drugs such as LSD and marijuana had been the staples of the San Francisco and LA music communities of the '60s, heroin and cocaine, with their more private cultures, became increasingly popular as the decade ended. Psychological trauma caused by bad acid trips also undermined the utopian claims made on LSD's behalf, and diluted the sense that it was a drug that could bring collective transcendence. Janis Joplin, Brian Jones of the Stones, Jim Morrison, Jimi Hendrix and The

Grateful Dead's Ron 'Pigpen' McKernan are just some of the stars who died of drug and/or alcohol-related causes between 1969 and 1973. Even where drugs didn't result in death, they could alter an artist's performance in ways that would alienate an audience: the emergence of punk rock groups like The New York Dolls and Detroit's Stooges and MC5, signified a reaction to the interminable jamming that preoccupied many West Coast bands. MC5 in particular, with their combination of short, musically aggressive songs and revolutionary ideology linked to the White Panthers, suggested a refutation of the self-indulgence that had beset the psychedelic generation.

Such self-indulgence was not confined to the stage: the incorporation of rock music resulted in the mounting separation of artists and their audience. Where once The Grateful Dead had been able to establish a commune in the heart of the Haight-Ashbury district, millionaire stars like Crosby, Stills & Nash made more and more outlandish demands from promoters, played in increasingly large venues rather than small clubs and halls and, at the end of their tours, headed off to their yachts and ranches. Although countercultural musicians had rarely been averse to making money, there was no longer any attempt to hide what now appeared to be shameless greed. Discussing Crosby, Stills, Nash & Young's 1974 stadium tour, Stephen Stills famously told Cameron Crowe, 'We did one for the art and music, one for the chicks. This one's for the cash.'[28] As early as 1970, the group had stipulated that a Persian carpet be placed on the stage for their performance at New York's Fillmore East; by 1974, they were demanding plates and pillowcases decorated with their tour logo.

Ironically, the self-immolation of the rock aristocracy was captured best by one of its own. The late 1960s and early 1970s were characterised by the emergence of two forms of music: on the one hand, singer-songwriters such as Joni Mitchell, James Taylor and Carole King produced soft, 'mature' and melodic albums that tended towards the introspective and appealed to broad swathes of the record-buying public, rather than being limited to the counterculture; on the other hand, bands such as the Allmans, The Doors, and the British group Led Zeppelin played various forms of heavy blues rock. Both genres generally avoided obvious referencing of the political turbulence that surrounded them, although Mitchell, in particular, did compose highly idiosyncratic songs that were almost Whitmanesque in their intermingling of the self and the nation within complex allegorical structures. It was Mitchell's fellow Canadian, Neil Young, however, who, as well as being one quarter of Crosby, Stills, Nash & Young moved between these two forms and emerged as the epitome of the countercultural artist of the 1970s.

Young's career in the period from around 1967 to 1979 illustrates an eclectic musical nature to match Dylan's. As a member of Buffalo Springfield, he was prominent almost from the start of the West Coast countercultural revolution; as a rocker backed by his long-time band Crazy Horse, he released material ranging from epic jams such as 'Cowgirl in the Sand' and 'Like a Hurricane' to the partly punk-inspired *Rust Never Sleeps* (1979); in addition, he produced 'classic' singer-songwriter material including *After the Gold Rush* (1970) and *Harvest* (1972), and made excursions into country. But, again like Dylan, Young has never been afraid to change musical direction with an abruptness that has brought periods of extreme critical and commercial rejection, such as when he followed *Harvest* with *Time Fades Away* (1973), a live collection of extremely raw new material.

Young's 1974 album, *On the Beach*, is probably the most damning musical assessment of what happened to the countercultural generation to be released by one of its inner circle. In some ways, it is a deeply introspective work that traces Young's own depression and his difficulties in coming to terms with superstardom, but it also serves as a commentary on the state of the nation at the time. The album cover's picture of a Thunderbird buried on what appears to be a Californian beach suggests (rather obviously) the demise of an ideology that has reached the end of the road, and has nowhere left to go. Two songs in particular, 'Revolution Blues' and 'Ambulance Blues', sum up Young's disillusionment with not only the prevailing political cynicism and corruption of the Watergate era, but also with the splintering of a counterculture now reduced to the pursuit of material abundance, or to acts of murder and terrorism. Implicitly, these acts collapsed the distinction between culture and counterculture, mirroring within the United States the atrocities being committed in Vietnam and elsewhere in the name of freedom.

In these songs, Young ranges from condemnatory attacks on Richard Nixon, through allusions to the Patty Hearst kidnapping and the Manson murders, and to rock stars living in luxurious seclusion in Laurel Canyon. The ambiguity surrounding his own ideological position in 'Revolution Blues' – sung from the perspective of a Manson-like revolutionary – was clearly disturbing to Young's superstar contemporaries (identified with 'lepers' to be killed in their cars in the lyric), and David Crosby, who plays guitar on the track, not only refused to play the song live, but even walked off stage when

Young performed it.[29] Whereas the protest songs of the 1960s and early '70s – including Young's own 'Ohio', recorded by Crosby, Stills, Nash & Young – tended to have clear ideological messages distancing the counterculture from the social injustices it attacked, 'Revolution Blues' is as critical of a counterculture that has lost its way as it is of the 'American' values espoused under Nixon.

The musical arrangements on *On the Beach* reflect Young's career-long capacity to veer between proto-grunge rock and acoustic melodies. A distorted electric guitar riff drives 'Revolution Blues'; 'Ambulance Blues' is a simple arrangement of acoustic guitar and fiddle, over which the vocals look back to the 'magic' of the 'old folkie days', the age of JFK's presidency and a moment when, for Young and many others of his generation, anything seemed possible. And, in a gesture characteristic of many of Young's songs, the lyric finally moves away from directly addressing the state of the nation, to focus instead on the collapse of an individual's relationships, his drift into alienation, spiritual meaninglessness and the search for redemption, as national malaise is allegorised through explorations of personal desolation.

But what is most interesting, in many ways, is Young's choice of musicians: The Band's Rick Danko and Levon Helm perform on 'Revolution Blues' in an echo of Dylan's own 'underground' take on America on his 'Basement Tapes'. Even more startling – within the context of the California rock culture of the time – is the use of guitarist and fiddler Rusty Kershaw, a Louisiana country musician with real claims to being one of Dylan's 'traditional people'. Although Kershaw doesn't play on 'Revolution Blues', there is no doubt that his mocking of Crosby and Stephen Stills in the studio helped create the mood for the recording. Moreover, in a moment surreal even by the standards of Young's lifestyle at the time, a stoned Kershaw (as he recounts in the liner notes to *On the Beach*) 'turned into a python and then an alligator . . . eating up the carpet and mike stands and such',[30] because he didn't feel that the musicians sounded like they knew how to start a revolution. The performance had the desired effect on Young, who, according to Kershaw, 'got it on the next take', and also on Crosby and Graham Nash, who were both spooked by the sight of an overweight swamp person in dungarees, and with 'dirty long underwear' on show, slithering across the floor like a snake.[31]

While the incident seems amusing in its undercutting of inflated rock star egos, it also clearly exposes the fact that members of the counterculture could be extremely disconcerted by aspects of American life outside either their own domain or the hegemonic institutions that they purported to challenge. Kershaw's drug-fuelled demonstration of how to start a revolution illustrates the multi-layered nature of the battles taking place over the future of the nation at the time. The 'traditional people' had appealed to the Newport audience because of their apparent innocence, their detachment from the complexities of the contemporary world and their provision of an 'authentic' alternative to the plastic America of 1960. Kershaw's performance rejects such reification and – while it is hard to imagine how his ideas about revolution-starting could be put into practice – reminds Young that there are alternatives to the counterculture's version of protest. In so doing, it enables him to step outside the singer-songwriter/hard rocker binary of mid-1970s countercultural music and generate an alternative critique of its own complicity in the nation's fragmentation at the time. With The Eagles' version of melodic country rock becoming the new sound of California culture, such rejuvenation – even from such an unlikely source – was much needed.

Notes

1. Marty Balin and Paul Kantner, 'Volunteers', taken from the Jefferson Airplane album, *Volunteers* (RCA, 1970). Copyright © 1969, Iceberg Corp.
2. Miles Davis with Quincy Troupe, *Miles: The Autobiography* (London: Picador, 1990), p. 262.
3. Jon Pankake, 'The Brotherhood of the Anthology', in 'A Booklet of Essays, Appreciations, and Annotations Pertaining to the *Anthology of American Folk Music* edited by Harry Smith', p. 26. The booklet accompanies the Smithsonian Folkways CD reissue of the *Anthology* (Washington, DC, 1997).
4. Greil Marcus, *Invisible Republic: Bob Dylan's Basement Tapes* (London: Picador, 1997), p. 98.
5. Quoted in Marcus, *Invisible Republic*, p. 195.
6. Robert Shelton, *No Direction Home: The Life and Music of Bob Dylan* (New York: Beech Tree Books, 1986), pp. 301–2.
7. See Martin Scorsese's documentary, *No Direction Home: Bob Dylan* (2005), for a chronicle of this period in Dylan's career. The film includes interviews with many of the key figures present at Newport that year.
8. David Crosby and Carl Gottlieb, *Long Time Gone: The Autobiography of David Crosby* (London: Mandarin, 1990), pp. 81–2.
9. See www.iamthebeatles.com/article1036.html
10. Bob Dylan, *Chronicles: Volume One* (New York: Simon and Schuster, 2004), p. 115.

11. Fred Goodman, *The Mansion on the Hill: Dylan, Young, Geffen, Springsteen and the Head-On Collision of Rock and Commerce* (London: Pimlico, 2003), p. 89.
12. Ralph Gleason quoted in Alice Echols, *Shaky Ground: The Sixties and Its Aftershocks* (New York: Columbia University Press, 2002), p. 26.
13. Dylan, *Chronicles*, p. 114.
14. Marcus, *Invisible Republic*, p. xv.
15. See the Introduction: 1960–72 for more on San Francisco and the 'Summer of Love'.
16. Jefferson Airplane, 'Somebody to Love' (written by Darby Slick), released as a single and on the album *Surrealistic Pillow* (RCA, 1967).
17. Jeff Tamarkin, *Got a Revolution! The Turbulent Flight of Jefferson Airplane* (London: Helter Skelter, 2003), p. 110; Todd Gitlin, *The Sixties: Years of Hope, Days of Rage* (New York: Bantam, 1987), p. 216.
18. See Goodman, *Mansion on the Hill*, p. 101.
19. Gordon Lightfoot, 'Black Day in July', released in edited form as a single and in full on the album *Did She Mention My Name?* (United Artists, 1968). The song was banned from the radio in Detroit and some other cities.
20. Richie Unterberger, *Eight Miles High: Folk Rock's Flight From Haight-Ashbury to Woodstock* (San Francisco: Backbeat Books, 2003) lists examples such as Austin, Texas' The 13th Floor Elevators, Chicago's H. P. Lovecraft and Kansas' The Blue Things. See pp. 55–7.
21. Tamarkin, *Got a Revolution!*, p. 145.
22. Quoted in Unterberger, *Eight Miles High*, p. 105.
23. See Goodman, *Mansion on the Hill*, pp. 68–71. Ironically, the band were not in LA when the 'riot' that inspired the song occurred.
24. Unterberger, *Eight Miles High*, p. 43.
25. The Doors, 'The End', from the album *The Doors* (Elektra, 1967).
26. Todd Gitlin, *The Sixties*, pp. 286–8.
27. I develop this point in my reading of *Woodstock* in Chapter 8.
28. Quoted in Jimmy McDonough, *Shaky: Neil Young's Biography* (London: Vintage, 2003), p. 452.
29. See McDonough, *Shaky*, p. 442.
30. Rusty Kershaw, liner notes for Neil Young, *On the Beach* (Reprise, 1974).
31. The description is by Johnny Talbot, brother of Crazy Horse bassist, Billy. See McDonough, *Shaky*, p. 441.

CHAPTER SEVEN

Painting

'Don't mourn for me, organise!'
    Joe Hill's last words before execution by firing squad
                                    (19 November 1915)

Perhaps the epitome of the alternative communal site was
Andy Warhol's Factory, a loft he began renting in November 1963 to use as a studio for painting and shooting films.
The Factory became a place where some Village people
actually lived . . . but where many more went simply to
hang out – to do drugs, listen to music, have sex, talk, and
meet people. By the late Sixties it was famous as a fashion-
able scene. The Factory was both site and symbol of the
alternative culture's disdain for the bourgeois ethic, from
work to sex to control of consciousness – a sanctified space
where leisure and pleasure reigned.
    Sally Banes, *Greenwich Village 1963* (1993)[1]

In my discussion of Abstract Expressionism, I highlighted tensions
inherent in the relationship between the New York avant-garde and the
counterculture of the 1950s. On the one hand, it is evident that there
are clear formal similarities between Action Painting, jazz and Beat
writing in the emphasis on 'spontaneity' and in the creation of works
that challenged traditional notions of artistic representation. On the
other, the ease with which the paintings of Jackson Pollock and many
other artists were incorporated and deployed by governmental and
private institutions keen to highlight American exceptionalism within

the climate of the Cold War is indicative of the limited challenge posed to political – if not artistic – orthodoxy by Abstract Expressionism.

Art is particularly vulnerable to such incorporation for reasons that I have also explored earlier in this book: because of a painting's uniqueness, it generally requires acceptance within the museum and gallery culture controlled by wealthy individuals and institutions and, once artists have established a critical reputation, their work is rapidly commodified – as 'a Pollock' or 'a Picasso' – whilst becoming an object to study or explain rather than to 'enjoy'. Despite loose affiliations such as the Studio 35 meetings, the Abstract Expressionists tended to be driven by careerist individualism and by a competitiveness that made institutional acceptance highly desirable. In contrast, West Coast artists, such as those responsible for San Francisco's Six Gallery, were more often amenable to collective projects, and to the creation of communal environments that enabled them to function outside traditional artistic controls.

But, if Abstract Expressionism had rapidly been incorporated as part of a wider State corporate Cold War agenda committed to establishing the superiority of American culture, the dominant art forms of the 1960s were even more closely – and immediately – tied to a dominant culture far removed from the counterculture of the time. As Robert Hughes has noted in *American Visions* (1997), his magisterial study of the history of United States art, the '60s 'ushered in the age of the blockbuster exhibition, the idea of the museum as the gee-whiz, populist, spectacular event . . . [which] deeply changed what the public expected from museums'.[2] While this culture began with the display of the *Mona Lisa* at the National Gallery of Art in Washington, DC and at the Metropolitan Museum of Art in New York in 1963–4, and also resulted in the exhibition of numerous other old-world historical treasures, it also had a profound impact on New York's contemporary art culture. Although Hughes overlooks the extent to which Abstract Expressionism had already (in the 1950s) precipitated the widespread acquisition of contemporary art by museums when he suggests that the 'institutionalization of the American avant-garde and the loss of its oppositional character' 'began' in the 1960s, there is no doubt that the process was greatly accelerated during the decade.[3]

The Pop art that dominated the institutional art community in the 1960s was the ideal form for this new culture: unlike Abstract Expressionism, which tended to avoid representation or direct engagement with the popular, Pop art was obsessed with brand names, commercial forms and – as Andy Warhol's famous *Campbell's Soup*

Cans (1961–2) indicates – with reproduction and with the elimination of the passionately individual drips and brush stokes of, for example, Pollock's work. Although Pop art bore some similarities to counter-cultural practice, especially in its dismantling of the divide between high and popular culture, there were also significant differences. Thus, although Warhol does have links to the counterculture, which I will return to later in this chapter, artists such as Roy Lichtenstein and James Rosenquist rapidly established profitable ties to wealthy collectors. Hughes makes the important point that the 'new-rich collectors who had missed out on Abstract Expressionism' found everything they needed in Pop: 'You made money from soap flakes and bought art based on soap-flake ads. There was no problem about difficult art anymore, and no lag between appearance and acceptance . . . Pop art was the first accessible style of international modernism; it was art about consumption that sat up and begged to be consumed.'[4]

In this chapter, I wish to explore three different ways in which artists in the 1960s sought effective ways to challenge this artistic establishment. This means that – unlike in my reading of Abstract Expressionism – I will initially be focusing on painters who do not feature in canonical histories of American art such as Hughes's. First, I will look at the role of artists operating within the countercultural iconography of Haight-Ashbury and beyond, assessing the significance of rock posters as symbols of a move to take art from the museum to the street and to make it a part of everyday life. The artists responsible for these posters – and for related forms such as psychedelic album covers – belonged to a more obviously inter-disciplinary counterculture than that of the 1940s and '50s, in which art, music and poetry, for example, were often brought together as part of a single 'happening' or experience. Next, I will offer a brief examination of more overtly political projects, focusing upon the 'Peace Tower' erected in Los Angeles in 1966. The Tower and similar events also challenge received wisdom about the function and practice of art both in the collective nature of their construction and in their appeal to the impermanent and immediate rather than to the memorialising ideology inherent in museum culture. Finally, I will return to New York to illustrate the workings of a space very different from that of Abstract Expressionism, but one that is equally well known. Andy Warhol's Factory deployed the tension between the individual and the collective in ways that invariably celebrated both cultural transgression and – in a manner echoed both in the media manipulation staged by the Yippies and the culture of celebrity of movies such as *Bonnie and Clyde* – encouraged forms of performance that made art more democratic, both in the sense that it removed the need for years of dedicated training required to become an 'artist' and generated forms that appeared to be accessible to spectators who lacked the vocabulary of conventional art criticism.

The Art of Noise

Although it would probably be an exaggeration to suggest that the covers of seminal countercultural albums of the 1960s and early 1970s are as well known as the music, there is no doubt that the artwork is integral to the total product. For example, Peter Blake's design for The Beatles' *Sgt. Pepper's Lonely Hearts Club Band* (1967), Andy Warhol's zipper cover for The Rolling Stones' *Sticky Fingers* (1971) and his design for *The Velvet Underground and Nico* (1966), and Stanley Mouse and Alton Kelley's sleeves for The Grateful Dead all break free of the traditional photograph-of-the band format, while Captain Beefheart/Don Van Vliet's career is marked by his intersecting interests in music, painting and poetry as parts of a multi-disciplinary whole. Blake and Warhol, for example, call attention to their designs in a number of ways: *Sgt. Pepper*'s gate-fold sleeve and the front of *Sticky Fingers* are both examples of covers that do more than merely contain the music, and the latter, with its zipper that was found to damage the vinyl inside, is perhaps the supreme example of impractical album art. The cover painting for *The Velvet Underground and Nico* also challenges conventional relationships between musicians and the designers who would promote their work, since the banana on the front cover of the first pressings could be peeled and – even more significantly – Andy Warhol's signature was at least as prominent as the band's name.

The covers for *Sgt. Pepper* and *Sticky Fingers* were dominated by photography rather than painting, but many of the most famous countercultural sleeves of the time did feature heavily stylised paintings that became inseparable from the music. Mati Klarwein's *Annunciation* (1961), reproduced on the cover of Santana's *Abraxas* (1970), represents forms of global multiculturalism, a fascination with mysticism and magic realism, and a celebration of sexuality that are all, of course, mainstays of late-1960s youth culture. Klarwein's art is also familiar from other album covers, such as for Miles Davis's *Bitches Brew* (1970), with the result that while his name is *relatively* unknown either inside or outside the art world, his work has received widespread attention.

185

Although Klarwein did have a significant reputation as a painter – and Andy Warhol even labelled him his favourite artist[5] – he generally avoided the traditional world of galleries and exhibitions and, especially after his move to New York in the early 1960s, socialised more with musicians than with fellow artists. By this time, he had also pre-empted the hippie trail in his travels through India, Bali, North Africa and Tibet, and the fusion not only of representations of different cultures but also of multiple formal practices offers a further twinning with the globally-inflected music of artists such as The Beatles, John Coltrane and The Byrds. In addition, he often worked in a barter economy where, for example, he would provide a painting in exchange for the publication of a book or for a car, thus establishing a lifestyle that matched the 'alternative' nature of his works and situated him outside the Pop art community that dominated the New York scene at the time.

In one way, Klarwein is representative of much 1960s counterculture in the equation of sex with freedom and, in particular, in the use of the naked female body as a marker of opposition to social and sexual norms. In a recent assessment of the decade's underground comix, Beth Bailey has pointed out that 'Transgressive sexuality offered a visual and verbal language with which to challenge the Establishment. Represented with purposeful, shocking vulgarity, sex served as a weapon against "straight," or non-hip culture.' As Bailey notes, 'in paper after alternative paper throughout the United States, the graphic representation of freedom was a naked woman'.[6] Nevertheless, as Bailey indirectly hints in this quote, Klarwein's use of the female nude also differs from a countercultural practice that depended upon what could also be read as the exploitation – rather than liberation – of women. Whereas many of the examples cited by Bailey offer misogynistic representations of women as either unpredictable beings or as the prizes promised to (generally clothed) men who drop out of the repressive society, Klarwein's work draws no distinctions according to race or gender: *Crucifixion (Freedom of Expression)* (1963–5), for example, offers what Conny C. Lindström and Peter Holmlund have accurately summarised as a 'blasphemic' representation of a 'myriad of people caught in a garden of earthly delights'.[7] *Crucifixion*, which Klarwein also described as 'the fucking tree',[8] epitomises a countercultural desire to transcend specific geographical, cultural or religious localities. It references not only Christianity, but also Eastern, African and, possibly, Native American religions and customs, all intertwined with the multi-racial orgy that dominates the picture. In *Crucifixion*, the images represent not so much Klarwein's abstract curiosity about the past, as an attempt to re-think what the present could be like if repressive Euro-American norms were removed. Although there is evidently an idealisation (also characteristic of other countercultural art such as Beat literature) of other cultures in the painting, *Crucifixion* also demonstrates an immersion in other cultures that moves beyond, for example, the more casual use of Indian and African instruments and scales in much 1960s rock music.[9]

Klarwein's work can thus be seen as an extreme example of what Sally Banes has usefully described as the representation of the 'eroticized antifamily'. Banes cites examples including Ron Rice's films *Chumlum* (1964) and *The Queen of Sheba Meets the Atom Man* (unfinished; completed by Taylor Mead in 1982), Jack Smith's film *Flaming Creatures* (1961) and Carolee Schneemann's dance/performance, *Meat Joy* (1964), 'all of which feature, more or less literally, group sex'. As Banes points out, these works offer radical critiques of hegemonic vales, since they 'not only flagrantly transgress the sexual codes of the bourgeois family, [but also suggest] one way to open up and extend the family – the most private of all social spheres – beyond the nuclear model of family-as-couple-cum-kids.'[10]

While Klarwein is an artist whose painting was adopted by musicians, there are other figures even more closely associated with work produced specifically for psychedelic rock bands. Stanley Mouse, Alton Kelley, Wes Wilson, Victor Moscoso, Bonnie McLean and Rick Griffin, for example, were at the heart of Haight-Ashbury counterculture and were largely responsible for the handbills (and also many of the album covers) that characterised the area's visual culture. These artists' posters – usually stuck on telephone poles, windows and street corners – for gigs by not only The Grateful Dead and Jefferson Airplane, but also bands such as The 13th Floor Elevators, The Charlatans, Quicksilver Messenger Service and Big Brother and the Holding Company at San Francisco's Avalon Ballroom and at the Fillmore Auditorium, marked a rejection of the traditional status – or, to use Walter Benjamin's apt term, 'aura'[11] – of the unique work of art, embracing mechanical reproduction and wide distribution and yet have, ironically, become valuable collector's items and the subject of major exhibitions.

When looking at these posters, it is impossible to separate them from the LSD culture that was at the heart of Haight-Ashbury psychedelia, and there is no doubt that the surrealism and colour of many of the designs are products of that world. Wes Wilson, for example, who was resident artist at the Fillmore until May 1967, as well as creating most of the early Family Dog posters, was a member of the community surrounding the San Francisco Mime Troup, the Diggers and the Merry Pranksters, and was involved at the very start of the San Francisco psychedelic scene as designer of the flyer for the Pranksters' January 1966 Trips Festival, a three-day acid party featuring The Grateful Dead, Allen Ginsberg and Big Brother and the Holding Company. Like several other leading countercultural artists, he did not have extensive formal training (and had studied horticulture and philosophy, rather than art), although, unusually, he achieved significant institutional and commercial recognition early in his career, receiving a $5000 National Endowment for the Arts award in 1968 and being featured in *Life*, *Time* and *Variety* magazines.[12] Wilson is probably the artist responsible for the widely copied emphasis on large, sweeping letters. His work regularly features the nude female form in a manner that is – as with Klarwein – more respectful towards women than in much countercultural representation. His art from the mid-1960s is, however, also occasionally more overtly political than that of most of his Haight-Ashbury contemporaries: *Are We Next?* (1965), for example, is a variation on the American flag that is as politically engaged as any of Wally Hedrick's flag series. Reshaping the banner's stars into the shape of a swastika and with the warning, 'Be Aware', at the bottom of the image, the poster is an early example of anti-Vietnam War art that, in some ways, acts as a visual antecedent to Jimi Hendrix's musical re-working of 'The Star-Spangled Banner' immortalised in *Woodstock* (1970).

Wilson's work, however, also illustrates the manner in which psychedelic handbills participated in a longer tradition of poster art. Wilson's designs resemble those of the Viennese Secessionist artist, Alfred Roller, and there is a wider connection between countercultural posters and those of the late nineteenth and early twentieth centuries. The pioneering poster historian, John Barnicoat, has illustrated the links between Art Nouveau and Symbolist designs and hippie art, and has highlighted the significance of the 1965 exhibition of 'Jugendstil and Expressionism in German Posters' at Berkeley's University Art Gallery in relation to the area's new art. Noting the manner in which psychedelic posters 'make full use of the past' – a point that can be identified, for example, in the Double-H Press handbill for the Golden Gate Park Human Be-In in January 1967 – Barnicoat observes that disillusion with materialism, the search for spiritual meaning, the use of 'long robes, flowing beards, drugs and unisex are expressions of both

Symbolist and Hippy'. Providing numerous examples to illustrate his argument, Barnicoat points out that while psychedelic poster artists of the 1960s 'exaggerated and . . . extended' the effects of their 1890s counterparts, their work often utilised similar elements, such as 'juxtaposing complementary colours and confusing the spectator by allowing one pattern to run into another'.[13] Significantly, of course, this effect epitomises one of the principal aspects of much counter-cultural art: on the one hand, the posters are clearly intended to convey information about a gig or other event; on the other, however, they also offer a visual experience whose meaning is deliberately opaque. Like the album covers that I discussed earlier in this chapter, the posters both fulfil and undermine their apparent function as the means to communicate a straightforward message, rejecting the simple and succinct styles used in advertising in the 1950s and replacing them with an appeal to sensory pleasure.

Stanley Mouse (born Stanley Miller) also stresses the influence of Art Nouveau, noting its focus on the human body and nature. Like Wilson, Mouse established himself in San Francisco through his poster art for the Avalon and the Fillmore and, with partner Alton Kelley, designed the famous Grateful Dead skull logo.[14] Mouse's history prior to his arrival in Haight-Ashbury is also indicative of the fusion of high and popular styles brought into countercultural art. His father was a drawer for Walt Disney and Mouse himself started as a cartoonist before becoming a highly successful T-shirt designer and later Hot-Rod painter in Detroit, whilst simultaneously attending art school. In an interview with Michael Erlewine, Mouse inadvertently reveals the extent to which Abstract Expressionism had already become – by the late 1950s – the new artistic orthodoxy, commenting that, in 'art school, they try to teach you that kind of abstract stuff',[15] while he was more interested in life study. Mouse was attracted to the West Coast psychedelic scene by California funk, by Wilson's poster designs and by acid (which he took copiously as a way of avoiding the draft).

Mouse is significant not just for his art as a finished article, but also for his approach to creating it: in some ways, his compositional style is reminiscent of Kerouac or of bebop musicians in that it is based upon rapid, improvised sketching that draws on years of dedication to his craft, both as a student of other artists' work and on to the point that drawing becomes virtual second nature. As with these artistic antecedents, the mastery of compositional skills enables total focus on the immediacy of production. In addition, Mouse's collaborative work with Alton Kelley marks a rejection of the individualism associated not only with Abstract Expressionism, but also with artistic production more generally, and relates to the collective practice often advocated – though not always enacted – by the counterculture. Mouse and Kelley's compositions appear to have been genuinely co-produced: according to Grateful Dead biographer Dennis McNally, 'they worked up designs together, trading licks like jazz musicians'.[16] Finally, as a trained and highly skilled artist, encouraged to develop his career as a 'serious' painter, Mouse's decision to reject the conventional pursuit of success via the production of individual, unique works constructed to be displayed in museums and galleries provides a significant example of the manner in which the counterculture was questioning traditional paths to success, even when these paths were engrained in earlier avant-garde practice. Furthermore, working with poster design relies upon another level of collaboration, absent from conventional painting and depending upon print technology and printer technicians. As with the musicians working out of San Francisco at the time, the use of this technology both indicates an acceptance of the innovations provided by the technocratic state – whether these are new amplification and recording equipment, or state-of-the-art print facilities – and a willingness to use these products in ways that were probably not intended by their designers. Like the feedback that introduces Jefferson Airplane's 'The Ballad of You and Me and Pooneil', much of the psychedelic art used on posters and record covers is blurred or distorted in a form of subversion of the clarity promised by modern technology.

Insisting on an art form that participated in the street theatre that characterised much of '60s counterculture, these posters re-imagine the function of art in ways that are similar to other forms of counter-cultural practice, such as the City Lights Pocket Poets series that helped to make poetry a part of a shared, public experience. Discussing the slightly different concept of poetry broadsides at the time, James D. Sullivan has suggested that 'one of the most common' uses of the broadside was 'to get the word out quickly', a point equally applicable to psychedelic rock handbills. While – unlike Sullivan's subject matter – the majority of these posters ultimately had the commercial imperative of attracting people to concerts, they shared the 'grass roots' approach that strove to avoid the 'institutional mediation' of the press or radio and television advertising.[17] Again, the effect of this is apparent even with the handbills advertising gigs rather than, for example, anti-war protest: the process is a clear assertion of the desire to drop out of the normal practices of a middle-class white America hostile to the lifestyle of the counterculture. With more overtly political works such as Wilson's *Are We Next?* or his acid-culture design for Allen Ginsberg's 'Who Be Kind To' (1965/1967), which illustrates Ginsberg's call for sexual freedom as an antidote to the violence unleashed in Vietnam, this withdrawal also assumes a direct moral imperative, highlighting the genocidal aggression at the core of American society and positing sex and drugs as liberating spiritual forms of behaviour. As Sullivan has noted, Ginsberg's words and Wilson's art combine, linking the 'desire to get high or get laid with an anarchist politics generally and . . . specifically with opposition to the Vietnam War. This poster encouraged young people to find political implications in their frustrated desires.'[18] By taking art into the streets, Wilson and Ginsberg encourage those seeing the broadside to take their own forms of anti-war and more general countercultural behaviour into those streets, and to imagine other ways to challenge or avoid identification with State aggression or oppression.

This should not be taken to indicate, however, that the handbills and posters produced by Wilson, Mouse and Kelley and others in the Bay region functioned entirely beyond the logic of the more traditional American marketplace. Much of the early psychedelic scene in the area had been coordinated by the Family Dog, fronted (on the whole) by Chet Helms, but operating as a four-person collective sharing a house on Pine Street, which rejected conventional business models. The very different Bill Graham, however, rapidly superseded the Family Dog as the leading Haight promoter. Although Graham had served as business manager for the San Francisco Mime Troupe, his subsequent career at the Fillmore Auditorium was marked by the application of ruthless commercial practice to the staging of profit-making countercultural entertainment. In this context, the artists working for Graham fulfilled a vital role: as Jefferson Airplane biographer Jeff Tamarkin has pointed out, the highly creative, professional materials produced by Wilson, Mouse and Kelley served a purpose that transcended simply selling out the venue on a particular night. Instead, they 'helped to promote an image of the Fillmore as *the* place to be' (emphasis in original).[19]

While it should be evident that art associated with Haight-Ashbury psychedelia is specific to a local and – in its original form – very brief moment of countercultural activity, the above discussion should also help to highlight its links with wider avant-garde and countercultural practice in the 1960s, and to show how these movements questioned not only cultural orthodoxy, but also earlier avant-garde ideology. In particular, I want to stress the manner in which these artists collapsed the distinction between high and popular cultures that had been at the heart of, for example, Clement Greenberg's defence of Abstract Expressionism in the face of 'kitsch' American culture. It is useful in this context to bear in mind Sally Banes's suggestion that – for the artistic avant-garde of the '60s – the distinction between high and low was less important than that between 'the artificial and the genuine'. Although, as I have suggested earlier, this shift functioned rather differently for a West Coast counterculture functioning outside the domain of museums and galleries, avant-garde and counterculture shared a desire to 'create an egalitarian meeting place of culture where high and low met on a two-way street . . . [standing] in opposition to a liberal, upwardly mobile cultural "melting pot" that would patronisingly raise all audiences up to appreciate high culture'.[20] Making art a part of people's everyday lives was clearly one, highly significant, element of the work produced for the Family Dog and the Fillmore. It was also, as I suggest in the following section, a strategy developed by artists more directly committed to political – largely anti-Vietnam War – protest than the majority of those working within the Haight-Ashbury community.

Art and Protest

> At noon on Saturday 26 February 1966, the 'Artists' Tower of Protest,' or 'Peace Tower,' at the junction of La Cienega and Sunset Boulevards was dedicated with speeches by the artist Irving Petlin, ex-Green-Beret Master-Sergeant Donald Duncan, writer Susan Sontag, and the releasing by children of six white doves to symbolise peace. Including work by 418 artists, this collective memorial had to be defended night and day against attacks by those who regarded such manifestations as un-American and at best a collusion with the 'Communist menace' in Vietnam.[21]

Although I have suggested that the leading figures of the New York Pop art scene operated at some distance (ideologically, as well as geographically) from the countercultural West Coast community, there were some points of contact, as well as moments when painters more commonly seen as part of the artistic 'establishment' went beyond their Haight-Ashbury counterparts in staging protests against American policy in Vietnam. The 'Peace Tower' erected in Los Angeles in

1966 was an expression of opposition to the war that united artists from America and Europe and from a multitude of 'schools' including Social Realism, Abstract Expressionism, Pop art and California Beat culture, but it was also a symbol of ruptures and tensions within the artistic avant-garde.

There is no space here to include a detailed description of the overall design of the tower and its surrounds – and, in any case, a full list of contributors no longer exists – but a brief description of its organisational principles is useful in suggesting the unusual nature of the project. The base of the tower was an octahedron seventeen feet six inches high, which supported a tetrahedron on its top triangle. Above this was a double stretched tetrahedron constructed in a diamond shape. Due to the need to construct a structure that would meet safety and planning regulations, as well as an original proposal to hang the works from the Tower itself, artists were invited to submit uniformly sized panels, two feet square, which should be weatherproof, but whose content was left entirely up to individual participants. The effect was two-fold: on the one hand, contributors were free to produce works each – as a promotional poster by Hardy Hanson suggested – 'uniquely symbolizing the individual protest of [the] artist';[22] on the other, the design had a clear democratic intent, with each artist offered the same space for their work and with the contributions arranged irrespective of the relative critical or commercial profile of the artist. Although the plan to hang the works from the Tower had to be abandoned for safety reasons, 'there remained' – as Francis Frascina has noted in a detailed and insightful analysis – 'a commitment to display works without regard to the status of the artist, to any formal criteria or to curatorial valuations'.[23] Thus, while by no means all the artists could be considered 'countercultural', the overall emphasis on collective practice, the sense that the work functioned as a form of street performance and the downplaying of egocentric divisions relate closely to countercultural ideals.

The collaborative aspect of the Tower is clearly integral to its significance as a work of protest and as an attempt to intervene in national political debate. The mix of artists from diverse backgrounds was important, since it guaranteed that audiences with different artistic preferences and ideological positions would be attracted to a project that was operating outside the norms of an art world reluctant to become involved with anti-Government protest. Moreover, as participating artist Irving Petlin pointed out, the 'growing realisation that the United States might be involved in genocide was a specific galvanising factor' in eliciting such unusual, perhaps unprecedented, collective and collaborative union across a diverse collection of interests, in a project that fused sculpture and painting.[24]

In addition, the Tower functioned outside traditional artistic paradigms in other ways. As an impermanent structure, which would be dismantled and sold in individual units at the end of the protest, it was clearly unlike works designed to be stored and displayed in museums and galleries, bringing an immediacy and sense of urgency to its existence. Given the close relationship between many of the wealthy benefactors of the art world and the Government – including those involved in the extensive scientific and military research industry in Southern California that combined profit with 'patriotism' – these factors suggested both a willingness (at least, for some of those involved) to jeopardise lucrative economic relationships and a recognition of art's potential role as a shaper of influential opinion.

Responses to the Tower do, however, demonstrate the power of hegemonic media to control news and manipulate public opinion. While the *Los Angeles Free Press* was keen to report anti-war and other forms of political protest, Frascina notes the lack of mainstream press coverage of the event and of similar attempts to use art to make anti-war statements.[25] Thus, while such displays could attract local interest and support (and the Tower received many visitors, both supportive of and opposed to its message), the potential for wider dissemination of oppositional, peaceful dissent was limited. Ironically, both the psychedelic hippie lifestyle surrounding Haight-Ashbury and the large violent confrontations staged by the Yippies were given much more attention, the former because its 'weirdness' appeared largely devoid of the desire for political intervention and the latter because it was easy to convince the majority of viewers that the protestors were violent revolutionary 'commies' who deserved whatever injuries they received at the hands of the police. At the same time, the mainstream newspapers were generally uncritical of the military propaganda that they reprinted, thus fuelling popular misconceptions about the war and generating additional hostility towards those who opposed it. In addition, there was no institutional support for art that sought to make political points: as I suggested in section one, Abstract Expressionism quickly became attractive to State and private institutions keen to promote American freedoms during the Cold War largely because its non-representational qualities and idiosyncratic formations could be deployed as exemplary instances of American freedoms. In contrast, the Peace Tower would be seen – from an institutional perspective – as an abuse of these freedoms, as well as an abnegation of the artistic responsibility to create enduring works.

Ultimately, the motives for and legacy of the Tower remain ambiguous. Frascina asks, 'Was the Tower the product of intellectuals who were, in terms of [Susan] Sontag's retrospective view, "too gullible, too prone to appeals to idealism to take in what was really happening" in Vietnam? Was the Tower merely an act of anti-war publicity, an act of protest, that at best was confused about the boundaries between "art", "morality" and politics and at worst a well-meaning "aesthetic" embarrassment?'[26] As suggested above, the hegemonic response to these issues was largely to ignore them and to focus on more conventional artistic displays. Where the consequences of protest could not be avoided, the corporate-sponsored art establishment would act in other ways. Thus, in a further signifier of institutional antipathy to politically controversial art and artists, the Chouinard Institute of Art (heavily endowed by Walt Disney) was relocated to an LA suburb and renamed as the California Institute of the Arts, in a response to a 1966 student rebellion.[27]

In countercultural terms, the Tower's legacy is also unclear. On the one hand, the focus on the power of performative protest resembles the street theatre of the Diggers, Pranksters and Yippies in its co-opting of public space as a site of political dissidence designed to make viewers question their preconceptions. On the other hand, while the Tower was meant to attract and challenge viewers from across the political spectrum, the Diggers generally performed to the like-minded, whilst the Pranksters' endorsement of psychedelic drugs encouraged transcendence of earthly political problems rather than engagement with them. Ultimately, the Tower represents a form that falls somewhere between the anti-war politics of the New Left and the theatricality of Bay area counterculture, but which cannot be comfortably accommodated to either. In these terms, the lack of emphasis on the celebrity of some of the participants – such as Mark Rothko, Robert Motherwell, Roy Lichtenstein, Larry Rivers and Claes Oldenburg – can even be seen to signify a lack of the promotional savvy surrounding countercultural protests advertised as featuring 'star' attractions such as Allen Ginsberg, or those organised by the Yippies in which the corporate media were tricked into drawing massive attention to what would otherwise have been small-scale activities.

Andy Warhol, The Factory and The Exploding Plastic Inevitable

While the Peace Tower clearly illustrates one set of overlaps between 1960s counterculture – as defined by the lifestyles and ideologies associated most famously with Haight-Ashbury and, more generally, the Bay area – and political performance art deployed utilising similar strategies, another set of (problematic) parallels is evident when the counterculture is set alongside Andy Warhol. Like elements of the West Coast counterculture, Warhol produced a series of works that satirised cornerstones of dominant American ideology and offered mirror images of attitudes to violence and to the star system. The 'death series' that Warhol produced around the time of John F. Kennedy's assassination challenged conventional attitudes towards violence, illustrating the extent to which the culture was fascinated with violent acts – whether these were car crashes, race riots or electric-chair executions – and serving as a critique of a society for which representations of death were simply another example of mass consumption. As Van M. Cagle has observed, the series tends to have the effect of 'humanizing objects, while dehumanising people', conveying the 'chilling impact of modernization and industrial life'.[28]

Warhol's approach to stardom is apparent both in his silkscreen mass images of Marilyn Monroe and other iconic Hollywood figures, and in his creation of his own stable of 'superstars', who featured in his movies and who tended to be beautiful and/or uninhibited non-actors such as Edie Sedgwick, Candy Darling and Eric Emerson.[29] The effect of these constructions is assessed effectively by Sally Banes, who argues that

> In the visual arts Andy Warhol developed a double-edged attack on the 'star' mystique. His homegrown crop of underground 'superstars,' created through his screen tests and 'home movies' at the Factory, were one side of this critique; his silk screen multiples of real stars like the Marilyn, Liz, Elvis and Marlon series (1962–64) were the other side. Both were ways to mass-produce notions of glamour, stardom and fame – with deadpan satire. The Factory films and superstars constituted a folk aspect of stardom, in which an alternative, grass-roots, underground Hollywood was constituted at a fraction of Hollywood's scale of operation. Anyone stumbling into the Factory scene was

incorporated into the mystique. Stardom was mass-produced here in the sense that it was available (although in an alternative arena) to almost anyone. Yet the multiples of actual Hollywood and popular music stars constituted a popular culture aspect of stardom in which people become icons and seem only to exist in multiple, mass-produced images.[30]

Elements of this process bear close resemblance to countercultural practice: the broad acceptance of anyone who does not fit comfortably within 'normal' American life and the rapidly developing cliques within The Factory are reminiscent of the counterculture's embrace of the 'freakish' and of the way in which it also rapidly generated hierarchal structures. More cynically, the often repeated suggestion that Warhol was manipulating those around him for his own advantage in his (successful) attempt to enter the world of New York socialites has also been levelled at sometime countercultural icons such as Mick Jagger and Warren Beatty. Given these similarities, it is unsurprising that Warhol's most ambitious multi-media event, The Exploding Plastic Inevitable, depended on the same combinations of psychedelic movies, lights and music (provided by The Velvet Underground) as those being developed both on the West Coast and in London. As Lewis Mac-Adams has suggested, The Exploding Plastic Inevitable was, for Warhol, the 'ultimate canvas. He was no longer just a painter, he was a conductor, a conduit for people's emotions and ideas.'[31]

When The Exploding Plastic Inevitable was taken to the West Coast in 1966, however, the reception was almost universally hostile. The Velvet Underground, in their tight jeans, did not look like the bell-bottomed hippies and their ultra-loud ironic songs did not sound like West Coast psychedelia. While Warhol's efforts to transform painterly techniques into multi-media performance appealed to the speed-fuelled, gay-inflected New York scene, the emphasis on sadomaso-chism and leather was out of place in the generally homophobic Californian counterculture. In addition, the show came across as being too controlled and at odds with the improvisation inherent to the lengthy acid-rock jams that dominated at the Fillmore. Warhol's own desire to become what MacAdams calls an 'emotionally efficient machine' (since, for Warhol, 'machines have less problems'[32]) also signalled a clear contrast to the countercultural stress on emotion and spontaneity that was as prevalent in the mid-1960s as it had been for the Beats, Action Painters and beboppers in the '40s and '50s. Although the trip did include the recording of much of the first Velvet

Underground album, the subsequent failure of the record was a further illustration of the gulf between California counterculture and New York avant-garde.

Both Warhol and the artists involved in the Peace Tower illustrate ways in which practices in painting were being re-deployed in other genres. Despite certain similarities to countercultural artistic experimentation, Warhol's multi-media Exploding Plastic Inevitable is probably more effectively identified as a harbinger of the punk rock, gay and synthesised disco cultures that became popular in the 1970s. It is notable that even exhibitions of Warhol's paintings were poorly received in Los Angeles in the mid-1960s; likewise, it was only when New York superseded the California of the counterculture as the hub of popular youth cultural production in the following decade that the (long-disbanded) Velvet Underground began to sell records in large quantities. While the cosmopolitan collection of artists involved in the Peace Tower were closer than Warhol to countercultural ideals – especially in their commitment to a cause driven by emotion as well as intellect – and possibly helped to generate anti-war sentiment and protest on the West Coast, their participation was, in many cases, a one-off undertaking rather than part of a calculated rejection of or withdrawal from the mainstream, as was the case for the Haight-Ashbury community.

Notes

1. Sally Banes, *Greenwich Village 1963: Avant-Garde Performance and the Effervescent Body* (Durham, NC and London: Duke University Press, 1993), p. 36.
2. Robert Hughes, *American Visions: The Epic History of Art in America* (London: Harvill Press, 1997), p. 523.
3. Ibid., p. 524.
4. Ibid., p. 525. Sally Banes makes the point that the New York avant-garde of the early 1960s 'saw in popular culture an enviable energy that was lacking in the correct, difficult (old) avant-garde art that [Clement] Greenberg championed. Instead of going down from Olympia to enlighten the masses, they wanted to bring the insights, skills, techniques, and pleasures of popular culture back home to high art.' *Greenwich Village 1963*, p. 106.
5. See, for example, Conny C. Lindström and Peter Holmlund, 'The Manic Landscape: Mati Klarwein', at http://art-bin.com/art/aklarwein.html

6. Beth Bailey, 'Sex as a Weapon: Underground Comix and the Paradox of Liberation', in Peter Braunstein and Michael William Doyle (eds), *Imagine Nation: The American Counterculture of the 1960s and '70s* (London: Routledge, 2002), p. 307, p. 308.

7. Lindström and Holmlund, 'The Manic Landscape: Mati Klarwein.' The painting became an integral part of Klarwein's Aleph Sanctuary, where Carlos Santana first saw *Annunciation.*

8. Quoted in L. Caruana, 'Mati Klarwein Remembered', *Visionary Revue: The On-Line Journal of Visionary Art*, Fall 2004, n.p., at http://vision-aryrevue.com/webtext3/klarwein4.html

9. I do not wish to suggest that all rock musicians were guilty of superficial appropriation of other cultures' art. While the widespread adoption of African-American jazz and blues by white artists did not generally lead to significantly deeper knowledge of black culture, and the faddish turn to sitars and ragas proved to be a temporary diversion for most artists, some figures developed more enduring interests. George Harrison, Roger McGuinn, Davy Graham, Ry Cooder and others have made not only long-term study of musical forms, but also, in many cases, have adopted elements of non-Western cultural or religious practice into their daily lives.

10. Banes, *Greenwich Village* 1963, p. 36. *Meat Joy*, in particular, is an extraordinary work, deploying raw fish, chickens, sausages, wet paint, transparent plastic, rope brushes and paper scraps in its representations of ecstatic eroticism. Stills from the performance can be viewed at www.caroleeschneemann.com/works.html

11. Walter Benjamin, 'The Work of Art in the Age of Mechanical Reproduction', in *Illuminations*, translated by Harry Zohn with an introduction by Hannah Arendt (London: Fontana, 1992), p. 215. Benjamin's essay is unquestionably the most famous approach to the topic and offers a damning attack on the extent to which the loss of the 'aura' of the work of art has resulted in 'a tremendous shattering of tradition' and 'the liquidation of the traditional value of the cultural heritage' (p. 215). Clearly, this is not a stance shared by artists working to make their original, highly skilled designs widely available through the use of reproductive technologies found so threatening by Benjamin.

12. See http://www.classicposters.com/eposter/showArtist.do?id=23932 for a useful biography of Wilson, especially during his time in San Francisco in the mid-1960s.

13. John Barnicoat, *Posters: A Concise History* (London: Thames and Hudson, 1972), pp. 57–8.

14. Dennis McNally notes that the iconic image was taken from Edmund Sullivan's illustrations for Edward Fitzgerald's 1859 translation of *The Rubáiyát of Omar Khayyám*. See Dennis McNally, *A Long Strange Trip: The Inside History of The Grateful Dead and the Making of Modern America* (London: Corgi, 2003), p. 223.

15. Michael Erlewine, 'Interview with Stanley Mouse', at www.classicposters.com/eposter/showArticle.do?id=CP000060&secId=001. I am drawing on this interview for much of the factual detail in this account of Mouse's background.
16. McNally, *A Long Strange Trip*, p. 223.
17. James D. Sullivan, *On the Walls and In the Streets: American Poetry Broadsides From the 1960s* (Urbana and Chicago: University of Illinois Press, 1997), p. 2.
18. Ibid., p. 139.
19. Jeff Tamarkin, *Got a Revolution! The Turbulent Flight of Jefferson Airplane* (London: Helter Skelter, 2003), p. 93.
20. Banes, *Greenwich Village 1963*, p. 107.
21. Francis Frascina, *Art, Politics and Dissent: Aspects of the Art Left in Sixties America* (Manchester and New York: Manchester University Press, 1999), p. 4. I am indebted to Frascina for the factual detail that follows.
22. Quoted in Frascina, *Art, Politics and Dissent*, p. 63.
23. Frascina, *Art, Politics and Dissent*, p. 64.
24. Ibid., p. 65.
25. Ibid., p. 31. Frascina also points out the extent to which the Tower has been erased from the history of art in America. It is largely unmentioned in textbooks and 'no longer exists to be curated, conserved and exhibited' (p. 18).
26. Ibid., p. 81.
27. Ibid., p. 91.
28. Van M. Cagle, *Reconstructing Pop/Subculture: Art, Rock, and Andy Warhol* (Thousand Oaks, CA and London: Sage, 1995), pp. 60–1.
29. See Lewis MacAdams, *Birth of the Cool: Beat, Bebop and the American Avant-Garde* (London: Scribner, 2002), p. 245.
30. Banes, *Greenwich Village 1963*, p. 112.
31. MacAdams, *Birth of the Cool*, p. 244.
32. Ibid., p. 242.

CHAPTER EIGHT

Film

Yeh, some folks inherit star spangled eyes,
Ooh, they send you down to war, Lord,
And when you ask them, how much should we give,
Oh, they only answer, more, more, more
    Creedence Clearwater Revival, 'Fortunate Son' (1969)[1]

This used to be a helluva good country. I don't know what
happened to it . . . people talking about freedom, but when
they see a really free individual it scares them.
    George Hanson (Jack Nicholson) in *Easy Rider* (1969)[2]

Great displays of war might were lined along Pennsylvania
Avenue as we rolled by in our battered boat. There were
B-29s, PT boats, artillery, all kinds of war material that
looked murderous in the snowy grass; . . . Dean slowed
down to look at it . . . 'What are these people up to?'
    Jack Kerouac, *On the Road* (1957)[3]

Whereas 1950s youth movies such as *Rebel Without a Cause* and *The
Wild One* appeared just too soon to be accompanied by a rock and roll
soundtrack and, retrospectively, seem bereft of the 'authenticating'
qualities that this would provide, the best-known Hollywood countercultural films of the late 1960s, such as *The Graduate* (1968), *Easy
Rider* (1969) and *Woodstock* (1970/1994), are all but defined by their
music. In the case of *Woodstock*, this is self-evident, since the movie is a
record of probably the most famous rock festival of all time; according

to Peter Fonda, *Easy Rider*'s central characters were based upon Roger McGuinn and David Crosby of The Byrds;[4] even *The Graduate*, although it lacks such direct connections and offers a rather weak attack on dominant culture, deploys an unusually close link between the lyrical content of Simon and Garfunkel's songs and its themes of youthful alienation and loss of innocence. In each case, it is clear that artistic cross-fertilisation has moved far beyond the overlaps discernible in the 1940s and '50s, when artists, musicians and writers lived alongside one another in Greenwich Village: Kerouac could describe the jazz inspirations for his prose but (bar in the recordings of his readings) the music is not part of the content; Jackson Pollock listened to jazz, but its sounds are not 'in' his paintings; even when a musician such as Ornette Coleman used a reproduction of a Pollock piece for the cover of *Free Jazz* (1960), it is unlikely that most listeners would have had this at the front of their minds as they listened to the album, although the Beat community of the time would certainly be familiar with the connections. Elvis Presley's move into acting – even allowing for the cult status surrounding *Jailhouse Rock* (1957) – signalled, for most observers, a shift towards the mainstream.

In contrast, although *Woodstock* is a record of the music that was performed at the festival, it is also much more. The film is constructed to represent a particular version of events that offers a summary of many of the central tenets of countercultural identity in the late 1960s, and the selection of musicians that it includes contributes to the narrative structure, rather than merely accompanying it. Although the soundtrack to *Easy Rider* emerged by chance (Peter Fonda had chosen songs to act as a guide for Crosby, Stills & Nash, who were to provide the 'real' music[5]), it is also an integral component of the storytelling process.

As with American music in the 1960s, the role of The Beatles is significant here: their films, *A Hard Day's Night* (1964) and *Help!* (1965), did nothing to undermine the band's status as the pre-eminent shaper of youth taste in the mid-'60s and also prompted not only the creation of NBC's *The Monkees* television series in 1966, but also many movies, including The Monkees' own *Head* (1968), understatedly advertised on its theatrical trailer as 'the most extraordinary adventure western comedy love story mystery drama musical documentary satire' ever made.[6] Although few of the US movies of the late 1960s were as shamelessly imitative as *The Monkees*, it is clear that *A Hard Day's Night* in particular demonstrated the artistic and commercial possibilities inherent in films featuring or about musicians.

For the majority of this chapter, I focus on films about the counter-culture, such as *Woodstock*, *Easy Rider* and Arthur Penn's *Alice's Restaurant* (1969), as well as the lesser-known *Psych-Out* (1968), as examples of the new power wielded by countercultural actors and directors in Hollywood in the 1960s. In my conclusion, I then extend this analysis through brief discussions of films that manifest counter-cultural ideologies in their representation of American life. Although Penn's *Bonnie and Clyde* (1967) is a revisionist gangster movie set in the 1930s, its romanticised construction of the anti-hero's attacks on the bastions of American capitalism functioned as an effective and popular symbol of 1960s rebellion. John Boorman's *Deliverance* (1972) is built around a narrative of male bonding that is a staple of the Hollywood cinematic tradition, but the film manipulates generic convention to critique dominant ideologies at a moment of supreme crisis for the nation at home and abroad.

As with my chapter on film in Part One, I concentrate on Hollywood rather than on independent alternatives, although the reasons for this focus are slightly different. Whereas in the 1950s, even the best independent films, such as *Shadows* and *Pull My Daisy*, emerged out of and chronicled pre-existing social movements – most notably, of course, the Beats – the non-Hollywood films of the 1960s were often designed to shape opinion and future events, and to challenge the accounts provided by an increasingly powerful hegemonic media. Unlike the Beats, who tended to distance themselves from overt participation in party politics, many sections of the '60s counterculture advocated direct action in efforts to change society and to offer alternatives to mainstream opinion. Thus, as David E. James has noted, 'new institutions had to be created: . . . underground news-papers to report antiwar activism, and eventually guerrilla video collectives where the biases of network television could be exposed and countered'.[7] This meant that, although there were significant experimental film-makers such as Sam Brakhage and (very differently) Andy Warhol producing radical alternatives to the aesthetics of pre-vailing cinematic language, Brakhage's highly personal experiments and Warhol's lengthy, near content-less films like *Sleep* (1963) and *Empire* (1964) remained peripheral to the interests of most youth movements.[8] Instead, especially in the period between 1966 and 1970, films with a strong social and political dimension rather than a commitment to aesthetic innovation came to dominate the independent arena. These productions focused not only on the Vietnam War, but also on events such as African-American uprisings in Northern cities, on campus protests and on the demonstrations surrounding the Democratic Convention in Chicago in 1968. The New York Newsreel, a co-operative of film-makers with strong commitment to social change rather than to profit, who later established branches in other major cities, produced the best-known examples of this type of film.

Newsreel's documentaries constitute an important element of the New Left of the late 1960s: as James has argued in a detailed and persuasive account, films like New York Newsreel's *Columbia Revolt* (1968) and *Summer of 68* (1969) – documentaries about the SDS-led student strike at Columbia University and the protests at the Chicago Democratic Convention, respectively – are 'fundamentally attempts to mobilize alternatives to the mass media's misrepresentation of radical social movements', and both films abandon the generic conventions of 'neutrality' associated with documentary film-making in order to articulate the views of militant participants and to highlight police abuses of their power. As James suggests of *Columbia Revolt*, the purpose of these films was 'to encourage students elsewhere to engage in insurrections of their own'.[9] Anyone screening the documentaries was advised to invite a member of Newsreel along to lead discussion afterwards, in an attempt not only to raise consciousness about particular issues, but also to challenge the culture of passive consumption engendered by hegemonic media. Ultimately, however, Newsreel's influence was short-lived: as a result of disagreements over how best to incorporate non-white and working-class members, the co-operative rapidly fragmented, splitting into what James describes as 'virtually autonomous white and Third World factions' in 1972.[10] At the risk of over-simplifying the relationship, its focus on content over style makes Newsreel tangential to the primary aims of this book, which focuses on the artistic dimensions of the counterculture. In consequence, I now turn to *Woodstock* – the record of an event that seems, for many people, to embody late-'60s counterculture.

On the Road Again: Woodstock Goes to Hollywood

There is an overly familiar narrative that sees Woodstock as the zenith of '60s counterculture, a moment when its ideals were (all too briefly) realised in, as the movie's subtitle asserts (following the festival's own promotional message), 'Three Days of Peace and Music'. The festival's events are contrasted with what occurred a few months later when The

Rolling Stones played at the Altamont Motor Speedway near San Francisco in December 1969, and the uneasy relationship between rock bands – most notably, the Stones and The Grateful Dead – and Hell's Angels collapsed into violent mayhem resulting in four deaths, including that of Meredith Hunter, an eighteen-year-old African-American killed by the Angels. For many commentators, this is the moment when, as Nick Aretakis sums up, 'the '60s effectively end'. Assessing the David and Albert Maysles film, *Gimme Shelter*, that records the Stones' 1969 US tour, Aretakis expands on this point, suggesting:

> But what raises the film to the level of great art are the contrasts between the start of the tour and the tragic events at Altamont. The images early in the film are of a band and its fans combining to form an ecstatic celebration. It's the exact opposite at Altamont, especially during the performances of 'Sympathy for the Devil' and 'Under My Thumb,' when the violence comes to a head. The pictures are unforgettable: a pretty young blonde girl in front of the stage with a look of fear on her face and tears rolling down her cheeks; a young man staring at Jagger, begging him to do something to curtail the violence as the singer stands looking at him, not knowing what to do next; a nude woman, clearly altered on drugs, fighting her way to the stage.[11]

Although there is no doubting the significance of the events at Altamont, establishing a bipolar opposition to Woodstock is reductive and misleading. As Michael Wadleigh's documentary[12] about the festival makes clear, this is also a site whose meanings are complex, contradictory and by no means utopian. Although Woodstock never exploded into violence in the manner of Altamont, its own moments of tension are probably even more valuable as a record of the contradictions at the heart of the counterculture at the end of the 1960s.

Woodstock begins as a eulogy to countercultural ideals: after a few seconds of Jimi Hendrix's rendition of 'The Star Spangled Banner', played over an explosion whose significance remains ambiguous, the film commences with interviews with residents who are generally supportive of what 'the kids' are doing. Contented hippies on horseback and locals in their gardens are represented in harmony, accompanied by Crosby, Stills & Nash's 'Long Time Gone', a song whose lyric makes explicit the counterculture's need to protest against the 'madness' of the Government's domestic and foreign policies. The contrast between 'Woodstock Nation' and the 'hassle' of politics and the city is epitomised by the emphasis on the preparation for the festival: the first shots of festival-goers show large numbers of children and create the sense of a single extended family, with vehicle owners willingly offering lifts to those without transportation. Likewise, the construction of the stage is portrayed as a communal activity in which artisan skills are pooled for the benefit of the community rather than divided in an economy driven by competitive individualism. The impression is clearly of authentic, meaningful work that is posited as a viable and desirable alternative to the alienation of daily urban existence.

This vision of a rural utopia continues to function as one narrative throughout the film: the split-screen style repeatedly twins footage of bands on stage with images of love-making, communal bathing, yoga, meditation and even – to illustrate the idyllic future promised by the 'Woodstock' lifestyle – shows a sheep playing contentedly with a dog. Both men and women, with none of the overt gender inequality present in Beat or bebop, espouse the discourse of free love. Although the weather is poor, this is also turned into an opportunity to demonstrate the power of collective thought, with a chant of 'No rain, no rain' conveying the impression that even the elements can be pacified by the will of a united community.

Nevertheless, there is a darker counter-narrative that runs in tandem with this vision, and which threatens to destroy it. Rural innocence is replaced by traffic jams and helicopters, and by the arrival of hordes without tickets, who are seen breaking down the fence around the festival. Although the organisers mouth hippie platitudes about the dollar being less important than welfare and music, the mood is better expressed in an old resident's complaint that the crowds trespass on property, steal milk and destroy the crops. The warnings about 'bad' brown acid, the paranoia expressed by an interviewee who believes that 'the fascist pigs have been seeding the clouds' and the 'scenes from a disaster area', with festival-goers phoning their parents while US Army medical teams provide assistance, all undermine the illusion of a community offering genuine alternatives to dominant American life-styles. Likewise, the selection of artists in the film suggests problematic ruptures within the counterculture. Many of the bands play an apolitical form of blues rock, and few are seen to be stating political opinions; the more overt anti-war content of Joan Baez's speech and resurrection of 'Old Joe Hill' thus seems to be an anachronistic legacy of an earlier age, her acoustic guitar and famously pure voice symbolically drowned out by The Who's aggressive follow-up. Even individual bands appear to be reaching the end of an epoch: while one half of Jefferson Airplane play 'Uncle Sam's Blues', Grace Slick and the others sit at the side of the stage in a foreshadowing of the band's subsequent split into Jefferson Starship, Hot Tuna and a series of solo projects.

Woodstock's utopia/dystopia dialectic reaches a crescendo – if not a resolution – with Hendrix's performance and, in particular, his interpretation of 'The Star Spangled Banner'. Hendrix's show has become one of the most studied moments in countercultural history, but readings have tended to view it either in isolation or within wider analyses of Hendrix's career rather than as a structured part of the movie's narrative. But within *Woodstock*, the top billing given to one of the few non-white performers at the festival – performing in front of an almost entirely white audience – assumes extra significance and irony, challenging many of the assumptions about protest and difference by which the counterculture defined itself.

Due to the festival being behind schedule, Hendrix's set is played out to a small Monday morning crowd surrounded by the garbage left by the masses who had already departed. The contrast to the ideals of the movie's opening scenes is clear and, whatever the protestations to the contrary, there is little sense of environmental responsibility inherent in the shots of a green field turned into a wasteland as desolate as those to be found in the urban centres abandoned by the white middle classes. Although a few volunteers – many bearing casts, bandages or plasters – are attempting to clean up, accompanied by Hendrix's instrumental jamming, their gesture seems futile in the face of so many symbols of the counterculture's complicity with the waste culture to which it claimed to be opposed.

In contrast to these scenes, the filming of the majority of Hendrix's performance concentrates on what *he* is doing. Whereas much of the movie is shot in split screen, this section serves as a study of a virtuoso musician delivering a highly charged message. At his early performances in the United States – in particular, at the Monterey Festival in 1967 – Hendrix had been accused by some of achieving success by pandering to racial stereotypes, with his flashy clothes and overtly sexual style. Robert Christgau charged him with being a 'psychedelic Uncle Tom,' and Charles Shaar Murray reports that some African-Americans saw Hendrix as a 'stoned clown acting like a nigger for the amusement of white folks'.[13] At Woodstock, however, Hendrix is focused on his music: apart from a brief moment when he plays the guitar with his teeth – a staple of his act when he started out on the black chitlin' circuit – his show is notable for the lack of the gestures for which he was famous. Indeed, during the lengthy solo on 'Voodoo Chile', he is almost motionless.

The camera's attention to Hendrix can be read in terms of its near-obsessive interest in the black body and the questions that its presence at Woodstock raises. As with the film's opening scenes, there is a concentration on a figure who – to use Carlo Rotella's term – is 'good with his hands'.[14] But, unlike the utopianism implicit in the collective artisanal craftsmanship required to build the festival stage, there are disturbing elements inherent in the filming of Hendrix. Although he is playing with a mixed-race band, they are hardly seen: instead, Hendrix appears to be a single black figure surrounded by a white audience that is polite, but hardly rhapsodic, about his performance. While the camera veers between the musician's hands and face, demonstrating the combination of passion and skill required to convey a complex message, it does not seem that this crowd is responsive to what he has to say. The dichotomy reaches a peak during Hendrix's rendition of 'The Star Spangled Banner', a moment that Lauren Onkey rightly identifies as 'symbolic of the counterculture'. Onkey's reading captures much of the significance of the performance:

> Hendrix began his instrumental version of the song by flashing a peace sign to the audience. Then accompanied only by Mitch Mitchell's psychedelic jazz drumming, he played the first few verses of the song, adhering closely to its familiar form. When he got to the line 'and the rockets red glare,' Hendrix let loose with a carefully orchestrated sonic assault on the audience in which his shrieking howling guitar riffs, modulated and distorted with feverish feedback, attained the aural equivalent of Armageddon. The bombs bursting in air and ear transformed Yasgur's placid cow pasture into the napalmed and shrapnel-battered jungles of Vietnam. As the song drew to a close, Hendrix solemnly intoned a few notes of 'Taps,' memorialising not just the slain but perhaps his own former pro-war stance that dated back a few years to his hitch in the army.

Onkey rightly concludes that this 'bravura deconstruction' of the national anthem manages simultaneously to 'evoke chauvinistic pride for and unbridled rage against the American way of life'.[15]

Despite the power of such a reading, there is no sense either of why those present seem so unmoved or of the kind of closure that Hendrix's performance brings to the film. In particular, there is insufficient focus on the clear difference in perspective between the African-American and middle-class white forms of resistance to the war. While disproportionately high numbers of the former were drafted and sent to Vietnam, many of the latter – including, implicitly, members of the gathering at Woodstock – were granted college deferments. Likewise, draft-dodging was a more straightforward operation for affluent whites who, while they could face police violence, imprisonment and short-term persecution, could usually later reintegrate into mainstream society without repercussions, and, as recent history has proved, even end up in the White House. In contrast, even as high profile an African-American as Muhammad Ali could suffer long-standing professional and financial consequences as a result of his refusal to go to Vietnam in 1967, while the racism that followed the riots that occurred after the assassination of Martin Luther King in 1968 affected both African-Americans at home and those who had gone to fight in the war. Hendrix's performance appears to be coupled to his move towards a 'blacker' sound in the final eighteen months of his life, when he jammed with Miles Davis and experimented increasingly with funk and the free-jazz legacy of John Coltrane, a spiritual father for African-American protest in the late '60s. In this context, his presence in the closing scene raises the paradoxical notion of a headliner whose emergent racial consciousness exposes tensions at the heart of countercultural practice.

Woodstock's narrative progression from innocence to a more complex representation of the contradictions and tensions inherent in the counterculture is indicative of the crisis confronting anti-Establishment groups at the end of the 1960s. Politically, the collapse of Students for a Democratic Society (SDS) and the emergence of violent organisations like the Weathermen (later, the Weather Underground) – whose four-day anti-war protest known as the 'Days of Rage' took place in Chicago two months after Woodstock – widened the gap between the vast majority of those who would identify themselves with the counterculture and radical factions who believed (as Weather Underground member Bernardine Dohrn put it) that non-violence was 'an excuse for not struggling'.[16] Todd Gitlin sums up the dilemma facing many in the New Left at the time when he recalls that 'to go with the Weathermen was to take flight from political reality. To go against them was to go – where?'[17]

Gitlin's point is a political one, underlining the extent to which the SDS and other avowedly non-violent protest movements seemed to be running out of ideas, especially after the Chicago Democratic Convention and with the emergence of Black Power. It can, however, be extended into the artistic wing of the counterculture: the increasing use of hard drugs, for example, was creating widespread social problems as well as an ever-lengthening list of rock star casualties. Brian Jones of The Rolling Stones drowned a month before Woodstock and Hendrix himself would die in September 1970. In cinema, too, *Woodstock*'s narrative is repeated in almost all the most significant films about the counterculture: *Psych-Out* commences with a montage of mushroom clouds, planes dropping bombs, Ku Klux Klansmen and other symbols of US racism and imperialism juxtaposed with a journey through an apparently egalitarian, communal Haight-Ashbury. The remainder of the film, however, deconstructs such binary oppositions, suggesting that the hippie counterculture is threatened as much by psychosis and internal conflicts driven by ambition and jealousy as by assaults from external hostile groups like the police and local short-haired hoodlums. Likewise, although *Easy Rider* famously concludes with all three male leads dead at the hands of rednecks, their journey also suggests that ideological advocation of equality often disguises exploitation, especially of women. Even *Alice's Restaurant*, a more complex hybrid of road movie, anti-war protest and rites-of-passage narrative travels a similar path, although the conclusion also hints at an ambiguous optimism largely absent from the other films.

Before moving to a more detailed examination of these movies, it is worth noting a further factor in the narrative enacted at Woodstock. On 9 August – that is, a week before the festival – Charles Manson's gang had murdered the eight-months-pregnant Sharon Tate and four other people in Benedict Canyon, Los Angeles. Whereas the war, racism and police attacks on students and other demonstrators could all be blamed on the Government, this was different: 'Manson', as Peter Biskind puts it, 'was themselves, a hippie, the essence of the '60s.' Biskind identifies a kind of closure on the West coast – and especially in the movie industry – that parallels the undercurrents detectable at Woodstock:

> It was as if, at the moment of ripeness, the dark blossoms of decay were already unfolding. Psychedelics were on their way out, acid had been laced with speed to make a paranoia-inducing drug called STP. Haight-Ashbury was already being decimated by speed and smack, and Hollywood was getting ready to take a fast ride down the cocaine highway.[18]

Echoing the stance implicit in Hendrix's rendition of 'The Star Spangled Banner', Dennis Hopper, the director and co-star of *Easy Rider*, has suggested that in the late '60s he felt 'conflicted' over America.[19] On the one hand, he was opposed to the war and had been involved in civil rights demonstrations; on the other, he celebrated the landscape and many aspects of the nation's history and ideals. *Easy Rider* is a kind of *On the Road* for the 1960s and, like the Beats, Hopper manifests a paradoxical antipathy to modernity coupled with a Dean Moriartyesque love of the freedom of travel across America's highways. Thus, the film contains numerous juxtapositions of motorbikes with horses and urban with rural life, without ever totally siding with one over the other. At one point, Wyatt (Peter Fonda) tells a farmer that he is lucky, since 'not every man . . . can live off the land . . . do [his] own thing', and yet the Americans native to the small communities through which Wyatt and Billy (Hopper) pass are invariably hostile to the travellers. In a visual equivalent to Hendrix's music, *Easy Rider* contains innumerable highly symbolic references to the American flag: Wyatt (also known as Captain America) wears it on his jacket and, significantly, has it painted on his bike's fuel tank, where he stores the profits from the pair's cocaine deal; many houses display it and it is prominent in the small towns through which they travel, even accidentally hanging upside down outside one Louisiana building, a detail indicative of the movie's subversive qualities.

Nationhood is also highlighted and challenged in the film's intertextual allusions: of course, Billy (the Kid) and Wyatt (Earp) are named after legendary Western individualists, and much of their early journey through Arizona's Monument Valley is a tribute to 'John Ford Country'. Nevertheless, these scenes are juxtaposed with elements antithetical to Hollywood conventions, such as the New Orleans collage shot on sixteen-millimetre film and the improvised passages and unconventional editing largely adapted from European cinema and independent American-based film-makers such as Jonas Mekas. For Buck Henry, *Easy Rider* 'looks like a couple of hundred outtakes from several other films all strung together with the soundtrack of the best of the '60s. But it opened up a path. Now the children of Dylan were in control.'[20]

There is much to be said in support of this argument: the film updates the portrayal of the provincial American values represented in *The Wild One*, suggesting a nation at odds with its professed celebration of diversity. It is clear that Wyatt and Billy are victims of the violence inherent in much American life at the time, and the film explores the institutional practices that facilitate ignorance and intolerance. The most explicit articulation of this position comes when George Hanson (Jack Nicholson) – an alcoholic lawyer who has rescued Wyatt and Billy from jail, but whose naivety about the effects of marijuana reflects state propaganda – explains why the counterculture is feared:

> They're scared of what you represent . . . freedom . . . Talking about it and being it, that's two different things . . . Don't ever tell anyone that they're not free cause then they're going to get real busy killing and maiming to prove to you that they are.

In this light – and given that all three men are killed because they are perceived by their murderers as representing freedom and difference – David E. James's suggestion that *Easy Rider* 'opened the door to the real exploitation of the counterculture' seems misguided. For James, contrasting the movie with East Coast independent films like those made by New York Newsreel, *Easy Rider* 'made sure' that the counterculture's ideals 'would be destroyed by reactionary elements, thereby ensuring that their energies would be neither validated nor sustained'.[21] Such readings, however, miss the extent to which the audience is invited to empathise with Billy and Wyatt and to be appalled by their murder, rather than to applaud their reining-in. The film's end contrasts their burning motorbikes with the wonders of the American landscape – which the men have appreciated throughout – and appears to offer an endorsement of their outlaw identities.

This is not to argue, however, that *Easy Rider* provides an unproblematic endorsement of Wyatt and Billy, or of the counterculture more generally. The latter, as depicted in a New Mexico commune, is seen to be strong on spirituality and idealism, but lacking in practical common sense. If anything, the city kids sowing seeds in the desert are as unable to look after themselves as their utopian Transcendentalist forebears at Brook Farm and Fruitlands more than a century before, and there is little sense that their endeavour will be any more successful than that of their spiritual American ancestors. More significant still is the manner in which Hopper's 'conflicted' ideas about America are played out by Wyatt and Billy: moments before they are shot, Wyatt famously tells a bemused Billy 'We blew it', in response to Billy's 'We're rich, man.' Although it is not entirely clear what Wyatt means – and he has already experienced a premonition of their deaths – the statement seems to be a belated recognition of the pair's complicity with hegemonic American values. By making a large profit from the coke deal and planning to retire to Florida, they have become part of the capitalist culture that they appeared to have renounced, living – rather than subverting – the American Dream. In this reading, Billy and Wyatt die not because (as James has it) they are too rebellious but rather because they are not rebellious enough. Even the outlaw element of their action that is inherent in drug dealing is incorporated within a corporate and political climate that the counterculture itself repeatedly exposes as criminal and corrupt. Although Wyatt and Billy confine their own drug taking to marijuana and acid, their participation in the cocaine trade implicates them in the promotion of hard drugs that was so damaging to the counterculture, making them the subjects of Steppenwolf's 'The Pusher' – which plays over their deal – instead of representatives of freedom.

These issues did nothing to undermine *Easy Rider*'s critical reception or commercial success, and it can be argued that the film is a nuanced representation of the crises confronting the counterculture rather than the kind of sell-out suggested by James. James's argument depends upon an overly simplistic independent-good/Hollywood-bad model that is at odds with the permeable relationships between dominant and countercultures demonstrated throughout this book. Although there are, of course, innumerable instances of 'exploitation' of youth cultures through the movie and music industries, constructing a bipolar divide is both unhelpful and inaccurate. Ultimately, such an argument depends upon a sense that hegemonic culture is an unchanging mono-lith that corrupts artists with promises of fortune and fame, whereas – as epitomised by Elvis Presley's career – many 'countercultural' icons appear to have desired these rewards from the start, and have helped to generate changes in the dominant culture itself. In addition, the argument takes for granted the sense that audiences are merely passive consumers of ideological messages handed down from above, a ques-tionable point at any time, but one made doubly unconvincing in the 1960s when a better educated generation was more willing to challenge social and political orthodoxies than ever before.

The modification of corporate entertainment in the 1960s is prob-ably illustrated most dramatically in Hollywood, where the relation-ships between actors, directors and producers provided the opportunity for greater control over decisions shaping the industry's future than, for example, in the music business, where even The Beatles' establishment of Apple Corps was a financial disaster. Although Peter Biskind overstates his case with the subtitle of *Easy Riders, Raging Bulls: How the Sex 'n' Drugs 'n' Rock 'n' Roll*

Generation Saved Hollywood, he is correct to identify the lack of direction within the major studios in the mid-1960s and to associate the industry's revival with the influence of 'countercultural' figures. Likewise, Mark Feeney discusses the eagerness with which the movie industry – noting the massive profits being made by a music business already catering for the youth market – rushed to embrace counter-cultural projects, especially after the 'stupendously' profitable *Easy Rider*, which was made on a 'shoestring' budget and took the 'fourth-biggest gross' of 1969.[22]

The ideology of the counterculture helped to shape many of the major Hollywood films of the 1970s and '80s: its presence is to the fore in the Vietnam genre, including Robert Altman's Korean War-staged *M*A*S*H* (1970), Michael Cimino's *The Deer Hunter* (1978), Francis Ford Coppola's *Apocalypse Now* (1979) and Oliver Stone's *Platoon* (1986); its political idealism and disillusion with a violent and corrupt nation contributes to Altman's *McCabe and Mrs Miller* (1971), Sidney Lumet's *Serpico* (1973) and Alan J. Pakula's *All the President's Men* (1976); environmental and anti-war sentiments are also blended in John Boorman's *Deliverance* (1972). Nevertheless, there are remark-ably few significant films that match *Easy Rider*'s representation of countercultural life, although Hopper's own *The Last Movie* and *The Hired Hand* (both 1971), as well as Stuart Hagmann's *The Strawberry Statement*, Michelangelo Antonioni's *Zabriskie Point* (both 1970) and Jack Nicholson's *Drive, He Said* (1971) bear strong similarities. In part, this paucity springs from the fact that *Easy Rider*'s commercial success was an anomaly and Hopper's own follow-ups, for example, were both flops.[23] In addition, too many of the films have flimsy plots that seemed dated remarkably quickly: for example, although both Richard Rush's *Psych-Out* and Roger Corman's *The Trip* (1967) contain scenes featuring breathtakingly imaginative use of colour, their narratives are simplistic and the techniques used to simulate hallucinogenic experience are unconvincing.

The most ambitious example of the genre is indubitably Arthur Penn's *Alice's Restaurant*, a film that attempts a bold combination of anti-war protest, coming-of-age narrative and examination of the counterculture's own weaknesses. In some ways, the film learns from earlier satirical attacks on American warmongering – most notably Stanley Kubrick's *Dr. Strangelove* (1964) and Joseph Heller's *Catch-22* (1961, made into a film by Mike Nichols in 1970) – and parallels novels like Kurt Vonnegut's *Slaughterhouse-5* (1969) in its use of a combination of different generic conventions to destabilise comfortable narratives. Thus, Arlo Guthrie's medical examination by the draft board at the Whitehall Street induction centre in Manhattan becomes an opportunity to parody the inverted logic underpinning Establishment American ideology. Arlo's demonic 'I want to kill' monologue elicits an enthusiastic 'You're our boy' response from his examiners until he reveals his recent conviction for littering (an offence that has brought an investigation involving a helicopter, three police cars and five officers at the scene of the crime), which means that he is deemed not 'moral enough to join the Army, burn women, kids, houses, and villages' in Vietnam.

Alice's Restaurant lampoons the usual targets – the army, the police, conservative university professors and rednecks – but also rewrites the more personal father/son narrative of *Rebel Without a Cause* in the relationship between Woody (played by Joseph Boley) and Arlo at a time when it seemed that most young men were at loggerheads with their fathers. As the musician son of the most famous countercultural songwriter of the previous generation – who was also the inspiration for Joan Baez, Bob Dylan and the folk boom of early 1960s – Arlo is searching for an identity that establishes difference as well as continuity, although there is none of the overt hostility demonstrated by the sons of more conventional fathers such as Jim Morrison of The Doors. At the start of the film, as he hitches to college in Montana, Arlo re-traces 'Woody's road', and his visits to his hospitalised father – who is paralysed and dying of the hereditary Huntingdon's chorea – are characterised by close identification with Woody's legacy. This identification also marks Arlo's search for his father's approval, most pertinently when he duets with Pete Seeger in a version of 'Pastures of Plenty' at Woody's bedside. Following Woody's death, however – and also that of Arlo's junkie friend, Shelly (Michael McClanathan) – Arlo recognises the need for 'some hard travelling to find [his own destiny] out for my own self'.

Arlo's narrative is both private – in his direct, personal relationship with Woody – and public. Because he is the son of Woody Guthrie, he shares his father with a generation raised on Woody's songs, and he always calls him 'Woody' rather than 'Dad'; more specifically, his genealogy has been 'stolen' (in life, if not explicitly in the film) in a highly public manner by Bob Dylan, who spent part of his apprenticeship playing nothing but Woody's music and continued to champion it – as well as visiting Woody in hospital – for several years, thus becoming, in the public's view, a kind of surrogate son. Arlo's act of paternal reclamation is even clearer in the reception of the song,

'Alice's Restaurant', which inspired the movie, and which would have been well known to many of its audience. Guthrie played the then largely unknown – and still unreleased – track at the Newport Folk Festival in July 1967. Although the first performance was at a song-writer's workshop, and the second in front of a relatively small audience, the impact was so pronounced that Guthrie was invited to perform the song again at the festival's climax, when he was joined on stage by around thirty well-known folk singers. The symbolic importance of the moment is obvious: in 1963, Dylan had received the same treatment when Pete Seeger, Joan Baez, Peter, Paul and Mary and others joined him for 'We Shall Overcome'. Woody Guthrie died a few weeks after his son's performance.[24]

In the movie, once Arlo has avoided the draft, he asks Woody, 'Now that they're not after me to do what I don't want to do, what do I want to do?', a question that resonates with the counterculture of the time's definition – stretching back at least to the Students for a Democratic Society's 'Port Huron Statement' (1962) – in terms of opposition or resistance rather than a coherent manifesto of its own alternatives. Arlo himself appears to have found some kind of resolution to his dilemma, but the film is more ambivalent about the members of the communal group that congregates in the Stockbridge, Massachusetts, church owned by Ray and Alice (James Broderick and Pat Quinn). Although Ray says that the church is 'a place to be the way we want to be', the dream of collective sanctuary is continually undermined from within, especially by Ray's own jealousy, violence and selfishness. At the end of the film, following Ray's 'remarriage' to Alice, the rest of the group have rejected his offer to sell the church and buy land in Vermont where there will be 'room to stretch out . . . in some kind of family', and Alice herself seems abandoned as she stares out at the now fragmented family as they depart. Likewise, Shelly's overdose alone in a motel room appears to be an indictment of the counterculture's increasing use of hard drugs, in which he is more of a victim of Billy and Wyatt's entrepreneurship than a brother in their freedom. In contrast to the positive message inherent in Arlo's spiritual – and, as a musician, professional – maturation, the collective narrative ends in a collapse that, like the conclusion to *Woodstock*, echoes the counterculture's wider crises at the end of the 1960s.

'In Wildness is the Preservation of the World':[25]
Bonnie and Clyde and *Deliverance*

Arthur Penn, the director of *Alice's Restaurant*, had already made a film that proved – against the expectations of studio bosses – extremely popular with both 'mainstream' and countercultural audiences. *Bonnie and Clyde* (1967), although it is set during the Depression rather than in the affluent mid-'60s, chronicles outlaws who anticipate *Easy Rider*'s Wyatt and Billy in their representation of what Todd Gitlin accurately summarises as a 'rhetoric of showdown and recklessness' that proved extremely attractive to many involved in youth movements.[26] Opening during the Summer of Love and a few weeks after major rioting in the ghettos of Newark and Detroit, *Bonnie and Clyde* was initially a critical and commercial flop, and was dismissively labelled a 'piece of fucking shit' by old-guard Warner Bros. executive, Benny Kamelson. The film was rescued by the combination of a lengthy *New Yorker* article by Pauline Kael that called it 'the most excitingly American American movie since *The Manchurian Candidate*', and by its success in Britain. This prompted its re-release in the US, following which it became an enormous financial success.[27]

Bonnie and Clyde is an unusually sensitive register of the changes occurring in America – and, more locally, in the Hollywood film industry – in the mid-1960s. Most obviously, its demonisation of institutional authority (the law and banks) and correspondingly romanticised celebration of the outlaw 'pits the hip and the cool against the old, straight and stuffy', saying (as Peter Biskind puts it) ' "fuck you" . . . to a generation of Americans who were on the wrong side of the generation gap, the wrong side of the war in Vietnam', and contemptuously dismissing the Hollywood establishment.[28] This is not all, however: in addition, the film represents the new culture of celebrity – Andy Warhol's 'fifteen minutes of fame' – in the couple's compulsive desire to photograph one another and send the results to the press, and carries implicit and explicit ties to sexual liberation. *Bonnie and Clyde*'s graphic, yet stylised, violence is a further innovation, creating a juxtaposition of an apparently rather sleazy story and a representational technique that transforms the material into a spectacle indebted to European experimental cinema, yet functioning as a critique of the United States of the 1960s. This process culminates in Clyde's slow-motion death (in which a piece of his brain flies across the screen), a scene reminiscent of the film of John F. Kennedy's assassination. Finally, the banjo and fiddle music that accompanies scenes of the outlaws driving away after shooting people deploys a satirical critique of Hollywood conventions, introducing a new, playful way of representing (and endorsing) the use of force against institutions that were already (in the mid-1960s) increasingly ready to deploy violence against young Americans.

Although *The Graduate*'s Mike Nichols beat Penn to the Best Director Oscar, *Bonnie and Clyde* is indubitably the most significant early example of the counterculture's impact on Hollywood, and of the degree to which that impact extended beyond films that are explicitly *about* the counterculture. In addition, its release pre-empted the re-emergence for the first time since HUAC's investigation of Hollywood in the late 1940s of highly chronicled political activism by stars now including Warren Beatty, Julie Christie and Jane Fonda, whose support for issues including the anti-war movement, Native American rights and Black Power raised awareness of politically 'sensitive' causes and, unsurprisingly, generated polarised reactions and enormous hostility in mainstream America.

If the banjo music accompanying the shootings in *Bonnie and Clyde* can be read as a teasingly subversive inversion of Hollywood's conventional approach to killing, the banjo-based soundtrack to *Deliverance* suggests something very different. While there was still considerable New Left and countercultural optimism about the possibility of political change when the former was made in 1967, that optimism had largely evaporated by 1972, when *Deliverance* was released. The assassinations of Martin Luther King and Bobby Kennedy, the Kent State shootings and the re-election of Richard Nixon, alongside internal fragmentation exemplified by the Manson killings, Altamont and the emergence of the Weathermen, help to explain the ideological confusion apparent in Boorman's film. What starts as an environmentalist lament for a soon-to-be-destroyed example of America's outstanding natural beauty becomes, next, a kind of *Easy Rider* in canoes coupled with Vietnam allegory and, finally, a critique of an America that has become over civilised and lost sight of what made it 'great' in the first place.

The opening scenes juxtapose what Lewis (Burt Reynolds) calls the 'last wild, untamed, unpolluted, unfucked-up river in the South' with examples of how humankind is destroying it: a hydroelectric dam is being constructed to meet the urban demand for power in what Lewis describes as the 'rape' of a landscape already scarred by rusting abandoned cars. For Lewis, however, who is depicted as a flawed, would-be Nietzschean *ubermensch*, nature is more significant as a testing ground for a manhood that is absent from daily life in the city. His three companions represent other versions of the urban male, ranging from Ed (John Voight), a capable family man who would rather 'go back to town, play golf', through the liberal, guitar-playing Drew (Ronny Cox), to Bobby (Ned Beatty), a flabby salesman. All are forced to examine the degree to which overcivilisation has distanced them from what Henry David Thoreau had, in the mid-nineteenth century, called the 'wildness' that could provide an antidote to modern alienation. In a world without women (bar in the closing moments), the only characters they encounter are backwoodsmen about to be relocated before the valley is flooded.

One of the movie's best-known scenes suggests that a harmonious relationship between self and significantly 'othered' people can exist, as Drew plays a rousing duet with a local banjo-player. The union brought about by the music returns, deceptively, to the heritage imagined in Harry Smith's *Anthology of American Music* (1952), but from this moment on, the four men are increasingly thrown into a battle with locals and unfamiliar natural forces that allegorises the defamiliarisation experienced by troops in Vietnam. Bobby is raped by a woodsman in a symbolic inversion of the 'rape' of the landscape in the construction of the dam and, following Lewis's killing of the perpetrator, the journey downstream becomes a retreat from alien country in which Drew is killed and Lewis incapacitated. As a result, the focus shifts from Lewis to Ed, who has to experience his own rite of passage in climbing a cliff and killing a man who might or might not be the rapist's partner. Having escaped to the local town, the three survivors have to lie repeatedly in order to persuade a suspicious local sheriff to allow them to leave. At a meal with local residents, Ed cries while Bobby represses all memory of what has occurred and, in the film's closing scenes, Ed returns to his wife and young son unable to recount the truth of what has happened and yet unable to forget it.

This brief summary only starts to convey the confused and ambiguous ideological position proposed through the film. On the one hand, the suggestion that the men will never be able to talk about their experiences – and that these events are too alien to be comprehended by their relatives – resonates with the experience of soldiers returning from Vietnam. Likewise, the need to lie to protect those at home anticipates *Apocalypse Now* in its appropriation of Joseph Conrad's *Heart of Darkness* (1902), even if the horror of this river journey occurs solely journeying downstream towards 'civilisation'. It is plain that an unproblematic return to Sunday golf is not an option for Ed. Less clear is the reason for his tears and nightmare: does what he has witnessed create an unbridgeable chasm between himself and his family, or is it what he has learned about his own capacity to kill that is so disturbing? Is it the realisation that – even in its horror – this has been the high point of his life and now he must return to an America built upon denial and the destruction of its landscape and its past? In any case, what is certain is that we have travelled far from the utopian union of humankind and nature at the start of *Woodstock*.

Implicit in *Deliverance* is a critique of a nation whose governmental policies have had disastrous consequences for nature – both human and material – at home and abroad. Where Transcendentalists such as Thoreau and Emerson had seen nature as an antidote to modernity – a point adopted and developed by the Beats and hippies to include a celebration of the sexuality repressed by dominant culture – the film suggests that uncontaminated regenerative natural spaces no longer exist, and, in the rape of Bobby, that idealised sexual freedom is no longer compatible with the natural spaces that do remain. Coupling the counterculture's revitalisation of environmentalism with its commitment to illuminating the damage done to human minds and bodies not only by war, but also by a corporate culture that strips people of their energy and dignity, the film implies that the classic American mythology of reinvigoration through nature is no longer realisable, and illustrates the speed with which natural spaces are being erased in the pursuit of an unsustainable culture of abundance. Like *Woodstock* and *Easy Rider*, *Deliverance* carries a 'conflicted' message about 'America', but the death of Drew (the counterculture-coded member of the group) implies a belief that the alternative nation imagined in the 1960s could not provide solutions to the country's crises. Although, given the fact that environmentalism and eco-criticism are among the most enduring legacies of the counterculture, there is considerable irony in this conclusion, *Deliverance* suggests that, by 1972, there was little sense of how to rescue the positive elements of national culture from the abuses carried out in pursuit of prosperity at home and an ironically named 'freedom' abroad.

Notes

1. John Fogerty, 'Fortunate Son', released as a single in 1969 and on the Creedence Clearwater Revival album *Willy and the Poorboys* (Fantasy, 1970). Copyright © 1969, Prestige Music, Ltd.
2. Throughout this chapter, I am using the 1999 Columbia DVD of *Easy Rider*, which includes invaluable extras such as Dennis Hopper's director's commentary.
3. Jack Kerouac, *On the Road* (London: Penguin, 1972), p. 128.
4. See Richie Unterberger, *Eight Miles High: Folk Rock's Flight From Haight-Ashbury to Woodstock* (San Francisco: Backbeat Books, 2003), p. 42.
5. See the documentary supplement to the DVD release of the film. According to Fonda, when Crosby, Stills & Nash saw the film they felt that they could not improve on the original selections. In his director's commentary, however, Dennis Hopper suggests that he vetoed the use of Crosby, Stills & Nash because they travelled in limousines.
6. See http://members.tripod.com/~ahiii/monkeesfilmTV.html for details of *Head*'s cast and – to use the term loosely – plot.
7. David E. James, ' "The Movies are a Revolution": Film and the Counter-culture', in Peter Braunstein and Michael William Doyle (eds), *Imagine Nation: The American Counterculture of the 1960s and '70s* (London: Routledge, 2002), p. 275.
8. See James, ' "The Movies are a Revolution" ', pp. 282–8 for a more detailed account of Brakhage and Warhol's films.
9. Ibid., p. 293.
10. Ibid., p. 297. The narrowness of Newsreel's approach – and its nervousness over more 'artistic' productions – had already been illustrated well before the 1972 schisms. Founder-member Robert Kramer's *Ice* (1970), set in a futuristic police-state America and representing the activities of armed revolutionaries, provided an astute and imaginative commentary on the tensions surrounding events such as the 1968 Chicago Democratic Convention and the 1969 People's Park Berkeley protest. Although the film was shot in standard Newsreel style, the group would not allow release under its name and was apparently perturbed by the more fantastical elements of the plot.
11. Nick Aretakis, 'Life and Death at Altamont', a 2000 *Sights* review of the reissued *Gimme Shelter*, at www.poppolitics.com/articles/2000-11-18-shelter.shtml
12. The following discussion uses the 1994 director's cut of the movie.
13. Quoted in Lauren Onkey, 'Voodoo Child: Jimi Hendrix and the Politics of Race in the Sixties', in Braunstein and Doyle, *Imagine Nation*, p. 192 and Alice Echols, *Shaky Ground: The Sixties and Its Aftershocks* (New York: Columbia University Press, 2002), p. 283, fn. 154.

14. See Carlo Rotella, *Good With Their Hands: Boxers, Bluesmen, and Other Characters From the Rust Belt* (Berkeley: University of California Press, 2002).
15. Onkey, 'Voodoo Child', p. 190.
16. See 'The Weathermen', at www.geocities.com/southernscene/edu3.html; Todd Gitlin, *The Sixties: Years of Hope, Days of Rage* (New York: Bantam, 1987), pp. 384–95.
17. Gitlin, *The Sixties*, p. 396.
18. Peter Biskind, *Easy Riders, Raging Bulls: How the Sex 'n' Drugs 'n' Rock 'n' Roll Generation Saved Hollywood* (London: Bloomsbury, 1998), p. 79.
19. See Hopper's director's commentary to the *Easy Rider* DVD.
20. Quoted in Biskind, *Easy Riders, Raging Bulls*, p. 75.
21. James, ' "The Movies are a Revolution" ', p. 299.
22. Mark Feeney, *Nixon at the Movies: A Book About Belief* (Chicago: University of Chicago Press, 2004), p. 226. The biggest-grossing film of 1969 was *Butch Cassidy and the Sundance Kid*, a revisionist Western with some striking similarities to *Easy Rider*, especially in its violent ending.
23. See Feeney, *Nixon at the Movies*, pp. 226–7.
24. See Charles Kaiser, *1968 in America: Music, Politics, Chaos, Counterculture, and the Shaping of a Generation* (New York: Grove Press, 1988), p. 40.
25. Henry David Thoreau, 'Walking', in Nina Baym et al. (eds), *The Norton Anthology of American Literature*, 6th edn (New York: Norton, 2003), B, p. 2004.
26. Gitlin, *The Sixties*, p. 287. Peter Braunstein notes that the 'very choice of the Depression-era 1930s was an act of provocation on the part of the filmmakers, for if there was one decade that traumatized the parents of Sixties youth, that explained their anxieties about financial security and their consequent privileging of the future over the present, it was the 1930s.' 'Forever Young: Insurgent Youth and the Sixties Culture of Rejuvenation', in Braunstein and Doyle, *Imagine Nation*, p. 261.
27. See Biskind, *Easy Riders, Raging Bulls*, pp. 40–1.
28. Ibid., p. 49. I am indebted to Biskind's reading throughout this paragraph.

Index